Christmas 2003

Ruby

Praise for aviation adventure in *Heroes of the Horizon:*

". . . A compelling, readable Alaska aviation classic. . . . You will enjoy this wealth of flying action, triumph, tragedy, courage, and determination. . . ." —*General Aviation News & Flyer*

". . . A particularly valuable collection of reminiscences of a bygone era." —*Library Journal*

". . . Harrowing and funny and rich with Alaskan history and the wonders of glacier flying." —*Booklist*

HEROES OF THE HORIZON

Flying Adventures of Alaska's Legendary Bush Pilots

Gerry Bruder

Alaska Northwest Books™
Anchorage • Seattle • Portland

Fourth printing 1998

Library of Congress Cataloging-in-Publication Data
Bruder, Gerry, 1944–
Heroes of the horizon : flying adventures of Alaska's legendary bush pilots / Gerry Bruder.
p. cm.
Includes bibliographical references and index.
ISBN 0-88240-363-X
1. Bush pilots—Alaska—Biography. 2. Aeronautics—Alaska—History. I. Title.
TL539.B79 1991
629.13'092—dc20
[B] 91-14326
CIP

Edited by Ellen Harkins Wheat
Book design by Cameron Mason
Photo editing by Carrie Seglin
Map by Cameron Mason and Carol Palmer

Cover Photos. *Front cover:* A Grumman Widgeon flies over the Arrigetch Peaks in the Brooks Range, Alaska. Photo by Fred Hirschmann.
Back cover: Author Gerry Bruder and Kenmore Air's Cessna 180 at Barkley Sound on the west coast of Vancouver Island, British Columbia. Photo by Larry Clinton.

Alaska Northwest Books™
An imprint of Graphic Arts Center Publishing Company
P.O. Box 10306, Portland, OR 97296-0306
800-452-3032

Contents

Pioneer bush pilot Joe Crosson flies a Fairchild 71 over Lynn Canal north of Juneau in the mid-1930s. *Photo by Lloyd Jarman*

ARCTIC OCEAN
Barrow
BEAUFORT SEA
Wainwright
Point Lay
Prudhoe
Cape Lisburne
Colville
River
Umiat
CHUKCHI SEA
BROOKS RANGE
Arctic Circle
SIBERIA
Anaktuvuk Pass
ALASKA
Shishmaref
Kotzebue
Walker Lake
Wiseman
Deering
River
Bettles
Candle
Fort Yu
Teller
SEWARD
PENINSULA
Koyukuk
Stevens Village
Nome
Moses Point
Rampart
ST. LAWRENCE
ISLAND
Koyukuk
Nulato
Galena
Manley
Hot Springs
Chena Ho
Springs
Ruby
Fairbanks
Norton Sound
Unalakleet
Nenana
North
Pole
Yukon River
Lake Minchumina
RANGE
Mountain
Village
Ophir
McGrath
Cape Romanzof
Saint Marys
ALASKA
MOUNT McKINLE
Fortuna Ledge
Holy Cross
River
Talkeetna
Kuskokwim
Glennalle
Bethel
Wasilla
Anchorage
Kuskokwim
Bay
Soldotna
Seward
Cook Inlet
BERING SEA
Iliamna
Lake
Cape Newenham
Dillingham
King Salmon
Bristol Bay
PENINSULA
Kodiak
KODIAK
ISLAND
GULF
ALASKA
CHAIN
ALEUTIAN
PACIFIC OCEA

N
Skagway
Haines
Lynn Canal
MOUNT
FAIRWEATHER
Cape
Fairweather
Glacier Bay
Juneau
Taku Inlet
Icy Strait
Stephens Passage
Chatham Strait
CHICHAGOF
ISLAND
SOUTHEAST ALASKA
ADMIRALTY
ISLAND
BARANOF
ISLAND
Sitka
Arctic Circle
Circle
Yukon River
Eagle
Chicken
Dawson City
Petersburg
KUIU
ISLAND
Wrangell
Clarence Strait
REVILLAGIGEDO
ISLAND
Northway
Pelly Crossing
PRINCE OF WALES
ISLAND
Klawock
Craig
Behm Canal
Ketchikan
YUKON
TERRITORY
Hydaburg
ANNETTE
ISLAND
Kennicott
Burwash Landing
Whitehorse
Dixon Entrance
COAST MOUNTAINS
Yakutat
Skagway
Juneau
CANADA
Sitka
Petersburg
Stewart
Hyder
BRITISH
COLUMBIA
Ketchikan
Prince Rupert

Foreword

Gerry Bruder has written a fine selection of profiles about some of the outstanding Alaskan pioneer aviators. I am privileged to have known most of these airmen, and my association with them has enriched my life.

Much has been written about the first to fly in Alaska, and justifiably so. Those flyers penetrated the uncertain skies of a vast, uncharted land. Some gave their lives. The course was set for a new generation of outstanding men and women, who continued to shape the future of Alaska and the aviation industry. The airplane served to open up a rich and beautiful frontier, as did the covered wagon a century before.

Many of the people who came to Alaska stayed, eager to accept the adventures of a new life. Others left, unable to cope with the inconveniences of a remote and harsh land. Still others were born and raised here, destined to leave their mark. When asked what they like about Alaska, some reply, "it's the people," while others say, "I love the challenge."

Visitors are often amazed at the challenges Alaskan aviators face. I am reminded of a flight to Gambell, on St. Lawrence Island, in the early 1960s. We were flying a C-46 and one of our passengers was an airline pilot from the South 48. I offered him the jump seat. It was a typical whiteout winter day. There was a 25-knot crosswind with drifting snow, which made it difficult to see the runway if you didn't know where it was. I don't think he liked the drift correction we were holding on final, either. In a C-46, sometimes it is necessary to land in a semi-crab angle with these conditions to keep from being blown off the runway. I have to admit, it would look a little scary if you hadn't been doing it for some time. After we landed, I noticed that he was no longer in the cockpit. Apparently he decided, somewhere on final approach, that the rear of the airplane was the place to be.

These kinds of adventures fill the pages of *Heroes of the Horizon.* The author has captured an excellent cross-section of some outstanding airmen during a very exciting period of aviation.

—Noel Merrill Wien

Noel Merrill Wien has flown over 28,500 hours as pilot in command of a variety of aircraft, from bush planes to helicopters to the Lockheed L-1011. He flew in the Air Force from 1951 to 1956. A member of the famous Wien family, he was a pilot for Wien Alaska Airlines (with time out for military service) from 1950 to 1985, when the company was dissolved. Wien Alaska Airlines was originally started in 1927 by his father, Noel Wien, legendary pioneer Alaskan aviator, who came north in 1924.

FRATERNITY OF FLYERS

TOWERING MOUNTAIN RANGES. Surging rivers. Junglelike forests. Waterways roiling with waves and swells. Mud flats. Grizzly bears. Mosquitoes so thick they stampede caribou. Endless miles of tundra. Alaska has always been an obstacle course for surface travel, but until the early 1920s people had no choice: you got around by dog sled, pack horse, boat, snowshoes, or foot, or you stayed home.

Then came the pioneer bush pilots. Flying rickety, underpowered biplanes, they took off without weather reports or radios. Gravel bars, meadows, and frozen rivers served as their runways. Engine failures and crashes hounded them almost as often as the fog and wind. Many sourdoughs scoffed, "We're not going up in those contraptions!"

But as the early aviators' experience broadened, they gradually demonstrated the airplane's potential in Alaska's rugged wilderness. The fur buyer who once needed weeks to travel among the trading stations could now simply charter an airplane, sit back, and cruise like magic at seventy knots *above* Mother Nature's gauntlet—all the while marveling at the awesome beauty he never knew lay over the next hill. The prospector could be dropped off right in gold country, the teacher at the village, the fisherman on the lake. The road engineer could minimize mistakes by taking an aerial survey of proposed routes. The kid suffering from acute appendicitis could be evacuated by air to the nearest hospital, sometimes hundreds of miles away.

Medicine, food, whiskey, ammunition, replacement parts, and today's newspaper could be ordered by telegraph in the morning and delivered that afternoon.

So quickly did the airplane revolutionize travel in Alaska that by the early 1930s every major community had at least one air service, and scheduled flights were available on some routes. Pilots and mechanics even had to get licenses. The pioneers had done their job, and they've since become legends.

At the other end of aviation evolution in Alaska, the modern era dates from the 1960s, when technology began making available high-performance workhorses such as the Cessna 185 and the de Havilland Twin Otter. Over the next few years, development of solid-state communications, Loran C navigation, and satellite-enhanced search-and-rescue operations gradually nudged contemporary pilots into the computer world. Increasingly tight federal control continues to render flying more regimented but also more professional.

Flying commercially in Alaska remains an exciting way to make a living. You can still find unnamed mountain lakes and hearty individuals who continue to follow much the same lifestyle as their ancestors did. Yet progress's encroaching fingers have brushed away a bit of the adventure, and the day of the true bush pilot is over.

Between the old and the new stretched a long transitional period that formed Alaska aviation's golden age. Pilots from the mid-1930s through the 1950s enjoyed a mix of romance and science, of innovation and routine. Destinations remained undisturbed by tourism yet more accessible, thanks to aircraft with greater speed and range. Short, unpaved village strips forced pilots to squeeze every ounce of performance from their airplanes and themselves, while high-frequency radios let them stay in touch with their dispatcher back home. Unstifled, individualism and idiosyncrasies could coexist with regulations.

During this epoch, construction workers hacked the Alaska (Alcan) Highway out of the wilderness. The military defended the remote, storm-swept Aleutian Islands from Japanese invaders. The Territory became the country's forty-ninth state. Government agencies brought services to outlying villages and resource management to the vast wilderness. In each project, the airplane played an indispensable part, transporting people, supplies, and equipment. By the start of modern aviation in Alaska, flying had become almost as common as driving in the Lower 48.

The aviators who started going aloft in the 1930s and 1940s are retired now, and in most cases their stories have yet to be told beyond a circle of friends and relatives and a few newspapers and regional magazines. In the pages that follow, thirty of them share their adventures, their observations, and their thoughts with a wider audience.

Many of these flyers had already stepped out of the cockpit for the final time when I started my first commercial flying job in Ketchikan in the early 1970s. Like seasoned skippers reminiscing about sailing the seas in the last of the square-riggers, the local retired pilots enthralled me with their tales. While all had met some of the great pioneers in their young years, to me they themselves were the heroes. The pioneers were gone, frozen forever in printed words and old photos. But the second-generation bush pilots were still sipping coffee, laughing, swearing, and telling story after story. I could look into eyes that had seen hundreds of snow squalls and thousands of takeoffs. Bush flying lived on in their reminiscences. I decided to write a book about these colorful characters and their peers around the state. Someday.

Meanwhile, I was busy following the skytrails they had blazed. Along with the scenery off my wingtips, the years slipped by. Suddenly, it seemed, the corps of old-timers had diminished. You'd better get going on this book while there's someone left to talk to, I told myself. Next year, maybe.

I still had made no definite plans for the project when my flying career brought me to Kenmore Air Harbor near Seattle. The largest commercial seaplane operation in the world, Kenmore regularly

Bill Lund learned to fly in 1935 in this two-seat, sixty-five-horsepower Aeromarine Klemm, owned by the Juneau Flying Club. The device on the right wing is an airspeed indicator. *Courtesy of the Lund Family*

attracted spectators. Singly or with friends, they arrived in cars, on bicycles, or on foot to stroll about, watching the seaplanes come and go. One of the most frequent visitors was a burly, elderly man with stringy white hair and a weathered face that always seemed to need a shave. He looked more like a tired grandfather than a veteran bush pilot.

But Bill Lund had logged thousands upon thousands of hours from the late thirties to the fifties flying bush planes all over the Alaskan Interior, usually with a stubby cigar stuck in his mouth. Eventually a young Alaska Airlines acquired him. When he retired in 1977, he was number one on the carrier's seniority list.

He had flown periodically out of Kenmore on ferry flights since 1946, and now in retirement he liked to hang out there. After tossing bread crumbs to the resident ducks, he would wander into the lounge to talk aviation with anyone who had time to listen. Blessed with a sharp wit and a vivid memory despite his age, Lund was an encyclopedia of bush flying anecdotes. He never ran dry.

"Sure, sure, anytime!" he answered, when I asked if he would spend an evening with me and a tape recorder. Someday.

Life finally ran out of patience. In the winter of 1989, Lund suffered a debilitating stroke, and a few weeks later he died. Among the shadows in my mind will always be the regret that I waited too long to spend an evening with him.

The next spring, I belatedly made "someday" now, flew to Alaska on a leave of absence, and traveled around the state talking with old-time pilots. Even then, the hourglass was draining. My list of pilots to interview included Art Woodley, who founded Woodley Airways in 1932 with service between Anchorage and Nome and the motto, "Have Plane, Will Travel." I noticed his obituary in the *Seattle Times* as my Alaska Airlines 727 taxied out from Sea-Tac Airport. A week later, I passed an entire day and part of an evening with octogenarian Jerry Jones in Petersburg, three months before he collapsed from a stroke. Four months after I met with seventy-five-year-old Norm Gerde of Ketchikan, he died. Rodger Elliott is also gone now. So are Bob Ellis, Sig Wien, Shell Simmons, and others. How fortunate I was to fly vicariously with them.

At my word processor afterward, my goal was not to compile complete biographies of these retired bush pilots, which would take many volumes. Instead, I wanted to create portraits that would collectively depict Alaska's greatest flying era, as it was experienced by the participants, in their own words. Convinced that only first-hand accounts would do, I restricted my subjects to pilots I could interview in person. That meant excluding some who, for one reason or another, were unavailable during my research, such as Talkeetna's Don Sheldon. A folk hero for performing dramatic rescues and pioneering high-altitude landings on Mount McKinley glaciers, Sheldon died in 1975.

I also chose to leave out pilots who started flying in Alaska late in the period and therefore belonged to more modern times. Their accomplishments were no less notable; they were simply too young for this book.

Dispatchers, mechanics, line crew, village agents, and others help indirectly to make flights successful, although bush flying itself is an individual effort. For that reason, I included two mechanics who flew regularly with pilots in the early days, lived lives of adventure, and contributed much to the development of Alaskan aviation.

Inevitably, a few pilots shook their heads at the opportunity to be part of the book. One was Ray Petersen, whose Petersen Flying Service eventually became part of Northern Consolidated Airlines and later Wien Air Alaska. Although Petersen said he regretted having declined Jean Potter's invitation in the 1940s to be the subject of a chapter in her classic *The Flying North,* he explained he was also going to turn me down because he was "tired of writers coming up here and getting rich off of me." A former Wien board chairman, Petersen is apparently unaware of the economics of the writing business. He called himself a curmudgeon and admonished me that his name is spelled "Petersen," not "Peterson." "I am not, and have never been, Swedish," he declared.

I tried to be attentive to such details in writing about the many pilots who welcomed a chance to share their experiences. Aviation is a sort of fraternity, and in Alaska most retired pilots know one another and are friends now, even if they were competitors in the past. Thus, as I visited with the aviators around the state I heard some stories five or six times, each version differing slightly from the others. I've verified facts as much as possible, but whenever an incident or anecdote exists only in a single memory, I've trusted the teller. The pilots and mechanics have read their profiles for accuracy.

Some apparent inconsistencies in this book actually reflect changed conditions and the passage of time. For instance, Bob Ellis founded Ellis Air Transport, but the company was called Ellis Air Lines when he merged it with Alaska Coastal Airlines. And although the Eskimo village of Ukivok on King Island is now deserted, people lived there when Orville Tosch served it in the early 1950s.

Aircraft engineers used to calibrate airspeeds in miles per hour—and mph airspeed indicators remain on the instrument panels of

An Alaska Air Transport Lockheed Vega piloted by Clarence Rhode near Juneau in the mid-1940s. *Photo by Lloyd Jarman*

many older planes—but the use of knots has become universal in aviation. To facilitate comparisons, I've converted all airspeeds in the narrative to knots, except in quoted remarks.

Because I wanted to offer a comprehensive overview in the profiles, I sought variety as I traveled about Alaska. It wasn't hard to find. Like every flight in the bush, every pilot I spoke with was unique and interesting. But whether they had specialized in seaplanes in Southeast or skiplanes in the Arctic, the aviators, most of whom were in their seventies, shared one intriguing trait: in both physical appearance and attitude, all seemed younger and more vibrant than their nonpilot peers. Several still flew their own planes, and most were active in various projects or enterprises. Typical was arctic pilot Bud Helmericks, born in 1917, who shuttles in his Cessna 180 between homes in Fairbanks and the Far North. He readily agreed to an interview, "if you can catch up with me." Luckily, I did.

From one end of Alaska to the other, the eyes of pilots I met reflected a common sparkle, a gratitude for a life of romance and adventure. Is it an innate joy of living that leads to bush flying, or does bush flying inspire such a spirit? Yes and yes. No one becomes a bush pilot without a yearning for excitement and a love of the outdoors. People who simply like to fly are content with the airlines or the commuters, or with private jaunts in good weather over relatively easy routes. But the hiker who chooses the less traveled trail at the fork, who a century and a half ago would have left the security of the East for the challenge of the West—there's the born bush pilot.

Once in the occupation, a pilot is energized by endless stimulation. Day after day, you fly in a land that humbles you with its grandeur, its immensity. You regularly visit places far off the tourists' routes or where an airplane may never have landed before. Eccentric passengers, peculiar freight, and spontaneous charters make each day as unpredictable as the weather. You handle your own navigation, make your own life-or-death decisions. Fear and joy race through your veins so closely together you sometimes can't tell one from the other. In such a job, just try to come home at day's end without an inner sparkle. After a while it shows.

Bush flying's finest years seem animated in the presence of the men and women whose stories follow. It would be foolishly sentimental to claim that while listening to them reminisce and looking at their albums and scrapbooks, I heard the distant rumble of a 1932 Lockheed Vega, or smelled the mixed fragrances of leather, oil, gas, and fabric that season old cockpits. And yet . . .

Jerry Jones

— *Old and Bold* —

A VENERABLE AVIATION ADAGE claims that there are old pilots and bold pilots, but no old, bold pilots. Walter John "Jerry" Jones illustrates the folly of making such categorical statements. Born on March 29, 1903, Jones is old by any chronological standard. And after you listen to his stories about early bush flying in Alaska, you realize that if he isn't bold, neither is Indiana Jones.

In a sense, when Jerry Jones came north in 1931, a pilot automatically qualified as bold by flying in Alaska at all. The state-of-the-art bush plane then was a radioless, wood-and-fabric crate with an unreliable engine. Less than a decade had passed since the advent of commercial aviation in the Territory, and bush flying was unrefined, a budding profession that pilots were learning by trial and error. You needed guts and spirit to fly in Alaska in the early 1930s.

As Jones strolls about the cabin of his forty-eight-foot power boat *Louel* in a Petersburg marina, describing bush flying back then, you can't quite picture him in scarf and goggles. A thick green sweater and baggy pants accentuate his stocky, five-foot-six-inch frame. Occasionally he runs a hand through his hair, white and ruffled, as if to nudge a name or place from his memory. He seems more like Spencer Tracy portraying a grizzled tugboat skipper.

Nor did the young Jerry Jones look much like a bush pilot. Yellowed, cracked photos show him with an innocent expression, a slight smile, and thick hair combed straight back, often the only person in the photo wearing sunglasses. Although there's little actual resemblance, you think of Mickey Rooney.

But prerequisites for the right stuff have never included an Errol Flynn image. People went up in an airplane in the flapper days for the same reason they ascend in a roller coaster today. Before Jones tightened his seat belt for the first time, while on a 1923 vacation in California, he had planned to study forestry in his native Syracuse, New York. After the flight, he was the wide-eyed kid who scurried back into line again and again.

To finance flying lessons at San Diego's Ryan Aircraft Company, he slept in a hangar and worked on the assembly line. Soon he had licenses as a mechanic as well as a pilot and was making a few charters for the company in open-cockpit biplanes. Southern California today contains some of the most congested airspace in the world; fly from San Diego up the coast toward San Francisco, and airliners, commuters, and private aircraft seem to whiz by constantly in the smog. But Jones had the region pretty much to himself. "Some days I never saw another airplane," he says.

As a major aircraft manufacturer, Ryan attracted a variety of people interested in aviation. One day at the hangar, Jones met a lanky young man named Charles A. Lindbergh, who had commissioned Ryan to build an airplane for a unique mission. Jones recalls that Lindbergh stayed up all one night fishing in the area to test his ability to go without sleep. "The next day, or maybe the second day, after Charlie landed in Paris, Claude Ryan got orders for thirty-three airplanes," Jones recalls. "It was taking us two and a half months to build just one!"

Among the flight students lured to the bustling company in the mid-1920s were future pioneer Alaskan bush pilots Joe Crosson and S. E. "Robbie" Robbins. After learning to fly, Crosson ventured to Alaska (in 1926) and eventually became manager of Alaskan Airways in Fairbanks. In need of pilots, he invited both Robbins and Jones to join him. Robbins went, but Jones resisted.

Ryan had made Jones chief pilot. Life for him was exciting

Jerry Jones (with sunglasses) poses with three well-known Interior aviation figures (left to right: mechanic Jim Hutchison, pilots S. E. Robbins and Ed Young) on Weeks Field by an Alaskan Airways mail plane in the early 1930s. *Courtesy of Jerry Jones*

enough, thank you. Yet Alaska has always tugged at the hearts of romantics, and in 1931 he finally succumbed.

Accustomed to the benevolent skies of southern California, Jones found a hostile world in Nome, where Alaskan Airways stationed him. "There was nothing up there," he says of the desolate, frozen coastline. "And you had awful weather out of Nome. There was snow, snow, snow all the time. It would catch you in a hurry and you were stuck."

No aeronautical institution offered a course on how to fly in snow. No publisher listed a textbook on it. Other bush pilots could provide a few tips, but they were still relative newcomers themselves. For the most part, you learned to fly in snow the same way you learn how to swim if you fall out of a boat.

And snow wasn't the only enemy. "One of the awfulest things was, you could leave in good weather and all of a sudden there'd be a fifty-mile-an-hour wind over the whole landscape," Jones continues, folding his arms and leaning against a wall of the *Louel*'s cabin. "Everything below seems to be moving. The first time you see it you say, 'What the hell's going on here? How am I going to get down?' Well, boy, get down as fast as you can before it gets worse—and tie the airplane down good!"

One month he counted thirteen forced landings, most of them weather-related. He needed no warning about the danger of being stranded in the wilderness. "It's hard to find a ship down in the snow. They [search pilots] won't see one person. If you're out in it, you're gone. You're dead. That's a hard thing to explain. People don't believe this stuff. They say, 'Well, how did you survive?' Well, some of them didn't survive. Play that on your piano."

Like other bush pilots who did survive, Jones learned to be resourceful. His wife, Eileen, had followed him to Nome, and she accompanied him on one flight to serve as a nurse for a passenger who had just been released from the hospital. The destination was Candle, a tiny settlement about 150 miles northeast.

"We got three-quarters of the way from Nome and were coming along right by a mountain called the Ass's Ears when all of a sudden the J-5 engine went [Jones groans to simulate a dying engine]. I landed. My wife said, 'Now what do we do?' I said, 'Oh, we have a nice little walk.' "

Fortunately, the patient was ambulatory. Darkness descended on the trio by midafternoon, but snowshoes and skis from the airplane's emergency supplies helped them plod through the snow toward Candle. After about twelve miles they came upon a mining camp. There they found a caretaker family who gave them shelter and food.

In the morning, a postman with a dog team arrived on a mail run, and Jones sent his wife and the passenger along to more convenient facilities in Deering, a hamlet to the northwest on Kotzebue Sound. Then he snowshoed back to the airplane, examined the engine, and found broken teeth in a gear that served the main cam drive. At the mining camp again, he waited several days for the next dog team to come through and gave the driver a message to be sent by radio to Fairbanks. A day or so later, an airplane dropped replacement parts by parachute. Jones repaired the engine, flew to Deering for Eileen and the convalescing passenger, and finally resumed the flight.

Despite—and a bit because of—engine failures, forced landings, and abominable weather, Jones relished his job. Flying in a wild, spectacular land made working for Ryan seem dull by comparison, and like the few pilots who had come before him and the thousands who would follow, he kept turning the kaleidoscope to find out what would happen next.

One day an MGM movie crew from Hollywood arrived in Nome to engage a pilot for a polar bear film project. They got Jones. "They didn't think much of me at first," he admits. "I was short, and young, too." But the crew quickly gained confidence in him as he shuttled them about and scouted for bears in a Fairchild 71.

The crew set up camp on the pack ice several miles out in the Bering Sea, relying on their curly-haired pilot for supplies from the mainland. Among Jones's memorabilia are several fuzzy snapshots of the eighty-by-forty-foot ice house they had built. Sometimes he joined the crew inside, watching silently through observation ports as the huge white bruins prowled just yards away.

Periodically, he flew the film canisters down to the port of Seward south of Anchorage for shipment to the States. Before returning to the pack ice, he picked up fresh film the crew had telegraphed for—"along with ten cases of good old Canadian booze."

At Seward and other settlements, Jones frequently encountered fellow pioneer pilots, many of whom were to become legends. If they had time, or if weather grounded them, they would sit around, drink coffee, smoke, and chat. "I knew all those guys," Jones says, staring out the *Louel*'s windows at the thickly timbered hills behind Petersburg. Noel Wien was "a quiet man, good character, real sensible." Russ Merrill was "a wonderful man," Frank Dorbandt "a great guy," Matt Nieminen "a hell of a flyer." He

Jerry Jones, center, mechanic Fred Milligan, left, and another mechanic stand by a Consolidated Fleetster at Tanana in 1934. The winter shutters in the plane's engine helped retain heat in cold temperatures.
Courtesy of Jerry Jones

describes Joe Crosson, who called him "Schmultz" because of his mother's German background, as "a mild, wonderful person, the very best friend I ever had."

Jones met Lindbergh again in Nome when the hero passed through in 1931 with his wife, Anne Morrow, on a survey flight to the Orient. While the Lindberghs bought supplies and waited for suitable weather, Jones and other local pilots took photos, examined their float-equipped Lockheed Sirius, and asked endless questions about both the 1927 transatlantic flight and the current mission.

But all the collective aviation lore in the North could provide little guidance for Alaskan Airways when five scientists chartered the outfit for transportation to Mount McKinley's Muldrow Glacier for a cosmic-ray study in the spring of 1932. No one had ever landed on a glacier; famed glacier pilot Bob Reeve's first glacier experience was still a year away.

Crosson, who two years earlier had discovered the missing Hamilton of pilot Carl Ben Eielson in one of Alaska's most noted searches, decided to make the flight himself. After taking off from the frozen Nenana River, he landed without incident in the middle of the glacier with three of the party, at just above the 6,000-foot level. At that altitude, his Fairchild 71 needed such a long takeoff run before lumbering into the air that he had to make an immediate emergency landing to avoid an approaching ridge. On the second attempt—after the four men finally rocked and pushed the airplane free from snow and ice—Crosson coaxed the 71 safely into the air.

Rather than return to the glacier alone with the rest of the party, Crosson asked Jones to carry one of the scientists in an open-cockpit Stearman and serve as a wingman in case he had more trouble. Before takeoff, this time from a frozen lake, the two consulted on glacier techniques. "Joe and I decided that the safest place was probably away from the middle, where we thought there would be snow bridges that could collapse with the weight of an airplane," Jones says.

Like a pair of gnats ascending the wall of a sloping skyscraper, the two aircraft flew through snow showers up North America's highest mountain. For this landing, Crosson chose a stretch closer to the side near a large rock formation. Jones then lined up for an approach, held his breath, and also got down okay.

Jones remembers Crosson's words to the scientists as the two of them turned to leave: "Fellows, we got you up here in lousy conditions, but you're on your own now. We can't carry you out of here; you're too heavy. We'll drop you some supplies, but you've got to come out on skis or showshoes about sixty miles down to the railroad at McKinley Park Station."

The pilots turned their machines downhill and took off, Jones's biplane becoming airborne much sooner than Crosson's heavier cabin monoplane. Jones assumed he had made his first and only visit to the Muldrow Glacier.

But about a week later, when he had returned to Nome from a flight to a goldfield, a message was waiting for him. "It said the guys are in a hell of a mess up on the mountain. Two of the men, Carpé and Koven, fell in a crevasse and they're gone. Beckwith, an older fellow, got pneumonia. Spadavecchia had gone down toward Minchumina, hoping to find a trapper with a radio, and Olton went the other way and he got to McKinley Park Station first."

Crosson was in New York on business, so Jones flew to Fairbanks to stage a rescue mission for the ailing scientist. There he found a problem. It was early May now, and "breakup," the annual transition from winter to summer, had enveloped interior Alaska in a quagmire of mud, slush, and melting snow. Jones needed to be on skis to land on the glacier, but the spring sun had left too little snow in Fairbanks to take off on skis. The previously frozen lake at which he and Crosson had changed from wheels to skis for the second flight to McKinley was now mostly liquid. The situation called for bold bush pilot ingenuity.

"I asked the fire department to wet down the field so I could get off on skis," Jones says. With Weeks Field soupy in mud, he climbed into the Stearman and pushed the throttle forward. "I held the stick back and the airplane started feeling a little light. The city dump was on the other end, and there was an awful lot of junk up there that you don't want to get into. I tried to lift the right ski off, and it felt a little lighter, and a little lighter. We were getting not too far from that dump now, but then it was in the air."

At McKinley, he encountered a ragged ring of snow showers, as if the mountain had drawn a curtain around itself. But bad weather was a familiar adversary, and Jones managed to zigzag his way up the glacier to the camp. "That sick man was happy to see me," Jones says.

The idling propeller sliced at the falling snow while he strapped his passenger into the rear of the two tandem seats, then refueled from a jerry jug he had brought. "You always leave the engine running," he cautions. "When you're in a pickle, don't ever shut it off."

Reluctant to try threading the Stearman back through the same treacherous clouds, he risked a different route off the mountain. The gamble worked, and soon they were on course for Fairbanks.

Landing at Fairbanks on the same muddy field, Jones completed the first rescue with an airplane on Mount McKinley. "The man recovered and was okay in two weeks," Jones reports. "But he never even thanked me. Play that on your piano!"

To escape the pressures of bush flying and the often cold, dreary weather, Alaskan pilots have long favored periodic getaways in the Lower 48. Even on a business trip there, they traditionally allow extra time for relaxing. Jones and Crosson had more on their minds than just picking up two new airplanes on a 1933 visit to the States. In Chicago, they toured the Century of Progress International Exposition, a forerunner of the World's Fair. "We went to every damn thing there," Jones says. At a hotel in Jones's hometown of Syracuse, they had drinks with their mutual friend, the famous one-eyed pilot Wiley Post. (Two years later, Post and humorist Will Rogers would die in an airplane crash near Point Barrow.) Over in Buffalo, they got a sneak look at the prototype of the Consolidated PBY flying boat, which was to earn distinction for performance and ruggedness in the tough Aleutian Islands campaign of World War II. The two also stopped at Crosson's hometown in Kansas. "They called school out for the day and had a big deal there because they thought so much of Joe," Jones says.

By now Jones had survived almost three years of bush flying, which made any pilot a veteran in the pioneer days of Alaskan aviation. Veterans would seem to enjoy a little extra protection against a crash because of the skills and judgment they've acquired. But veterans are also more likely to take chances, more likely to be bold.

Through a merger, Alaskan Airways had become Pacific Alaska Airways and a subsidiary of Pan American Airways (later Pan American World Airways). One company mail contract included a stop at Eagle, a tiny community on the Yukon River near the Canadian border. "You couldn't land on the regular field there due to seven or eight feet of snow," Jones says. "When you get that much snow, skis are no good. So the only place you can land is on a beach." The beach at Eagle presented a short, narrow, curving "runway."

While Jones was waiting there for a favorable takeoff wind one winter day in 1934, the postmaster's daughter ran up and told him her dog team had just attacked her beau, biting him savagely before she beat the animals off with a chain. Could Jones fly him downriver to Fort Yukon right away? "It was snowing and going to get dark," Jones says, frowning. "What I should have told her was, 'No, we can't do it.' "

Yet in the demanding world of bush flying, it's hard to shake your head, to say, "No, I can't," especially when an attractive young woman is pleading in an emergency. As the Fairchild 71 roared across the snow-covered beach, struggling to attain takeoff speed, an alarm bell clanged in Jones's brain. Too late, he cut the ignition. "The river was broken with great big cakes of ice, and the first cake we hit the left ski went off, and that let the wing down. God, we weren't going over twenty-five miles an hour, but it knocked about four feet off the left wing and dinged the prop all up. Finally we stopped."

It was the only serious accident in Jones's 27,550-hour flying career. Both pilot and passenger climbed out uninjured (from the accident, that is). That night Jones helped sew up the man's seventy-seven dog-bite wounds, and a day or two later another airplane flew them to Fairbanks.

Jones welcomed a respite from the Interior winter in 1940 when Pan American assigned him and Robbie Robbins to make ten survey flights in large, two-pilot Sikorsky flying boats. The flights up and down the Inside Passage were in preparation for twice-weekly scheduled runs between Southeast and Seattle. But Southeast's banana-belt climate offered a few nasty substitutes for the Interior's frigid cold.

On the first northbound flight with passengers, heavy fog forced the men to land at the mouth of Taku Inlet south of Juneau and taxi eight miles up Gastineau Channel into town. The weather relented a bit two days later for the inaugural southbound leg, with territorial governor Ernest Gruening and 22,000 cacheted airmail letters from all over Alaska on board. But fog, stratus, and wind often plagued subsequent flights. If conditions ahead permitted, Jones and Robbins climbed to 10,000 feet or higher to escape. As often, they had to follow shorelines a few feet above the water, squinting through the windshield.

"Robbie and I got tired of shaking hands with all those islands," Jones says. "These fellows today have a lot of navigational aids we didn't have, and they can't understand how we flew it. Well, I kind of wonder how we did it, too. We didn't like it."

Neither did Pan American. After a year, the company substituted DC-3s for the flying boats and shifted the routing inland, away from the coastal weather. Soon the exigencies of World War II curtailed the run altogether.

The war also ended Jones's Alaskan adventures: Pan American sent him to South America, where he spent the rest of his career flying large transports around the Caribbean and South Atlantic. Once smitten with the romance of Alaska, however, a pilot is haunted by the sirens no matter how far abroad he roams. Several years after retiring in 1963 as the most senior captain in the company's Latin American division (number four in its international system), Jones returned and has lived in Petersburg ever since.

"Bob Ellis and I are the two oldest old goats in Alaska now," he boasts on the subject of surviving pioneer bush pilots.

Old *and* bold. Play that on your piano.

Bill English

— *Cherishing Two Cultures* —

WILLIAM D. ENGLISH says he doesn't know what career he might have pursued other than flying, but certainly he would have made a successful professional storyteller. While other pilots use ordinary prose when they talk about their Alaskan experiences, Bill English speaks with an almost poetic reverence—not just for aviation, but also for the land, the wildlife, and the people that filled his thirty-seven years of flying. It's subtle; there are no grandiose adjectives, no overt tributes. You don't listen for rhyme or rhythm. But his enthusiastic tone and melodic, youthful voice captivate you nonetheless. Sit with him in the living room of his Anchorage home, and the coffee table becomes a campfire. In the flames you can see a herd of caribou grazing on the tundra or a canoe gliding down a river.

A handsome, distinguished-looking man with mixed gray and black hair, English began absorbing material for such vignettes through early exposure to a vanishing grass-roots Alaska. Only a couple of dozen people lived in the old gold-mining town of Wiseman, 200 miles north of Fairbanks, when he was born there on January 31, 1923. As the son of an Inupiat Eskimo woman and a white Californian who ran the general store, English grew up amid two cultures. He learned to follow conversations in the Inupiat language, attended a one-room log-cabin school, and helped his family gather food.

At age four, he went aloft for the first time—before he had even seen his first car or train. English was too young to recall the air service or the airplane type on that flight from Wiseman to Fairbanks, but other memories linger. "I can remember looking down over Fairbanks at all those tiny people, and at so many strange things like cars and bridges," he muses. "And I was filled with wonder." Fantasizing about the flight later, he fashioned a squadron of toy airplanes from sticks.

Seven years Outside augmented his formal education, but home was always Alaska, and flying there his dream. When he returned to the Territory as a twenty-one-year-old, he worked at various jobs in Fairbanks to finance flying lessons and airplane rentals. Eventually his logbook recorded 200 hours.

In looking for a cockpit position, English faced two obstacles. First, air services in Alaska look askance at low-time pilots. A novice can't always tell whether the wind-whipped water below is too rough for his floatplane, or if he can stuff another twenty-pound mail sack into his wheelplane and still get off the strip. Anxious to prove himself, the novice sometimes takes foolish chances, or, afraid of establishing a bad reputation, he shies away from gentle wavelets and leaves half the payload behind to make sure he can clear the trees. Either way, the inexperienced pilot costs an air service money.

English's ethnic background became his second hurdle. In the Alaska of the mid-1940s, Natives, even those of mixed blood, were unwelcome in many restaurants and theaters. Few air services had yet entrusted them with their airplanes, passengers, and image.

But English's local knowledge worked in his favor. Expanding Wien Airlines needed more pilots, and many of the high-time Lower 48 cheechakos looking for flying jobs seemed helpless in the bush. The company had recently hired its first Native pilot, David Johnson, partly because he had grown up with the winter cold and summer mosquitoes.

This boy from Wiseman also had a commercial license and bush savvy. On a recent private flight he had shown good judgment by landing on a sandbar rather than remaining aloft in deteriorating

Bill English, right, and a gravity-meter reader on the Colville River by Umiat in 1948. *Courtesy of William English*

weather. And although it took eight days to walk out, he had emerged in fine condition. Maybe he'd learn quickly, despite his paltry flight hours. Still, English acknowledges, "Signing us on took a certain amount of courage."

At first, Wien turned him loose on only an hourly pay basis in a two-place Taylorcraft carrying mail and cargo. After he brought the airplane back from his village runs undamaged night after night, the company began including an occasional passenger.

Eventually satisfied with his apprenticeship, Wien offered him a salary of $300 a month, with no days off (employee benefits were then as scant in the Territory as civil rights). Junior pilots, Native or not, traditionally got the least desirable assignments, and English spent three summers and a winter landing a Cessna 140 every three to five miles on the North Slope so a scientist could step out with a gravity meter to geologically map potential oil fields.

As tedious as it was, all that landing practice may have saved his life one day in 1949, when the engine of his Cessna 170 lost power between Wiseman and Stevens Village. English had time to radio for help but insufficient altitude to glide to a good emergency-landing site. Only the side of a hill was available, and most pilots who come down on the side of a hill don't walk away. Because of the rising slope, you have to time the flare just right, and of course there's no second chance if you flub it.

English stopped the 170 undamaged in 100 feet.

The adventure had only begun. As an Air Force rescue helicopter was descending, a crewman prepared to toss out a phosphorus bomb to determine wind direction. Suddenly, the bomb ignited prematurely, shredding the crewman's hand and spraying him and the pilot with the poisonous phosphorus. The helicopter slammed onto the ground. A horrified English rushed forward and pulled the men out.

A second helicopter had only two empty seats, so English stayed behind after helping the injured men on board. Finally, with the Air Force balking at further participation, Wien sent out a mechanic, who poked around until he found a safe place to land his Cub.

When the two restarted the 170's engine, it seemed to run normally. English elected to take off, but the engine soon began sputtering again. This time he struggled into Stevens Village, left the airplane there, and returned to Fairbanks as a passenger in a Cessna 195 floatplane. Mechanics later discovered a partially plugged fuel screen in the 170.

A couple of years later, English was first at the scene of another crash, one that brought a startling discovery. By then Wien had checked him out in the line's DC-3s, and he was flying one of the big twins that day on a scheduled flight to Barrow. After holding outside the community until snow squalls passed, he proceeded in and landed. There, he frowned at some disturbing news: a company 170 from Wainwright was overdue. The pilot had radioed his position from twenty miles southwest, then . . . nothing.

A local pilot with a ski-equipped Super Cub offered to take a look, and English, deciding to delay the DC-3's departure, climbed in as an observer. They found pieces of the 170 scattered across a frozen lake several miles away, not far from where Wiley Post and Will Rogers had crashed sixteen years earlier. The pilot apparently had tried to squeeze through one of the snow squalls, lost visibility, and flown onto the lake at high speed. He and a female passenger were dead.

At first English and the local pilot thought they were the only occupants. "Then we heard a baby cry," English says, his voice hushed. "He was on his mother's back, which must have protected him during the crash. I cut open her parka and cradled the youngster, and we flew him to the hospital at Barrow." The baby had suffered a head injury but survived.

As his experience broadened, English moved up to larger airplanes such as the C-46, the F-27 turboprop, and the 737 jet. However, larger planes did not guarantee trouble-free flying. On the return portion of a cargo flight to a White Alice radar site in the early 1950s, his C-46 lost the generator first on one engine, then on the other (both turned out to be faulty). To conserve what power remained in the batteries for landing, he and the other pilot shut off their navigational radios and dead-reckoned on top of a solid undercast to Bettles, the nearest community with decent weather. As they let down through the clouds, they held their breath, hoping their crude navigation had been accurate. A serious error could take them into a mountain peak. They broke out at about 6,000 feet, and Bettles was right where it should be.

English remembers the time in the late fifties when unexpected fog closed most airports in the Arctic as he and his crew were returning from a supply drop to scientists on the other side of the North Pole. They had planned to refuel at Barrow but now had to continue all the way across the Brooks Range to Fairbanks. After a fifteen-and-a-half-hour round-trip flight, they landed the big four-engine Lockheed Constellation with just ten minutes' fuel left in the tanks.

On two occasions, locked brakes on one side of an F-27 created a serious steering problem on landing, and in 1974 a 737 nosewheel that refused to extend made for an anxious hour (and a frantic phone

Bill English on an Arctic lake with a Wien Air Cessna 140 floatplane in 1948. *Courtesy of William English*

call by Wien to Boeing engineers).

But English handled these and other emergencies with professionalism. By the time his sixtieth birthday forced his retirement in 1983, he was number two in Wien's seniority system and the best-known Native pilot in the state. He was the first Native in Alaska to earn an airline transport rating (now called an airline transport pilot certificate), and the first to be designated an FAA pilot examiner. He was also a check pilot for Wien and a member of the company's board of directors.

After his retirement, the Alaska State Legislature presented him with a citation applauding his aviation achievements, noting that he had taken time during his career to earn bachelor's degrees in business and transportation.

For young Natives struggling to adapt to encroaching cultural changes, few people could serve as a greater inspiration than Bill English. Yet, as he reflects on his career today, he minimizes the high-paying, status-filled years when he wore a gold-braided captain's uniform on a sleek 737. His thoughts dwell instead on the early days: "In jets up at 30,000 feet you get a broad perspective of what the world looks like, but there's no detail. And after the FAA banned passengers from the cockpit, a distance was put between crew members and passengers which we didn't have in the old days. On trips in smaller planes to Nome, Barrow, Kotzebue, and other places, we frequently had visitors come to the cockpit for a while, and we were able to see moose and sheep and of course lots of caribou. I can remember seeing whales between Nome and Saint Lawrence Island. Rarely did we see them while flying the jets.

"In the villages you'd get a lot of help from people. That was one of the enjoyable things about flying in the bush in those days. Of course, people were dependent on air transportation; it was their contact with the outside world. But in the spirit of being friendly and helpful, you knew you always had a place to stay, regardless of where you were. You were always well taken care of. The spirit was there. I liked that. Villages are still dependent on the airplane, but now they have telephones and TV, and there are a lot more air services. So people do have contact with the outside world in other forms. And they have their own snow machines and outboard motors. Many of the villagers have airplanes, too, so the relationship has changed. Help is still available, but before, they were eager to help.

"I remember one day I was trying to bring a floatplane from Barrow to Fairbanks. It was the end of the summer season in 1948, and when I got into the Brooks Range I ran into a snowstorm. Chandler Lake was nearby, so I landed there by a small Eskimo village to wait it out. It was getting dark, and the shoreline was very rocky. I could see some villagers watching from the shore as I tried to find a place to park the airplane so it wouldn't get battered in the wind and waves. All of a sudden I ran onto a sandbar. I tried to power it off, but it wouldn't move. I was stuck there, maybe two hundred feet offshore, and it was cold. 'What am I going to do now?' I asked myself.

"Soon I saw two men walking out toward the airplane along a narrow sandspit. They may not have known how to swim, and the water was frigid. They were really risking their lives for me. But they reached the airplane and pushed me off the sandbar and told me where to find a sheltered spot. They were Nunamiut—inland Eskimos—and one of them, Frank Rullund, turned out to be a cousin of mine. He invited me into his hut. It was a skin hut, which they made by tying willows together and covering them with caribou skins. For these people lived off the land. They caught fish in the lake and shot sheep in the mountains and caribou in the pass. There were no trees in that area, so to get the willows they had to go sixty miles down to a river. It was a nomadic way of life, a way that had changed little over hundreds of years.

"Frank's hut was warm and cozy, with Frank and his wife, and two children and two dogs. His wife fixed a dinner of tenderloin and biscuits—very tasty. I slept quite comfortably while the storm raged outside, and in the morning the weather was fine and I continued on my way.

"But it's an Alaska we won't see again, for those people now live in permanent buildings at Anaktuvuk Pass with a school, an airstrip, a post office. And of course, those conveniences are welcome to them. But regrettable changes have come to many villages, especially the introduction of alcohol. In the old bush pilot days, we delivered mail, medical supplies, and food, and it was a service we were happy to engage in. We knew what we had on board and could control it. But now people can ship pretty much anything they want. I've seen villages that were virtually liquor-free, with people who were healthy and living happy, useful lives, that now have liquor and drugs in abundance, and it's been all downhill.

"Natives more and more have come to grips with the issue. Some villages have banned liquor, and there are efforts to revive some of the old culture. That sort of pride is good to see, as long as people remember to keep the best parts of the new culture. No one wants to get out of the airplane to go back to the dogsled."

English, who throughout his career refused to transport alcohol, continues to look to the future as he cherishes the past. Since retiring from Wien, he has earned his mechanic's license ("just to stay busy") and has accepted several contract positions as jet flight instructor or director of operations for airlines. He occasionally flies a business jet on charters, and he sits on the boards of directors of several non-aviation corporations.

He also speaks to various school and civic groups about bush flying. For the listeners, the experience is a lesson in both history and storytelling.

Bud Bodding

— Father Goose —

RETIRED PILOTS usually associate their peers with certain characteristics or incidents. One might be especially remembered for pushing the weather hard, another for the time a black bear chased him off the airport at Ruby.

Mention the name Bud Bodding to fellow pilots and two things come to their minds: an incredible survival story, and the Grumman Goose. The associations are unrelated except in the sense that Bodding probably would not have lived to become the world's premier Goose pilot were it not for a remarkable coincidence after an emergency landing.

A lifelong Southeast resident, Gerald A. "Bud" Bodding was a twenty-four-year-old pilot for Ketchikan's Ellis Air Transport in October 1941 when he took a steamship south to Seattle to relax after the busy season. He had planned to return on the ship, but Tony Schwamm of Petersburg Air Service phoned and asked him to ferry a four-place Waco floatplane he had purchased up the Inside Passage instead. Always eager for a chance to fly, Bodding enthusiastically accepted. Harry Sherman, brother of Ellis chief mechanic Jack Sherman, was also in Seattle on vacation and rode along in the right front seat.

The two spent the first night at Alert Bay, British Columbia, then took off in the morning for Petersburg. As they worked their way up the coast, Bodding began to worry about finding the right channels in the thickening drizzle and fog. Navigation would soon be the least of his worries, however: over Milbanke Sound, an exposed body of water that often gives boats a rough passage, the Waco's 225-horsepower Jacobs engine suddenly quit, possibly from carburetor icing.

Bodding's voice remains calm today as he relates the story; after all, it's been fifty years. But anyone who has flown a small, single-engine seaplane along the North Pacific coast and glanced at the deep, rolling swells in the exposed sections can imagine the fear that must have surged through the men's veins after the abrupt silence up front. "I turned toward a little island and tried to land parallel to the swells," says Bodding, whose bifocal, wire-frame glasses, neatly combed-back gray hair, and composed manner seem to befit a retired businessman. "We hit hard downwind, and over we went in the swells."

The impact slammed both men into the instrument panel. Bodding stayed conscious, but Sherman was dazed. Bodding unbuckled his passenger's seat belt and pulled him from the Waco. "I was afraid he'd drift away, so I tied him to one of the upside-down floats with my belt."

As Bodding clung to the other float, the swells and waves slowly pushed the plane closer and closer to the island—Salal Island, they would later learn—about a hundred yards away. Gradually Sherman, who had broken a wrist, regained alertness. The men exchanged few words; there was little to say, but a lot to think about. The Waco had carried no radio to scream "Mayday!" into, even if the emergency had granted enough time. They were alone. Searchers would have hundreds of miles of remote, undeveloped coast to scour. Meanwhile, the two would face hypothermia in the October air, for all their emergency supplies were under water. They had no matches, no dry clothing, no sleeping bags. Already they shivered in the chilly ocean.

Suddenly, the men detected the droning of an airplane engine above the slapping of the waves and the screeching of the sea gulls. The sound grew louder and louder. "We couldn't see the plane because of the fog," Bodding says, "but we heard it fly by pretty close. Then it faded away. But a minute or so later we heard it coming back; the pilot must have turned around when the visibility got too low. This time we just caught a glimpse of it. Then we heard it crash on the island."

Powerless to help, Bodding and Sherman could only speculate on the occupants' fate—and their own.

After about a half hour, the Waco met a current that countered the push of the waves. It stopped drifting. A mere twenty or thirty yards separated the men from the island at that point, so they swam to shore. Numb from cold, they began working their way over the beach rocks toward the area where the plane had crashed.

"Pretty soon we came onto a duck that just sat there without fear of us," Bodding says. "We knew we'd need food to survive, so I sneaked up to it, grabbed it, and wrung its neck."

Close to the crash site now, the men entered the dense rain forest and located the wreck. "It was Livingston Wernecke's Bellanca Skyrocket," Bodding continues. "He was a mining engineer, and he and his pilot, Slim Gropstis, were dead." Based in Mayo, Yukon Territory, the two apparently had been bound for Seattle.

Bodding and Sherman could do nothing for Wernecke and Gropstis, but in a sense the victims could help them. The Waco pair salvaged everything from the wreck that could improve their chances of staying alive: clothing, matches, a rifle, tents, sleeping bags, food. Then they set up a camp well away from the wreck and hunkered down to wait for searchers.

On the fourth day, a Royal Canadian Mounted Police patrol boat looking for the Bellanca (the search for the Waco had been abandoned) sighted the survivors' signal fire and picked them up. The crew took them to the cannery town of Klemtu, on Swindle Island, where a nurse gave them medical attention. The next day, a U.S. Coast Guard cutter shuttled them to Ketchikan, pausing at Salal Island to collect the bodies of Wernecke and Gropstis.

Bud Bodding was not yet a pilot in the late 1930s, when he worked as a mechanic's helper for Alaska Air Transport in Juneau for $90 a month. Here he's standing on a float of ATA's Lockheed Vega. In 1940, before starting his career with Ellis Air in Ketchikan, he worked briefly for famous bush pilot Bob Reeve in Valdez.
Photo by Lloyd Jarman

What if the Bellanca had crashed elsewhere along the coast, or if it had burned, or if better visibility had averted a crash at all, or if the Waco's engine had quit a couple of minutes earlier or later? Bodding still wonders.

The next July, with the United States embroiled in war, Bodding joined the Navy and began his long affair with the Goose.

Today you might still find a Goose in southeastern Alaska. Maybe even two. Before newer airplanes began replacing the Goose in the 1970s, however, Southeast's fleet included twenty or more of the Grumman JRF twin-engine amphibians. All day, every day, they roared off waterways or runways on scheduled flights or charters, lugging up to nine passengers and an assortment of cargo and mail, bound for camps, villages, towns, and lakes. Until Ketchikan got its own airport in 1973, airline travelers coming or going had to use the old military field on Annette Island, twenty-three miles away. It was the Goose that shuttled them. Longtime Southeasterners know the Goose real well.

Bodding eventually logged a record 18,000 hours in the airplane (out of a total flight time of 23,500) during his career with Ellis and its successors. Not that you'll tally that much Goose experience if you line-item his logbooks: he quit making entries after 12,000 hours or so. But he figures 18,000 is a conservative estimate, and people in the knowledgeable community of Alaskan aviation have dubbed him "Father Goose." If a pilot somewhere else figures *he* deserves that title, let him step forward.

Nonpilots can't imagine how anyone could spend 18,000 hours in the cockpit of an airplane that sprawls in the water like a bug and squats on land like a bulldog. But nonpilots know nothing about romance. Incorporated into the Goose's beef and bulk are two rumbling radial engines, rugged workhorse dependability, and the taste of both land and sea.

"The Goose is the most wonderful airplane ever built," Bodding says quietly. A touch of melancholy is evident in his voice, as if he's reminiscing about a mistress from long ago. "It was a very stable airplane, very forgiving, probably one of the best rough-water airplanes."

Rough-water capability is crucial in coastal Alaska, where North Pacific gales often join a waiting line to howl in; try driving your car at the Goose's takeoff speed of fifty-nine knots (about sixty-eight miles an hour) for a couple of hundred yards over a road ridden with potholes and ridges. Thanks to its battleshiplike construction, the Goose can frolic in water that would bend a Cessna.

But no airplane can hold together during an emergency landing on coastal Alaska's cliffs and glaciers or in its forests. Engine reliability was especially important because, as Bodding observes, "the Goose wasn't an airplane you'd bring home on one engine." There's little streamlining in that thick wing, wide hull, and the round cowlings. Lose one engine and parasite drag makes quicksand for the other. If you've got a moderate load, you'll probably be unable to maintain altitude and will have to make an unscheduled landing.

Getting down safely in any relatively small piston-engine twin with one engine out can produce sweat on the brows of even veteran pilots such as Bodding. Asymmetrical thrust creates control problems, and if the speed drops too low, the airplane will roll over toward the inoperative engine. People who think a twin provides twice the safety of a single-engine plane had better take a look at National Transportation Safety Board statistics, which consistently show that after an engine failure, the fatality rate in the twin is actually higher.

Fortunately, Goose pilots seldom have to contend with such problems. Grumman engineers developing the Goose selected the 450-horsepower Pratt & Whitney R-985 Wasp, which turned out to be one of history's most successful powerplants, the same engine that pulls another renowned bush plane, the de Havilland Beaver. Bodding practiced single-engine work in a Goose during his training, but never once in 18,000 hours did he have to bring one home like that.

The Navy chose wisely, then, when it detailed the Goose as a personnel and mail carrier between bases in Alaska during World War II. Bodding was an ensign stationed at Kodiak when he got his introduction to the airplane. He had spent the previous weeks in a Grumman Duck, a single-engine amphibian infamous for tough handling, and by comparison the Goose seemed "quite an upgrade."

A native of Juneau, Bodding might have found himself in fighters or bombers overseas if he hadn't begun flying for Ellis before the war. When he joined in 1942, the Navy decided he could fly well enough already to skip formal military flight school. To utilize his civilian talents and training, the brass kept him in the Territory rather than waste his three years of local experience in Europe or the South Pacific. Too many Lower 48 greenhorns assigned to Alaska were wrecking planes or aborting flights because of weather.

By the time he returned to Ellis after V-J Day, Bodding had

amassed plenty of Goose hours. The relationship promptly resumed. For its postwar expansion plans, the company needed a seaplane that could safely haul lots of people and gear, something Bodding had regularly done in the Navy. "We'd fill up the gas tanks, then stuff mail into the baggage compartments and fill up all the seats, and away we'd go," he says, smiling slightly. "I never saw the day when we could stick a Goose." (You "stick" a seaplane by loading it so heavily that it can't get off the water.) He and Ellis founder Bob Ellis, who had also worn Navy wings in Alaska during the war, agreed that only the Goose would do.

Ellis bought its first war-surplus Goose in 1945. By 1959 it owned nine, and a merger with Alaska Coastal Airlines of Juneau in 1962 boosted the number to seventeen (out of a total fleet of twenty-four aircraft). Yes, longtime Southeasterners know the Goose real well.

Like his employer, Bodding appreciated the Goose enough to remain with the airplane and the company for the rest of his career, rather than follow the usual bush pilot route of moving on after a few years to larger machines and fancier uniforms. Serving as chief pilot and a director as well as a line pilot lent extra responsibility to the job for Bodding. And Southeast was home.

Like every aircraft model, the Goose has a few personality flaws, beyond generic ones such as single-engine unwieldiness. For instance, a pilot naturally wants to keep track of rocks, trees, or water if he has to make a sudden tight turn in low visibility. But no matter how close to the windshield you stretch your neck during a turn in a Goose, a cowling blocks your view.

The Goose can also be unruly on wheel landings due to its tail-wheel-gear configuration and narrow wheelbase. Ironically, while Bodding never ground-looped a Goose, the wheels were down during his worst career landing.

Returning to Ketchikan from the Annette Island airport one day in 1947, he had just one passenger, who sat up front in the right-hand seat. The weather was great, and the two spent much of the fifteen-minute flight chatting—or yelling, as you must if you wish to communicate verbally in a Goose cockpit without headphones and an intercom system. They were still bantering as Bodding throttled back and lined up on Tongass Narrows. Lower and lower the Goose descended. Absorbed in the conversation, Bodding failed to notice several fellow Ellis employees jumping up and down on the dock and frantically waving their arms at him.

Although an amphibian like the Goose provides the flexibility of operating from land or sea, the pilot has to put the gear in the appropriate position for landing: up for water, down for land. Touching down on a runway with the wheels retracted scrapes the bottom of the hull, perhaps damages a wing float, and makes one hell of a noise. Usually that's it—embarrassing but not excessively expensive.

Landing on water with the wheels extended, however, is a major error. The wheels connect first and cause such an abrupt deceleration that the nose pitches down, usually resulting in a flip. Sometimes alert bystanders can get the pilot's attention in time; sometimes a rearward center of gravity will keep the plane from going all the way over. But on that day, the bystanders gestured in vain, and Bodding had no weight in the rear.

Splash. The passenger scrambled out the upside-down cabin door first, followed by a chagrined Bodding. Both got wet but were unhurt. The company pulled the Goose out of the water and eventually sold most of it to a Seattle salvage dealer. Airplanes dunked in the ocean aren't often worth renovating because of pervasive, corrosive salt.

Never again did Bodding forget to raise the gear after takeoff from a runway or to check for retraction before landing on water. Even so, "There are still people who remind me of that day," he adds, smiling self-consciously.

Occasionally, passengers who stepped off an airliner at Annette and climbed on board the waiting Goose for the shuttle to Ketchikan would be unaware of the airplane's amphibious nature. As the plane would land in Tongass Narrows—well, more than once a pilot heard

An Alaska Coastal Airlines Grumman Goose taxis along the Juneau waterfront in 1946. *Photo by Lloyd Jarman*

a sudden scream in back. During a normal water landing, water typically cascades over the cabin windows, confirming the neophyte Goose passenger's impression of a crash. Bodding claims he dutifully informed arriving Annette passengers that the landing at the Ketchikan end would be on water, but other Goose pilots acknowledge they sometimes kept mischievously silent.

Besides being unfriendly to the careless and the naive, the Goose was "rather chilly at times in the winter." You'd think that for all the noise and power they produce, a pair of 450-horsepower engines could also supply enough heat to keep the whole airplane toasty. Of course, R-985s generate plenty of heat, but in the Goose, as in many other World War II–era aircraft, the heat is largely untapped. Back then, aeronautical engineers thought more about performance than plumbing and insulation.

"In the old days we furnished blankets to passengers," Bodding says. "Later we also used gas heaters, which improved the comfort somewhat, but even so on real cold winter days it was not warm."

You can almost see him shiver as he recalls the winter afternoon in 1948 when heavy snow forced him down on upper Seymour Canal with a full load of Juneau men bound for Ketchikan. Snow continued to drape a murky curtain around the Goose as dusk descended several hours later. No chance even to sneak back into Juneau, just seventeen miles to the north. They were stuck for the night.

Bodding grounded the airplane on a beach on an outgoing tide, then passed out the blankets. Periodically during the night, he fired up the engines to make sure they would start in the morning. At those times, the gas heater could also be run. But the cold kept everyone cringing in his seat. "It was the longest night I've ever spent, because I could see the luminous dial on that clock and watch that hand tick, tick, tick every second," he says.

Dawn revealed a foot of snow on the Goose, and fresh snow was still falling. When Bodding radioed the company to check in, he learned that the Coast Guard had dispatched a cutter from Base Juneau to the vicinity. To locate the airplane in the heavy snow, the crew had to take a bearing on it with the on-board direction-finding equipment. By then, however, the snow had finally relented a bit, allowing just enough visibility for flight. The passengers elected to remain with Bodding rather than ride into Juneau on the cutter.

The entire group climbed back on board for the continuation of the flight the following day, when conditions were better. "The experience didn't discourage any of them," Bodding says. "People had a lot of faith in us in those days. Everybody looked up to a pilot; everybody knew you. Consequently, you had a lot of friends."

Such loyalty worked two ways. One night in the mid-1950s, Bodding had already gone to bed when the phone rang: a pregnant woman in Hydaburg on Prince of Wales Island was in labor and needed immediate evacuation. Ellis had shut down hours earlier, because the night obscures reefs, logs, and other objects that can damage a seaplane. But Bodding called a company mechanic for assistance, then rushed down to the waterfront. The two got a Goose into the water and took off.

Good weather helped Bodding navigate by darkened islands and waterways to the village, where the woman and her mother were waiting on the dock. He landed at daybreak. "We took off with them and headed for Ketchikan," he relates. "About ten minutes out of Hydaburg this girl's mother came forward and said, 'She's having the baby!' So I poured a little more coal to it and called for a doctor to meet the airplane."

Streaking through the dawn sky at a high-cruise speed of 160 knots, the Goose (Stork?) reached Ketchikan in fifteen minutes. There, an ambulance whisked the woman and her child to the hospital, where both were admitted in excellent condition. But the mother—now grandmother—stayed behind for an important mission. While Bodding was filling out his flight log for the trip, she tapped him on the shoulder. "I hope you don't tell the papers about this," she whispered, "because we don't know who the father is."

In the 1962 merger with Alaska Coastal, Bodding retained the title of vice-president of operations. He continued to fly the line most days, however, preferring the cockpit to an office where "I just twiddled my thumbs." Another merger with Alaska Airlines in 1968 burdened him with additional office duties, so he resigned his vice-presidency.

He also declined an opportunity to qualify on Alaska's jets. Computers, autopilot, regimentation, cruising in the clouds miles above the deer in the muskeg meadows—he'd stick with the Goose, thank you. But by then the Goose had become an endangered species in Southeast. Alaska Airlines wanted to modernize its fleet and was already replacing some of the Grummans with new, two-pilot, turbine-powered Twin Otters. Soon Ketchikan would have its own airport on Gravina Island on the other side of Tongass Narrows, and ferryboats would eliminate the Goose shuttles. Routes to the bush communities would be subcontracted to a local air taxi that used Beavers and Cessnas.

It was time to get out.

On October 28, 1972, Bodding made his last flight, a scheduled run to the Prince of Wales communities of Hydaburg, Craig, and Klawock. At each stop, residents gathered on the dock to thank Father Goose for his years of service. Friends, family, and fellow pilots greeted him at the Ketchikan terminal with more gifts and best wishes.

Then fifty-five, Bodding bought the forty-foot cruiser *Mytime* and spent the next eleven years running charters in it. These days he's busy with landlubber projects such as working on the house he's lived in since 1952.

Most of the 345 Gooses the Grumman Corporation built at Bethpage, New York, between 1937 and 1945 have also retired. Whereas Gooses once thronged the Ketchikan waterfront, Bodding now has to turn to his photo albums or a painting on the north wall of his living room to see one. After a twenty-year absence from the cockpit, he'd probably even have to take a couple of lessons to renew his acquaintance with the airplane if he decided to fly one again.

But in the annals of Southeast aviation, the term Father Goose will forever belong only to Bud Bodding.

Sig Wien

— *The Eskimos' Friend* —

AT THE *ANAKTUVUK PASS* village airport in May 1987, an elderly man with glasses stepped off a Frontier Flying Service Piper Cheyenne to a hero's welcome. The entire ambulatory population of 270 Nunamiut Eskimos had gathered to greet Sigurd Wien. Many residents had never met him. Some forty years had passed since he had flown his Bellanca there regularly, and he had visited the village only occasionally since retiring from commercial flying in 1948. Wien was now eighty-four.

Yet all but the toddlers had heard about the quiet pilot who long ago had assumed the role of father protector and regularly brought the village food, ammunition, medicine, and other supplies, on credit, in snow, fog, and bitter cold. They knew he had helped the Nunamiut move from a nomadic camp at Chandler Lake to the permanent settlement at Anaktuvuk Pass, and that he had learned their names and their customs. He had been a friend as well as a lifeline.

So the village decided the time had come to thank him officially. Frontier Flying Service provided free transportation for Wien to the Brooks Range community from Fairbanks, 260 miles southeast. At least one of the Eskimo greeters at the airport bore the middle name Wien, in honor of Sig. After taking the guest on a tour of the village, the hosts staged a banquet that included caribou stew and dancing. Then they presented him with a pair of exquisitely fashioned homemade snowshoes.

There's more to the Wien legacy than Sig. His brother Noel, four years older, was one of Alaska's earliest and best-known pioneer pilots. Wien Airways, which Noel founded in 1927, endured through several mergers and name changes for more than half a century as northern Alaska's most successful and beloved airline.

Among the Natives, however, Wien means Sig—"Sigwien," as many called him, unaware the name was two words. Not only at Anaktuvuk Pass, but at villages along the Arctic Coast—Kotzebue, Point Hope, Wainwright, Barrow, and others—Eskimos revered Sig Wien as their link to the outside world, their guardian angel in troubled times. He seemed to have an innate affinity with them, as if he belonged more to their world than his own.

Although other pilots flew to the villages in summer, for years he alone provided regular air service during the winters. The sound of an engine would intrude on the frigid silence, prompting residents to come out of their shacks. "Airplane!" (or its Eskimo equivalent), someone would yell. All eyes would scan the horizon. "There it is!" Moments later, a skiplane would circle, then thump across the snow next to the village. From the late 1930s through much of the '40s, the pilot who emerged in a heavy fur parka was usually Sig Wien.

Daily service was impossible. The villages lay dozens of miles apart, and unless clear skies prevailed along the route, Wien had to restrict his flying to the daytime, which in the darkest part of winter consisted of just a few hours of twilight. Even when the sun had crept above the horizon, navigating could be challenging due to the desolate, almost featureless landscape and seascape, cloaked in a relentless white that stretched in all directions like endless sand on a desert.

When fog or a snowstorm blanketed the coast, visibility shrank to a few feet and Wien tied down the airplane. Sometimes traveling from one village to the next took days—or weeks.

In early February 1944, an axle on the landing gear broke as Wien was taxiing his Bellanca into position for takeoff from Point Lay, a small coastal community of sixteen huts and a schoolhouse.

He used the village radio to relay a request to Fairbanks for replacement parts, but for more than a week snow and clouds grounded pilots in the Interior. At last an airplane with the new axle on board took off. It crashed in the ocean at Nome. Renewed bad weather delayed a second plane's departure from Fairbanks.

Meanwhile, Wien and his three passengers were struggling to survive more than just boredom. The supply ship from Seattle had been unable to reach the coastal villages that fall because of unusually thick ice. "There was a shortage of supplies and fuel," Wien says laconically. "The schoolteacher we stayed with was totally out of fuel and virtually out of food. So it was interesting."

With temperatures as low as twenty-four below inside the school, the teacher canceled classes indefinitely. Frost coated the desks, the floor, sleeping bags, everything.

Finally, thirty-six days after the Bellanca's mishap at Point Lay, the second airplane got through and delivered the new parts.

While the Eskimos could not count on Wien to arrive on a specific date, they knew he would show up eventually, that he would keep trying. Whether or not a supply ship had reached them in a particular year, the isolated villagers greeted each landing like kids waking up on Christmas Day. What had Sig brought this time? A letter from a relative? The new rifle ordered from Fairbanks? Magazines to read?

For his part, Wien, who at different times was based at Nome, Kotzebue, and Barrow and thus knew the Eskimos from a resident's viewpoint as well as a pilot's, enjoyed playing the Santa Claus role. With no family of his own, he cherished the Eskimos' company. "It was virtually a continuous visit, going from village to village," he says. "I knew all the people, and the people looked forward to the plane coming."

Among peers and passengers, Wien was notorious for his reticence and shyness. One fur buyer who traveled with him to several villages reported that in hours of flying the pilot uttered just two words: "Five wolves," after banking to point out the animals. You

Sig Wien stands before a single-seat, forty-five-horsepower Buhl LA-1 Flying Bull Pup at Fairbanks' Weeks Field in 1936. *Photo by Noel Wien*

still notice those traits in him today. He grants few requests for interviews, and while he dutifully answers questions, he volunteers little information and is slow to smile. The Eskimos have always liked him despite his introversion, or perhaps because of it. They appreciate his polite, gentle, patient manner.

Wien's aversion to the limelight extended to his official capacity as manager of the airline, a responsibility he acquired in 1940 when Noel sold him controlling stock in the company for $15,000. Noel needed the money to finance a convalescence trip Outside for his ailing wife. Preferring the cockpit to a desk and the Arctic's solitude to the bustle of a flight-operations headquarters, Sig continued to fly. For several years he lived in Barrow to make North Slope oil exploration flights for the U.S. Bureau of Mines and the

Navy. Not until 1948, when the growing airline demanded more managerial attention, did he return permanently to Fairbanks.

His move to management actually constituted the third major element of his aviation experience. Wien had studied maintenance as well as flying at the Boeing School of Aeronautics at Oakland, and he worked as a mechanic for Noel from 1935 to 1937, when he earned his commercial license and turned to full-time bush flying.

Of course, knowledge of mechanics was essential to an arctic pilot in the early days. Even if the Bellanca could have accommodated a regular mechanic in addition to piles of mail and supplies, keeping him on the payroll might have bankrupted the company. Flying out a mechanic every time something broke made no more sense because of the time involved and the difficulty in contacting civilization in the first place; not every place in the bush had a radio.

It was Wien himself who installed the new axle at Point Lay, working outside in the arctic winter. On another occasion, he mended an oil cooler with borrowed soldering equipment at Little Diomede Island in the Bering Strait. Returning to the mainland from the island, which lies within shooting distance of the Soviet border, Wien noticed the oil-pressure needle had dropped to zero. Below lay the open Bering Strait, with its deadly cold water. No place to land the Bellanca if the engine seized. "There were a few minutes of tension not knowing whether I was going to make it back to Diomede," Wien comments unemotionally. "But these things were just routine. Flying then was a continuing adventure."

Aerial adventure had enveloped Wien on his initial trip to Alaska in December 1930. Noel came to the States for a visit, and Sig, not yet a pilot, rode back to Fairbanks with him as a passenger in his brother's Stinson from the family farm in northern Minnesota. The fourteen-day flight apparently was the first anyone had made over the inland route in winter between the States and Alaska, and it involved many weather-related detours.

But adventure can quickly turn to tragedy in north country aviation. Two months before that flight, brother Ralph had died in the crash of a diesel-powered Bellanca at Kotzebue.

That Sig survived 15,000 hours ("kind of tough hours," he notes) intact testifies to his skill, judgment, and, to some extent, luck. Ingenuity, too. One summer day, while he was landing at Cross Island off the Arctic Ocean in the late 1940s, his Noorduyn Norseman decelerated too quickly on the soft beach, and the airplane went up on its nose, damaging the prop. Two days later a new propeller arrived at Barrow up the coast, and Wien pilot Cliff Everts flew it and a mechanic to the island in a Norseman floatplane. They brought along an empty fuel barrel to use as a ladder.

After beaching, a floatplane pilot normally secures the airplane by tying the float's mooring line to some object on shore—a stump, a boulder, a tree, a derelict boat. But the Cross Island beach afforded no anchor within the length of the line; all the men could do was push the plane a few inches farther onto the beach, leaving the line loose.

Wien had joined them, and the three carried the new prop and rolled the barrel up the beach toward the damaged Norseman. They bantered in good spirits, for the Arctic basked in seventy-degree sunshine. At one point, Wien turned around and saw the floatplane drifting away, probably sucked off the beach by the current. Everts and the mechanic ran to the plane, hoping to grab the mooring line, but it had already been pulled into the sea beyond reach. In southern Alaska, a pilot could charge into the water and swim a few yards without risking hypothermia. But even in summer, the frigid Arctic Ocean tolerates no such tactic; although the bay in which the floatplane had landed was ice-free, floes caked the water on the other side of the island.

Everts and the mechanic ran around the island onto a spit on the chance that the Norseman would drift within their grasp. It didn't. Meanwhile, Wien had rolled the barrel back down the beach and was fashioning it into a raft. Several logs that had spewed into the ocean from a nearby river had washed up on shore. He tied two on either side of the barrel to prevent it from rolling, then, with the help of

Everts and the mechanic, who had returned from the spit, pushed the rig into the water. Each of the others offered to ride the makeshift raft, but Wien insisted on handling the risky mission himself. Straddling the barrel as if it were a fat horse, he paddled out to the errant Norseman with a shovel, climbed on, and taxied it back.

Wien brought the same ingenuity and leadership to the business side of the company after he retired from flying. In 1968, Wien Air Alaska merged with Northern Consolidated Airlines to become Wien Consolidated Airlines, with Sig as chairman. By the early 1970s the company, again called Wien Air Alaska, employed more than 800 people and operated Boeing 737 airliners as well as a variety of smaller aircraft.

That was enough success for him to begin relaxing, to start thinking about retirement—and other things. At age seventy he married for the first time, and two years later he became a father. Today he's the last of the famous Wien brothers (a fourth, Fritz, had also worked for the company as a pilot and mechanic and served on the board of directors), the last of the pioneer arctic bush pilots. Besides raising a belated family at his home in North Pole, down the road from Fairbanks, he spends hours in his garden. You can't help thinking of Voltaire's Candide, who also turned to reflecting in a garden after traveling a long road of adventure and challenge.

"I don't find life boring at all," Wien says. "This is probably the best part of it." As our conversation becomes philosophical, his reticence begins to melt and he smiles kindly. "Get old enough to get wise. The best years are ahead of you."

Fred Chambers

— Lost on the Nulato —

Among the disappointments wrought by the December 1989 eruptions of Redoubt Volcano, west of Anchorage, was the cancellation of a special reunion flight to mark the anniversary of an event that had occurred half a century before. On December 19, 1939, pilot Fred Chambers and three passengers made a forced landing on the frozen Nulato River after an oil line vibrated loose in their single-engine Fairchild 24 skiplane. They spent the next three days together waiting for help in the winter wilderness.

Chambers, still an active pilot, has kept in touch with his fellow castaways throughout the years, and to commemorate the fiftieth anniversary he had planned to fly them over the scene ("with two engines this time," he wryly notes), then treat them to a dinner in Nome, the original departure point.

How characteristic of Chambers. An effervescent, optimistic gentleman, he's every host's ideal party guest: an organizer, a volunteer, a stalled-conversation rescuer. Meeting him, you'd be surprised to learn that he was born in 1917—but not that he made his 564th parachute jump on his seventieth birthday. He seems dashing. Maybe it's his easy smile and laugh, his trim, hale figure, the sparkle in his eyes. Maybe it's the way he strides across the living room of his Soldotna home to hold out a chair for a woman.

Eruption or not, Chambers was not the sort to let the golden anniversary of the most momentous event in his 35,000-hour flying

Fred Chambers at the Nome airport in 1939 with the Fairchild 24 in which he later made a forced landing. *Courtesy of Fred Chambers*

career slip by without a celebration. Nor would he allow Redoubt's acidic fallout to ground his enthusiasm as well as the reunion flight.

So, he put Plan B into effect. First, a trip to the exhibition area of the Alaska Aviation Heritage Museum by Lake Hood to gaze at a Fairchild 24. "We wondered how in the world we survived for three days in that little thing," he muses. Then, an elaborate dinner at an Anchorage restaurant. As the group reminisced about their grand adventure so long ago, looking at photos, reading old newspaper clippings aloud, and toasting their survival, eavesdropping diners at an adjacent table bought them a second bottle of champagne.

Chambers was a twenty-two-year-old pilot for Nome's Mirow Air Service when he took off that December morning in 1939 with Madge Jefford, nineteen, her fifteen-month-old son, Billy, and twenty-eight-year-old Joe Walsh. All were bound for Fairbanks, a long flight even in summer. Because of the short winter day, Chambers planned to overnight at Koyukuk, on the north bend of the Yukon River.

It happened 200 miles into the flight, at 4,500 feet on top of a stratus layer covering the Nulato Hills east of the Seward Peninsula: blue smoke suddenly began pouring from under the cowling. The oil pressure needle promptly dropped to zero; in moments, Chambers realized, the engine would seize. Remembering that the valleys in the area ran northeast/southwest, he turned to a heading of sixty degrees and descended into the clouds.

For a minute the adults sat rigid, holding their breath, cringing against a violent meeting with trees and rocks. But Chambers' strategy worked—they broke out over the middle of a river valley.

"I figured it had to be the main branch of the Nulato," he says. "I flew down the river for several minutes. Then the engine started smelling hot, and the oil smoke quit pouring out, so I knew the oil was gone and that the engine was about to freeze up. I throttled back. Up ahead I spotted a bend in the river with an open spot."

The Fairchild's equipment included the first voice communications radio of the era, a high-frequency Lear T-30, and Chambers had been broadcasting the predicament from the time it began. Even while the airplane was still in the air, Mirow Air Service owner Hans Mirow and a few employees had gathered around the radio in Nome, listening. When Chambers stopped transmitting to concentrate on the emergency landing, the Nome crew cocked their heads and waited tensely.

At Koyukuk, the station operator's family had been cooking dinner for the inbound Fairchild people. They too leaned toward the radio.

Then, at both places and others where Alaskans were monitoring the aviation frequency, receivers crackled again, bringing welcome news: the Fairchild was down safely at the headwaters of the river, twenty-five miles from the village of Nulato, Chambers thought. In fact, they were about thirty-five miles away.

Mirow wired a telegram to Nulato, and mushers set out immediately toward the scene with dog teams in the midafternoon nightfall. But they turned around several miles from the airplane, figuring they had traveled far enough to conclude that the pilot had estimated his position inaccurately. "I didn't know why they didn't hear me," Chambers says, shaking his head and smiling. "I knew they were on the way from the radio, and every two hours I'd go out and fire my rifle, and oh, the sound just echoed up and down that canyon."

News in Alaska spreads like rumors at a boarding school; by dawn most of the Territory knew about the missing airplane. Because the passengers included a baby, the news quickly fanned across the Lower 48, too. In his hometown of Mifflinburg, Pennsylvania, Chambers' parents first learned their son was "lost in the wilds of Alaska" from Lowell Thomas's national radio program. Thomas broadcast updates until the rescue.

Interest in the story deepened when Hans Mirow and a mechanic, searching in a Gullwing Stinson, themselves disappeared.

Meanwhile, the Fairchild occupants were surviving with the minimum of discomfort despite six feet of new snowfall. The airplane's emergency supplies contained sweet chocolate, Eagle brand condensed milk, dried eggs, and dried vegetables, and with fuel he drained from the tank, Chambers ran the firepot (for preheating the engine) to warm the food and make cups of hot chocolate.

At night, when temperatures dropped to a relatively mild minus-fifteen, the adults huddled in the rear of the Fairchild beneath a heavy-duty sleeping bag Walsh was taking to Fairbanks for cleaning. Little Billy stayed warm in his mother's sealskin coat as he slept on the ledge above the baggage compartment.

"We just ran out of most of our food and fuel by the time they got to us, so we never really suffered," Chambers says. "But if we had been there any longer it would have been quite grim."

During the day, Chambers kept in touch with fellow Mirow pilot Jack Jefford (Madge's brother-in-law), who was at search headquarters in Nulato. Searchers were scouting other rivers because of the mushers' negative report on the Nulato River, but the strength of the radio transmissions convinced both Chambers and Jefford that the Fairchild was indeed close to Nulato.

Cloud cover and snow showers during the day continued to

The Stinson SR-5 was a favorite with air services in the 1930s and '40s. *Photo by Lloyd Jarman*

hamper efforts to investigate further, but the weather cleared at night. Jefford decided to try a late-night search and told Chambers to light a fire if he heard his Stinson-A Trimotor wheelplane approaching.

Shortly after 2:00 A.M. on December 21, the drone of engines interrupted the still night air. Chambers snapped on the Fairchild's running lights and lit a pile of pine boughs. Nulato villagers riding as observers spotted the lights instantly, and Jefford air-dropped additional supplies, including a steak.

About 1:00 P.M. the next day, mushers reached the group and evacuated them.

Chambers then joined the search for Mirow, and on Christmas Eve the wreckage of the Stinson along with the bodies of the two occupants were found in the trees about six miles west of Kaltag. Mirow apparently had been trying to follow telephone lines into the village in a thick snow shower and descended a little too low. The ruddy glow on Chambers' face seems to dim as he talks about this aspect of the adventure, recalling once more that two men died looking for him.

Jefford, one of Alaska's best-known early bush pilots, again figured prominently in Chambers' aviation career two years later, when Chambers decided to get an instrument rating. Jefford (who by then had begun an illustrious career with the Civil Aeronautics Authority/Federal Aviation Administration) recommended American Airlines for that purpose and wrote a reference letter for Chambers to a vice-president he knew in the company.

"My idea was, okay, I'll go to work for American and get my instrument rating and pick their brain for six months and then come back to my beloved Alaska," Chambers says. But soon he decided that flying for a large airline made more sense for a career-minded pilot. The six months turned into thirty-seven years.

Yet the call of Alaskan aviation remained in his blood. He took a leave of absence in the winter of 1946 to fly for Bill Munz's Northern Airways in Nome and returned periodically throughout the rest of his career for brief flying stints. After his eleven-year marriage to a Nome woman ended in divorce, she returned home with their four children, giving him even more reason for visits to Nome.

Chambers was there in May 1957 to see his kids when a telegram arrived from Wales, a village up the coast. A ten-year-old girl had stomach pains, possibly appendicitis, and needed evacuation to Nome, the message read. Northern Airways asked Chambers to make the flight. How fortunate for both him and the girl that he had kept his hand in bush flying. "The weather was bad," he says. "It was snowing and blowing, with about a quarter-mile visibility at Wales. But I was able to come down through a hole and land on the sea ice. The villagers brought her out with a dog team."

Were it not for the gravity of the situation, the mushers might have laughed at him; he hadn't had time to don bush pilot garb and greeted them in his Lower-48 big-city tweed suit and crushable hat.

Back in the air, Chambers maneuvered the Gullwing Stinson around areas he knew to be turbulence-prone to give the girl as smooth a ride as possible. "I looked back at her now and then to reassure her, and we smiled at each other. At the Nome hospital, it turned out that she didn't have appendicitis after all; she had just eaten too much walrus."

During other breaks from his airline routine, Chambers flew for missionary organizations. (His brother, John, served as a flying missionary in arctic Alaska and wrote the book *Alaska Bush Mission.*) On one missionary project, he parachuted into the Colombian jungle and helped hack out a 1,600-foot landing strip on a plateau near the equator. The strip is still officially named Chambers Field.

After retiring as a senior 747 captain in 1977, Chambers came back to Alaska for good to volunteer his pilot services for Missionary Aviation Repair Center in Soldotna. He had arranged to use MARC's Navajo for the 1989 reunion flight, but because of the uncooperative volcano, Madge, Billy, and Joe will have to retrace the 1939 route in their memories or imaginations.

On his MARC flights, Chambers had already looked down on the Nulato River emergency-landing site several times before the anniversary, and he's viewed it at least twice since. "The river course has changed considerably since 1939," he reports. "If I dropped down into the valley and made a low pass, though, I could pinpoint the place within a quarter-mile."

By now he probably has.

RUTH JEFFORD

— *Wings and Strings* —

AT *JUST FIVE FEET TALL*, Ruth Jefford has to sit on a cushion to see over the instrument panel of her V-tail Bonanza. The cushion is well used, and she fits snugly on it behind the controls. Jefford is comfortable with the surrounding geography as well. We're cruising at 1,800 feet above nondescript streams and mud flats on the upper Kenai Peninsula, en route to Soldotna, sixty-five miles southwest of Anchorage. Although haze cuts visibility to ten or fifteen miles and few landmarks stand out below, Jefford uses no chart or navigational radio.

In more than fifty years of flying, she's ridden that cushion in several dozen airplanes over lots of familiar routes in southcentral Alaska. But it's no paradox that such a diminutive woman might challenge the skies in a land that has claimed many strong men.

Jefford was the first woman in Alaska to earn a commercial pilot's license, the first woman instructor at Anchorage's Merrill Field, and the first woman air taxi operator at Anchorage International (for nine years she ran the business alone). Today she rides a motorcycle, sails an iceboat in winter, and flies the Bonanza to school reunions in the Lower 48. She's signed on with a group of pilots from around the country who plan to fly their own aircraft to Provideniya and Anadyr on an upcoming tour of Siberia.

No, Ruth Jefford isn't too small for Alaska.

"It's a shame it's so hazy today," she calls above the roar of the 250-horsepower engine. Her large, intense gray-blue eyes scan the east, toward the Chugach Mountains, and the northwest, toward the Alaska Range. "The mountains are pretty. Usually you can see Mount McKinley from here."

Various flights have taken Jefford through passes in those and other mountains, partially fulfilling a childhood fantasy. At the age of four, as she was swimming one day on Lake George in upstate New York (where her father was headmaster of a prep school), she noticed a Curtiss flying boat land and taxi to shore. It was the first airplane she had ever seen, and she stared at it, transfixed. In a dream that recurred for weeks afterward, she flew her brown rocking chair over the Adirondack Mountains.

Studying her resolute mouth and chin, one can easily imagine Jefford as a plucky teenager hanging around the local airport after school, wheedling rides from freshly soloed students and accepting the inevitable late-for-dinner scolding at home. One can also picture her pedaling a bicycle out to a Nebraska field where an airplane has just landed. It's 1937, and her father has become president of a small college in Fremont. Pilot Jim Hurst stays airborne so long trying to impress the young woman who has asked for a ride that his Arrow Sport runs out of fuel in the middle of the field just after landing.

Hurst became her instructor. "I couldn't afford goggles right away, and my left eye was bloodshot all the time from leaning out in the windstream to see," Jefford says with a hearty laugh. "I was so nervous before my checkride that I went into the ladies' room and threw up. Then I went out and passed it." Her blond hair bobbles as she laughs again. It's a pleasant, ingratiating laugh, one of the reasons acquaintances greet her enthusiastically on the ground.

Hurst also became Jefford's husband and, in early 1942, her ticket to Alaska when his employer, the Civil Aeronautics Administration, transferred him to Anchorage.

"On our arrival here it was January and raining and pretty dismal, but I gradually fell in love with the beauty," she says, waving a hand at scenery that today hides behind the murky air. "The first time I saw the northern lights, I must have watched them for two

Ruth Jefford learned to fly in this Arrow Sport in Nebraska in 1937. She got up at 4:00 A.M. and drove fifty miles to take lessons before 8:00 A.M., when her instructor taught army cadets. *Photo by Jim Hurst*

hours out the back-door window. I had never *seen* anything so beautiful."

The prevalence of aviation in the Territory also intrigued her. Soon she had her commercial and instructor certificates.

But Jefford brought to Alaska more than a romantic inclination. The same fingers that are now fine-tuning the prop control and changing frequencies on the radio once flitted across the strings of a violin, producing concert-quality tones. She studied music under scholarships at the American Conservatory in Chicago, the Cité Universitaire in Paris, and the Mannes College of Music in New York.

To inject a little culture into what in 1942 was a frontier town of 3,500 people, she helped found the Anchorage Symphony Orchestra. For thirty-eight years she served as its concertmaster. She also played in the Anchorage Symphony Quartet and a string quartet of her own, gave music lessons, and during breaks in flying went on concert tours, including one to Russia. Finger stiffness in the late 1980s finally forced her to stow her violin permanently. Fortunately, she can still play the two pianos in her home. Jefford remains active in music associations as a nonplaying member, and she sits on two museum boards of directors.

As the only woman instructor on Merrill Field, and such a tiny one—she had to stand on the tire to check the oil in some aircraft—Jefford probably seemed unimpressive to some members of the aviation community at first. In Alaska more than most places, however, performance and character melt prejudices, and she quickly found acceptance. Using her own 1941 Taylorcraft and customers' aircraft, she taught on wheels, skis, and floats. Her students included the CAA regional administrator and the president of the National Bank of Alaska. At least three students eventually became airline pilots.

"I used to carry a knife, and when I instructed in other people's floatplanes I'd go to every exposed attach point in the tail and scrape through the rust to see how far it went down," Jefford says, grimacing as she laughs. She picks up the microphone and radios the Soldotna flight service station for advisories at the airport, ten miles away now.

Rust never did create a problem in the air, but on one winter instructional flight carburetor icing did. The Piper PA-11 she was teaching in had an experimental 115-horsepower engine that, she subsequently learned, lacked an adequate carburetor-heat control. Icing suddenly choked off power to the engine, and Jefford made an uneventful touchdown on frozen Lake Spenard near the present international airport.

With another student, heavy snowfall forced a precautionary landing on a road in Canada. The student had asked Jefford to keep him out of trouble in his Super Cub on a flight from Anchorage to St. Louis, Missouri, and she took over the controls when the snow began between Watson Lake, Yukon Territory, and Fort Nelson, British Columbia. Unable to reach an airport, she set the Cub down by a gas station. Relentless snow showers grounded them there for the next four days.

Snow again forced Jefford to take over while they were passing through the Edmonton, Alberta, area. "I had to get down to 250 feet and follow the railroad tracks," she says. "The tower over at Industrial Airport [now Edmonton Municipal] cleared us to land, but the weather was so bad I couldn't see the approach lights." When she told the controller she was going to land in a field instead, he advised against the idea and suggested that she contact Namao Air Force Base. A controller there provided radar vectors to a runway at that military airport. She and the student spent the night in a nearby motel while the Cub sat parked beneath the wing of a B-36 bomber.

Jefford continued instructing part time for several years after she and Hurst started International Air Taxi in 1957. By 1961, they had divorced, though their business association continued. Hurst, diabetic and no longer eligible for a pilot's medical certificate, asked Jefford to handle the flying. In compensation two years later, he signed over the airport lease and air taxi certificate.

Ruth Jefford logged about 600 hours in this Cessna 175 before buying a Cessna 180 to meet a new rule for FAA contracts.

Photo by Stan McCutcheon

Jefford was on her own.

Twelve customers who rented aircraft-tiedown spaces paid for the lease, and charters and government contracts made her a successful businesswoman. One contract, a weekly mail run to the village of Skwentna, seventy miles northwest of Anchorage, provided steady income for twenty years. She enjoyed being a one-person operation and resisted expanding. Answering the phone, typing up government reports, pulling on wing covers, pumping fuel into the tanks of her aircraft (first a Cessna 175, later a Cessna 180), shoveling snow off the apron—she did it all, save maintenance and tax returns.

Because Jefford was an operator rather than a hired hand, she encountered little male chauvinism beyond some initial skeptical expressions from passengers. Composed and confident, she would have brushed off wisecracks anyway. But the question of chauvinism inspires an anecdote: "Once, over the Alaska Range, I had a seven-year-old boy on board. He had gotten some stick time flying his parents' Super Cub, so I let him handle the controls for a while. Then it started getting quite turbulent, and I asked him if he wanted me to take over. He said, 'Do you think you can handle it?' " She erupts in laughter.

Often, her professional attitude toward flying helped hesitant passengers relax even before she started the engine. Two men seemed a little nervous one day when they climbed into the 175 for a sightseeing flight. "As I went about my usual preflight routine, they kept watching me, I guess to see if I knew what I was doing," Jefford says. "As I was checking the oil I heard one of them tell the other, 'Gosh, you don't see a Northwest Airlines captain out there looking at the dipstick.' "

Jefford never asked for special treatment, but occasionally she got it anyway, like the time she flew a radar technician to a Distant Early Warning station at Cape Newenham on the Bering Sea and a doting sergeant in the club restaurant offered to prepare dinner for them. Her meal: a thick steak, French fries, and a salad stuffed with freshly cooked shrimp. The technician's: a ham sandwich. "I don't think male pilots were treated to such a feast," she notes with a chuckle.

A cautious, skilled pilot, Jefford avoided serious accidents in her career, although several contracts took her to mountainside strips with an incline so steep she had to land uphill and take off downhill, regardless of wind.

On the only occasion when her airplane was damaged, the culprit was an unfortunate combination of factors. Flying a charter to Skwentna in 1968, she had a very heavy load of three men and an outboard motor, which gave the 180 a rearward center of gravity and rendered the tail especially susceptible to ground-looping. When she touched down at the strip, a stiff crosswind from the right forced the tail to the left. Ordinarily, she would have been able to hold the tail straight with rudder. Unknown to her, though, the tailwheel mechanism had broken, and the 180 ground-looped. Everyone escaped harm, but the left wing and tail scraped across the ground. "My pride was hurt, too," she admits.

As the Bonanza crosses the Kenai River, she cancels her flight plan, which she files for every trip, even on short hops in good weather. "There's great fishing in the river," she calls. "Very famous for salmon."

She acquired a figurative copilot in 1972 when she married Jack Jefford, a well-known Alaskan pilot who had retired from a distinguished career in the CAA/FAA. They ran International Air Taxi until 1975, then sold it, moved to Wasilla thirty miles north of Anchorage, and founded Valley Air Transport at the Wasilla airport. After Jack died in 1979, she continued the operation herself for another two years. Skyrocketing insurance premiums finally persuaded her to get out of commercial aviation. In addition to the Bonanza, she kept the Cessna 180, which is now on floats and ramped behind her lakeside home in Wasilla.

Because both husbands worked for the CAA/FAA, her friends include many others who did, too. She joins them for a traditional weekly luncheon in downtown Anchorage.

The landing gear thumps into place, and Jefford lines up on Soldotna's Runway 25. Although any pilot would rate the touchdown as excellent, she comments, "I don't deserve much applause for that one."

There's been no shortage of applause from other arenas. In 1972, the Ninety-Nines, an organization of women pilots formed in 1929, awarded her its annual Amelia Earhart Memorial Scholarship; Jefford is a charter member of the Alaska chapter. In 1988, the Alaska Airmen's Association presented her with a citation that "recognizes the excellent contributions made to Alaska general aviation by Ruth Jefford." And she was the recipient of the 1990 annual pioneer women's award of the OX-5 Aviation Pioneers, whose members have to have flown or worked on an airplane powered by the OX-5 engine before 1940. A Travel Air biplane she flew in Nebraska qualifies her for membership.

On the apron, she steps to the ground and exchanges warm hugs with the pilot we have come to visit. After sitting beside her in an airplane for a while, standing next to her is a bit startling, because it's easy to forget how petite she is. In other ways she seems so lofty.

Ray Renshaw

— *Everybody's Favorite* —

RAY RENSHAW doesn't seem to have changed much over the years. While many retired pilots bear only a vague resemblance to their youthful selves, Renshaw's tall, willowy frame and angular features stand out instantly in a group photo taken half a century ago. He just looks a little more seasoned today.

The same holds for his personality. Pilots who flew with him back then all agree: "Ray was the nicest guy you'd ever want to meet." He still is. Call him up for an interview, and sight unseen he'll invite you to his modern, spacious home overlooking Juneau's Fritz Cove.

Renshaw greets you with the grace and friendliness of a gentle civil servant. Right after seating you on his living room sofa, he fetches his aviation photo album. There's no need to ask questions about this scene or that. Although he last handled the controls in 1980, his enthusiasm for flying hasn't changed, and he provides a fascinating commentary on practically every photo.

Renshaw built his career in southeastern Alaska, but the first few pages in the album show him as an aviator in western Washington State. Unlike most of his Southeast contemporaries, who learned bush flying on the job, he came to the Territory already well versed in the art. Born in Seattle in 1909, he turned to flying after a succession of boring post–high school stints in a picture-frame store, a specialty coffee store, a machine shop, and a dry-battery company.

At the Olympus Flying Club on Boeing Field in 1928,

Renshaw's ground school instructor turned out to be Bob Ellis, who would soon become one of Southeast's best-known pilots. Ellis headed for Alaska the next year, but Renshaw stuck around to continue flight training. Under a special arrangement, he did odd jobs at the club for compensation in both flying lessons and pay. When the club folded owing him a lot of both, he settled for one of the club's assets, an OX-5–powered Command-Aire biplane.

"I barnstormed around the state for a while," Renshaw says in a distinctive voice that reflects his pleasant personality. "And I remember helping a guy with his milk run down at Centralia in between. Finally, I traded the airplane for a car and went back to Seattle."

That's when his bush training really began. He got a job flying for Gorst Air Transport, a seaplane operation based at the old Pier 3 on Elliott Bay by downtown Seattle, and spent the next four years flying customers to Victoria, British Columbia, and various islands and mountain lakes. He also air-dropped supplies to winter mining camps in the Cascades. The supplies included more than just food and toilet paper. "One camp wanted several cases of dynamite," Renshaw recalls with a chuckle (he says almost everything with a chuckle). "We were a little dubious the first time we took this powder up, because we had asked the guy at the powder house if this stuff would blow up if it hit a rock, and he had said, 'I don't know.' Well, we heaved the dynamite out into the snow, away from the cabins, and one of the cases hit in the creek and smashed all to hell." As he tells the story, you can picture him cringing in the cockpit and shielding his head with his hands. Then he adds, "But it didn't go off. You need a real detonator to set off powder."

Gorst used ancient single-engine Loening, Boeing, and Eastman flying boats. This type of aircraft floats on its hull instead of pontoons and has a few operational quirks. Of a photo showing him sitting in the Boeing, looking tall in the saddle, Renshaw says, "Once you got onto it, flying it wasn't so bad. But notice where the engine is [on top of the fuselage]. It's a pusher, and there was so much torque on takeoff your foot couldn't hold it straight, so we had to

Ray Renshaw (right) and an assistant unload containers of trout fingerlings from Herb Munter's Aircraft Charter Service's Bellanca Pacemaker on floats at a Southeast Alaska lake in the late 1930s. *Courtesy of Ray Renshaw*

get a bungee to hook the rudder pedal down. It also had a flat bottom, and if you didn't know how to set it down right it would just leap like crazy."

His fingers, long and thin, turn the album pages to scenes of the Ketchikan waterfront and of old floatplanes on tree-lined lakes in southern Southeast. Renshaw was too busy lumbering around western Washington to give the North Country much thought until 1935, when Ketchikan's new Aircraft Charter Service offered him a flying job.

Western Washington and Southeast share North Pacific coastal weather. Southeast's variety is a little more intense, but Renshaw had flown through enough drizzle and squalls in those cumbersome flying boats to fit right into the Ketchikan aviation world. He felt so much at home, in fact, that he's remained in Southeast ever since.

His new assignment called for doing maintenance on as well as flying Aircraft Charter's Waco, Bellanca, and Stinson floatplanes. For a while he slept in an apartment he'd set up in the hangar. "Sometimes I'd work half the night fixing planes after flying all day," he says. "I'd just be falling asleep about 4:00 A.M. and the phone would ring, and someone would say, 'We want to go fishing,' not knowing I had been up most of the night. It was summer and daylight already, and they'd have to be at their own jobs at eight. So I'd take them out." It's hard to imagine easygoing Renshaw turning down eager sport fishermen, regardless of how bleary-eyed he felt. After dropping his passengers at the lake, he'd catch up on his sleep by napping in the airplane while waiting for them.

People in the thriving commercial fishing industry also frequently called on Aircraft Charter Service. Besides flying to the thirteen canneries operating in southern Southeast in those preconservation years (decimated salmon runs eventually forced most to close), Renshaw flew night patrols to hunt for pirates trying to rob fish traps. A licensed mechanic, he fashioned a searchlight out of a Ford auto headlight for the Bellanca and would flick on the light when over a fish trap.

He points to a shot of one of these traps. "Everybody knew each other in those days, and when they [fish pirates] saw me on the street during the day they'd say, 'Ray, you're not playing fair with those night flights!' We could fly at night only when it was clear, so the guys learned to go out in stormy weather."

Some of the pirates apparently took the patrols seriously: Renshaw occasionally found what he suspected were bullet holes in the Bellanca.

The Ketchikan pages of the album include a photo of a Stearman wheelplane on a mud flat at Bostwick Inlet on nearby Gravina Island. The pilot was ferrying the biplane from the Lower 48 to Skagway, and Renshaw took off to help that day in 1938 as the plane circled town, obviously looking for a safe place to touch down amid the area's thick forests and spongy muskeg. Ketchikan would have no airport until 1973, and the (now-closed) Annette Island airport twenty-three miles away hadn't yet been built. Like a shepherd he led the Stearman to Bostwick Inlet, where low tide had exposed the mud flat.

Renshaw himself had to look for an emergency landing site three years later. He had picked up a new Monocoupe in the Lower 48 in late November, 1941, and was ferrying it to Fairbanks for the Alaska Game Commission. He knew the airplane's magnetic compass was inaccurate because of an installation error, but he figured he could navigate without it by using a chart. That strategy worked fine until he got to Watson Lake in the Yukon. "I had a map for that part of the area but nothing between there and Whitehorse. So I started following river valleys, assuming they were heading west and that eventually I'd hit the Yukon River. But I ran into fog and couldn't tell what was below me. Then it started to snow, and the visibility really dropped."

Problems in flying often seem to pile on top of one another, almost conspiratorially. As if Renshaw needed more of them, dusk had begun to settle over the wilderness around him, and the Monocoupe's fuel supply was dwindling. Suddenly the engine

Ray Renshaw flew this Eastman Flying Boat as a pilot for Gorst Air Transport in Seattle in the early 1930s. *Courtesy of Ray Renshaw*

coughed and sputtered, possibly from ice in the fuel lines.

What had been worry turned immediately to fear. Through the fog and snow he spotted a frozen stretch of river up ahead and managed to land safely there without damage to the airplane. The parade of emotions continued. First, relief at being safely on the ground. Then loneliness as he listened to the engine pinging from dissipating heat, the only sound other than the crunching of his boots on the snow. And finally hope, for he was not entirely alone: the Monocoupe had a radio.

"I called out that I was down and raised a station in Anchorage. I told them I wasn't sure of my position but that I was down on some river."

The next day he saw a twin-engine airplane pass by in the

distance, too far away to identify or attempt to hail. Again he radioed Anchorage and reported the sighting. That was his last transmission. The icy cold sapped the battery of its remaining power.

While he waited for search planes to find him, Renshaw struggled to stay alive. He built a lean-to and converted an empty gas drum he found into a stove to combat temperatures that dropped to thirty below over the next several days. "I found out why animals go underground to stay warm," he says with his habitual gentle laugh. His only company was a persistent bluejay that wanted a share of the airplane's emergency food.

Meanwhile, rescuers had finally figured out from Renshaw's sighting of the twin that he must be on the Pelly River. An Electra flew up the river, spotted the pilot waving his arms, and dropped a sleeping bag, food, and a note informing him he had come down ten miles from the village of Pelly Crossing. Renshaw thawed out the Monocoupe, which had just enough takeoff room and fuel for the short flight.

Although the bombing of Pearl Harbor happened less than a month after his return to Ketchikan, the album shows no photos of Renshaw in uniform. Like many Alaskan pilots who tried to enlist, he found that his flying services were considered essential at home. Still, he contributed to the national defense through dozens of chartered offshore patrols with Navy and Coast Guard personnel, hunting for Japanese submarines. Renshaw also spent one of the war years flying for Ketchikan's Ellis Air Transport after pilots Bob Ellis and Bud Bodding were called to active duty in the Navy within Alaska. When Ellis returned to Ketchikan, he discovered that his niece had become Mrs. Ray Renshaw.

More pages turn, revealing photos of the Alaska Coastal Airlines Gooses, PBYs, and other aircraft Renshaw spent most of his working hours in after moving to Juneau in 1945. Ten years in Southeast had made him a senior member of the region's flying fraternity, and the company soon acknowledged that experience by naming him chief pilot. Like a first sergeant, a chief pilot has to come down hard on his charges when they make mistakes. A line pilot who wrinkles a float in excessively rough water or snaps at a tardy passenger will probably do it again unless his chief pilot disciplines him. That Renshaw held the position until his retirement from the company in 1969 proves a nice guy can be tough, too.

He would like to have kept his chief pilot status indefinitely, but in 1968 Alaska Coastal merged with Alaska Airlines, subjecting the company to a ridiculous FAA rule that proclaims a pilot too old for major airline flying at the arbitrary age of sixty. Obviously, some pilots are unfit for the cockpit at forty-five, while others can continue doing the job safely at seventy-five. Renshaw had had no accidents or incidents during his twenty-four years with Alaska Coastal, could pass all required tests, and had years of valuable experience left to offer. Yet, when he turned sixty he suddenly became too old to fly, in the judgment of the FAA.

"I wasn't quite ready for a desk job yet," Renshaw says with no trace of the bitterness many pilots would feel toward involuntary retirement. The rule applies only to outfits that operate schedules with large aircraft, so he became a corporate pilot for Champion International, which planned to construct a lumber and pulp mill at Echo Cove in Juneau.

He taps a photo of the airplane he flew for four years in that job, the "Super Goose," a turbine-powered version of the standard Goose. "That was fun to fly," he says. And different. After years of taking loggers and fishermen on relatively short hops in well-worn piston Gooses and other bush planes, he now was transporting businesspeople on nonstop flights to Fairbanks and Portland in a posh, high-performance conversion. To carry enough fuel for such long missions, Renshaw persuaded the FAA to authorize a 3,300-pound increase in gross weight.

When a Sierra Club lawsuit prompted Champion to drop its Juneau program, Renshaw became an air service chief pilot again, this time for Southeast Skyways in Juneau. He intended to stay only a year to help Skyways revamp its flight operation. But pilots have a way of hanging around, and the job stretched into six years, ending when he married for the second time.

His first wife had died in 1973. While visiting her in a Seattle hospital, he had met a woman whose husband was hospitalized there, also for a terminal illness. The two stayed in touch, and after six years they decided to marry. Renshaw gave up flying to spend more time with her.

"Well, that's the end of my story," he says, laughing softly as he closes the album. At that point, it's pretty hard to avoid the same kind of bittersweet feeling that comes after the last page of a great book.

DON HULSHIZER

— Day of the Lunatic —

RECLUSIVE WOODSMEN, seiner skippers, tobacco-chewing loggers, prospectors, Eskimos—colorful are the people of the bush, people who usually travel by air to get a dose of civilization. When the conveyance is a single-engine bush plane, such characters can rub shoulders with the pilot. They can exchange quips about the weather with him, ask him questions about the world, tell him stories about the bush.

Or pump up his pulse like the nastiest blizzard.

Forty years have passed since Don Hulshizer endured an hour with a passenger who proved to be a bit too memorable, but during our conversation in Fairbanks I can see him shudder a couple of times, as he relives that bizarre flight.

It was June 8, 1951, and Hulshizer was a thirty-two-year-old Wien Alaska Airlines pilot who had come north with his wife five years earlier to escape a tedious flight-instructing job in Oregon. He had just landed at the Yukon River community of Fort Yukon on a scheduled mail run from Fairbanks. He smiled as he taxied the Noorduyn Norseman off the strip to the ramp. In those days, as now, bush pilots often had to fly well into the evening during the busy season, sometimes not getting home until 10:00 P.M. or later. Today, however, had been unusually easy. This was his last flight and Fort Yukon his only stop. The Interior glimmered in balmy, late-spring sunshine, threatening no weather delays.

As he pulled mail and freight from the Norseman, Hulshizer

calculated he would be back in Fairbanks in time for dinner, with a couple of hours to spare. Imagine sitting down to dinner at home in June!

Then Wien's Fort Yukon representative walked up and told him that two passengers at Circle Hot Springs needed transportation to Fairbanks. A small resort with naturally heated mineral water, Circle Hot Springs lay about eighty-five miles to the south. A fairly minor detour; it should still be an easy day. Hulshizer loaded the 300 pounds of outgoing Fort Yukon mail into the Norseman and took off.

After landing in Circle Hot Springs, he learned that his passengers were a married Fairbanks couple, and that the husband was mentally ill. A Fairbanks doctor had prescribed several days of rest for the man at the spa, but the management had ended up asking him to leave. He apparently had neither slept nor eaten, spending his time instead wandering about bare-footed, praying, and preaching to the other guests.

"He appeared to be about twenty-five and probably weighed 200 pounds," Hulshizer says. A trim, serious-looking Nebraska native who wears wire-frame glasses, he speaks rapidly with a resonant voice. "I judged the woman to be a little younger. The U.S. commissioner brought them out to the airfield with their luggage and a couple of boxes of canned goods, which belonged to them. I asked the commissioner about someone escorting them to town, but he told me that the fellow was harmless and that his wife would watch over him." Satisfied, Hulshizer placed the two in the rear of the plane, behind the pile of outgoing mail.

A Norseman takes about an hour to fly from Circle Hot Springs to Fairbanks. Hulshizer soon began counting the minutes. "Not too long after takeoff the man unfastened his seat belt, crawled forward, and asked if he could smoke a cigarette. I told him I would rather he didn't; the airplane was fabric-covered and could burn readily. He said that was okay and went back to his seat."

Glancing over his shoulder a moment later, Hulshizer saw that the passenger was raving to his wife with strange, wild hand gestures. Periodically he would hit his head with his palms, then resume the gesturing.

By now Hulshizer had leveled the Norseman at 5,000 feet over the snowcapped White Mountains. "Everything went along nicely for about fifteen minutes. Then I felt the trim of the plane change. I looked back and saw him crawling forward over the mail sacks again. He stopped right behind my seat and started making writing motions with his finger on the side of the cabin. After a minute he asked if I knew the Bible. I said yes, I did. He asked if I remembered the part about the handwriting on the wall. I told him that I did. Then he told me to read what he had just 'written,' so I looked at the place and pretended that I was reading. I nodded my head several times and tried to look pleased."

Like an impassioned street preacher, the passenger began pontificating about God. Hulshizer kept nodding and smiling, trying to ward off hellfire and brimstone.

"Next, he decided that he wanted to put me into a trance, and he started to wave his hands in front of my face. I let him do that for a short time, then told him that I was too busy flying the plane, but that if he would wait until we reached Fairbanks where I could relax, he could then put me into a trance. That seemed to satisfy him for the time being. He smiled, patted my shoulder, and crawled back to the rear of the plane."

Hulshizer stole glances over his shoulder every few minutes to check on the would-be evangelist, who was again ranting to his wife and frantically waving his hands. Hulshizer also glanced out the window at the surrounding peaks, wondering where he could land if getting on the ground suddenly became urgent.

Having a lunatic on board is high on any pilot's list of nightmares because, as when there's structural failure, the pilot loses much of his control. Fuel-gauge needles nudging the "E" zone or fog and dusk blocking the way home limit your options, but you still make the decisions, decisions based on fairly predictable scenarios.

A crazed passenger, however, is a question mark. He can determine as much of the flight's fate as he wants. He might shoot holes in the fuselage, attack other passengers, start a fire, grab the wheel. Calling for help on the radio provides some psychological comfort, but a tower controller or flight service station specialist can do nothing to restrain the lunatic. Intervention by other passengers could merely open the tiger's cage.

For a while it seemed the man had lost interest in Hulshizer, for he remained in the rear of the Norseman. Hulshizer began to relax. Then, he felt the trim change once more.

"I looked around and there he was, crawling forward again, with a pretty serious look on his face. He stood up behind my seat, slightly to the right, and began again on his favorite subject, God. Again he wanted to put me in a trance, and again I tried to reason with him to wait until we reached Fairbanks. But every time I opened my mouth he told me to shut up. He started waving his hands in front of my face, like magicians do when they're trying to put a subject into a trance, and he would point at my eyes and then at his, meaning for me to look into his eyes. He reached out twice and pulled my eyelids down, and then pulled his eyelids down, and continued to wave his hands in front of my face. Once in a while I looked forward to see if we were still on course, but each time he hit my shoulder and shouted at me to stop turning away."

Hulshizer's heart was pounding now with both anger and fear. The situation was getting out of hand. He considered trying to bash the man's head with the small fire extinguisher beneath his seat, but that would have required an awkward left-handed swing. He also rejected a sudden aerobatic maneuver such as a snap roll to dislodge the evangelist, for fear that it might enrage him. The Norseman was not an aerobatic airplane anyway.

As Hulshizer tried to think of another tactic, the man put one arm around him, held the control wheel with the other hand, and screamed in his ear about God. Understanding hardly a word, Hulshizer nodded and forced himself to smile. Suddenly, the passenger began pounding his fists on the aircraft clipboard, breaking it into pieces and strewing the papers it held about the cockpit.

"After that outburst, he asked me if I believed in God again, and I replied that I surely did. He then told me to get up and come to the rear with him and let God fly the plane. I knew that I was really in trouble if he insisted. He didn't, though, and he turned around and crawled back over the mail sacks. He then reached into one of his boxes and brought out a salad fork and spoon and began drumming on a mail package, like a drummer in a boogie band."

While the lunatic was entertaining himself, Hulshizer tried to radio Fairbanks, but either high terrain or unfavorable atmospheric conditions interfered. Just as he rehooked the microphone, he heard a crash behind him. The man was throwing cans of food from his baggage out a window. One can missed, ricocheted off the cabin wall, and struck Hulshizer on the head, bruising him. Soon three windows were broken, and out of them was being jettisoned everything that would fit, including the mail sacks.

"His wife was in her seat with her hands over her face. I guessed she was as scared as I was. I was glad she didn't try to stop him, as he might have tried throwing her out also."

Fairbanks was on the horizon now, and this time Hulshizer contacted both Fairbanks Radio and the Wien dispatcher. If he could land, help would be instantly at his side. Ladd Field, a military base, lay three miles closer than the civilian Weeks Field, and at first Hulshizer planned to land there even though he was unable to contact the tower for authorization. But by now the strange passenger had exhausted his supply of throwables and had quieted, so Hulshizer decided to push on to Weeks.

"After a long few minutes I reached Weeks Field and landed. I taxied up in front of the hangar, cut the engine, and jumped out of the cockpit. One of the mechanics standing by opened the door and the man fell out. He lay flat on the ground for a few minutes. Suddenly he got up, ran down the runway, and took off all of his clothes. He ran toward us stark naked, changed his mind, and ran toward the hangar, where he picked up a piece of pipe and started swinging. He hit a small plane and broke the windshield. Then he began swinging the pipe at the mechanics who were trying to get a hold of him. Finally, they managed to throw him to the ground and hold him there."

Following another struggle, city police handcuffed the man and took him to the hospital. Orderlies were unable to restrain him, so police transferred him to jail and put him in a padded cell. There, he tore up the padding and shouted an endless stream of obscenities at the guards. Authorities eventually put him in a straitjacket, sedated him, and flew him to an institution in the Lower 48.

A witness who had seen an object fall from the Norseman tracked it down and turned it in—one of the mail sacks. The six or seven others presumably are still scattered around the White Mountains.

Ever afterward, Hulshizer looked askance at any passenger who seemed a little odd. Except for obnoxious drunks—the perennial bane of bush pilots—he had no further trouble with passengers during his career.

At least, none who made nuisances of themselves on board the airplane. But passengers can create dilemmas for bush pilots in other ways, even when they're miles over the horizon. "I had a rule to never go into the short strips in the Fortymile country before six o'clock in the evening," says Hulshizer, "because the air was usually too unstable. One day the dispatcher told me a couple of prospectors at Seventymile Falls had to get out real bad. I said I didn't want to do it—it was the middle of the day. But I was in a hurry to get back for something and didn't want to wait till later, so I went."

The Fortymile Mining District lies east of Fairbanks near the Yukon Territory border and contains some of the richest gold deposits in Alaska. Perhaps the two prospectors had hit a strike and were impatient to file a claim. Perhaps they simply yearned for a hot bath and a night on the town after a long spell in the bush. Whatever their reason for wanting immediate transportation out, they were

After Don Hulshizer joined Alaska Airlines in the late 1940s, among the aircraft he flew was this Pilgrim, seen here at Weeks Field in 1949. *Courtesy of Don Hulshizer*

glad to see Hulshizer's Cessna 180 land.

The pilot, however, was concerned. "I stepped off the strip and counted 700 or 800 feet. I had been in there before and it was adequate, but on that day it was about one o'clock, and the wind was kind of squirrelly, coming off the Seventymile River."

Skeptical of the conditions, Hulshizer decided to depart with part of the prospectors' gear and ferry it to a longer strip nearby, then return for another load.

"I took off and got into the air all right, but there was brush about ten feet high off the end of the field. I kept on full power. The flaps were already partly down for takeoff, and I put on full flaps to try to clear the brush. I let the nose up a little, but I knew I was going to crash in there."

He was right. The wheels clipped the top of the brush, slowing the 180 and causing a stall. After plowing through some spruce treetops, it came down on tundra on the far side of the strip. One landing gear collapsed, spinning the airplane. By the time the plane bounced to a stop, fire had erupted. Hulshizer burned an arm getting out, but he was otherwise unhurt.

"That airplane never flew again," he says wryly. "This happened because I gave in against my better judgment. I got pressured into it."

It was a lesson the bush has taught many pilots, a lesson Hulshizer fortunately never had to relearn. Despite the accident, Wien had enough faith in his judgment to elevate him to chief pilot of the bush operation, with hiring and firing authority. (The company also had a large-airplane division that concentrated on scheduled flights to established airports.)

Most of Hulshizer's associations with passengers left pleasant memories. He especially enjoyed pointing out the sights to tourists who rode on his mail runs to villages along the Yukon River. In the 1950s, the Alaskan tourism industry was unrefined, and visitors had to tolerate rather informal accommodations.

"There was usually no seat for them on the mail flights," Hulshizer admits. "They sat on top of the freight. At each stop they'd get off and take a tour of the village. The pilot was the tour guide; you'd walk them around, then get back on the plane and go on to the next stop. The company wasn't really promoting tourism, but these fellows just showed up and wanted to go for a ride."

As more and more tourists spent vacations in the North Country, Wien began offering sightseeing flights. Hulshizer developed some personal touches. "Often we'd be in a Norseman, which made so much noise it was hard to talk. So I wrote up little cards with descriptions of where we were, numbered them, and passed them out. When we'd reach a certain spot, I'd hold up my fingers to correspond to the number on the card and point out the window. When we crossed the Arctic Circle I'd make a big dip or something. They got a bang out of that."

After twenty-three years with Wien, Hulshizer decided he wanted a change and quit to become a captain on twin-engine transports for Interior Airways. Several other flying jobs followed, mostly hauling freight and oil in C-46s. There was also a stint driving trucks and buses for the trans-Alaska oil pipeline project ("and making three or four times as much money as I ever did in the cockpit").

Hulshizer retired at sixty-five, but after five years of relaxation and recreation he was ready to return to work. Today he's a part-time C-46 pilot for Everts Air Fuel in Fairbanks. Sometimes a flight takes him northwest over the White Mountains toward Circle Hot Springs. Remembering the lunatic he carried that day in 1951 can still make him cringe. Sometimes he even looks over his shoulder.

Bob Ellis

— Southeast Pioneer —

ROBERT E. ELLIS'S condominium juts out over Tongass Narrows in Ketchikan smack in the path of the prevailing southeast wind. To keep out the winter gales, Ellis has had to install thermal glass four panes thick on that side of his home.

The location offers a superb view, though, and on nice days Ellis, who still bears the handsome looks and boyish smile that endeared him to passengers sixty years ago, often lounges on his porch to gaze at the sights: heavily forested Deer Mountain behind the town, Pennoch and Gravina Islands, a hodgepodge of boats plowing through the water, the mix of old and new buildings along the waterfront, the screeching sea gulls.

And the seaplanes. Here in southeastern Alaska, they are still the taxicab of the bush. All day, a fairly steady flow of 185s, Beavers, and Otters roars off and splashes down, many coming to or going from the Temsco Airlines complex only a few hundred yards down the shore. A generation ago, the planes were Grumman Gooses and their logo bore a different name: Ellis Air Lines.

As he watches the seaplanes, Ellis reminisces about the postwar years, when he operated Ketchikan's most successful fixed-wing air service, with more than a hundred employees. He was a businessman then, concerned about aircraft acquisitions, public relations, and other administrative matters.

To be sure, building a business brings excitement and satisfaction, and for some, including Ellis, financial security. Yet, excitement

Built in 1934, the Sitka Pioneers Home in the background was just three years old at the time of this photo of Bob Ellis and his Cabin Waco. *Photo by Lloyd Jarman*

and satisfaction are relative. If you flew as a pioneer bush pilot in your youth, running an airline in middle age can seem a little unromantic by comparison.

So the seaplanes taking off and landing in front of his porch also trigger memories of an earlier era—"the glamour years," Ellis calls them. For example, 1929, when he served as navigator on a Lockheed Vega floatplane on the first nonstop flight between Seattle and Juneau. Pilot Anscel Eckmann had asked Ellis, then a twenty-six-year-old Naval Reserve aviator, to plot a course for him. Ellis had just started his first commercial flying job at Renton near Seattle, but Alaska beckoned, and he purposely complicated the navigation plan so much that Eckmann agreed to take him along on the historic flight.

"The cabin was loaded with cans of gas, some of which spilled," Ellis says, chuckling. His native Vermont twang has long since disappeared, but the naval officer's training shows in his poised, confident manner. In the early days, the government required pilots to have perfect vision, and like so many retired pilots, he still needs no glasses for myopia. "The gas saturated my pants, burning the skin, and I arrived in Juneau as the 'red-assed kid.' "

Watching the professional routine the seaplanes follow on Tongass Narrows, Ellis shudders at the ignorance he and other pioneer pilots had to shed as they gradually adapted to the country, the weather, and their machines. "Once we got our license at 200 hours, we were on our own, and the only thing you learned was something you discovered by yourself or you gained by conversation with other pilots," he says. "And there usually wasn't another pilot around to talk things over with. Things like a wingtip stall, which is important to know about, but when I discovered it I didn't even know the name for it. I flew all one summer with an icing carburetor. I didn't know what was wrong with it, and the mechanic didn't know."

Ellis smiles and points at a taxiing Beaver that makes a tight right turn toward the dock. "We didn't have water rudders when I started flying up here. We couldn't make turns like that. It was a real handicap. Half the time you taxied up to wherever you were going to moor and you stopped the engine and got out and paddled. You didn't dare approach the thing downwind."

That reminds him of the day in 1930 when he flew several miners up the Taku River to battle a forest fire. With limited maneuverability after landing in the river, he had no way to reach a sheltered slough or bight. Instead, he could only taxi upstream, using bursts of power on the air rudder to slide the Vega toward one bank. When the float nudged shore, he jumped out, and his flight mechanic (many pilots carried one in those days) tossed him a line.

But the swift current pulled the line out of Ellis's hands, and the Vega drifted out of sight around a bend, stranding him. Moments later he heard the engine start; abruptly it stopped. Then it started again, and again stopped. Trying to taxi back to Ellis, the mechanic had to keep shutting down as the airplane turned toward the bank.

Finally the Vega reappeared around the corner and taxied past Ellis onto a nearby sandbar. The mechanic kept the engine running, and a passenger scrambled out and tied one end of a line around a log. But he had forgotten to tie the other end to the airplane. When the mechanic turned off the engine, the Vega drifted rapidly away once more.

Ellis, who by now had torn through the bushes to the sandbar, at least had company this time. Behind the bend, the mechanic started and stopped the engine again and again as he tried to battle the current back upstream. Eventually he managed to reach a bank close to the two men. They rushed over, and while the spinning prop clipped bushes they at last secured the Vega.

Back in the middle of the river for takeoff, the airplane turned broadside in the current when Ellis applied power. He yanked back the throttle, and the Vega drifted downstream for several hundred yards. Now what, he wondered? Desperate, he firewalled the throttle again, discovered that handy seaplane maneuver the 180-degree step-turn, got the nose pointed downstream, and took off.

A breeze ruffles Ellis's white hair. Almost losing an airplane on the Taku revives thoughts of the only occasion when he did lose one; he tells the story as if he were describing a minor fender-bender on Ketchikan's Tongass Avenue. Although he spent the bulk of his career in Southeast, Ellis made mail runs along the Kuskokwim River in southwestern Alaska in 1931. One overcast November day that year, he took off from Anchorage to deliver a J-5 Standard biplane to McGrath. There, he was to pick up a Fairchild 71 and return it to Anchorage.

Suddenly, over a valley eighty miles from McGrath, the 225-horsepower engine quit, apparently because of a fuel problem. Ellis glided to a clearing, but when he touched down the soft snow caused such an abrupt deceleration that the Standard flipped. "I ended upside down hanging by my seat belt," he says.

Unhurt, Ellis crawled out, salvaged emergency supplies, and camped there for the night. He knew the Knik-Iditarod Trail was only eight miles away, and early the next morning he hiked to it. At a roadhouse along the trail, a trapper cooked some moose steaks for him. The following morning a search plane from McGrath landed on nearby Farewell Lake and picked him up. "I was back in Anchorage before anyone there knew I was lost." The J-5 Standard never flew again, although the engine and other parts were salvaged.

Despite close calls, relatively crude aircraft, and the lack of a bush pilot instructional manual to consult, Ellis left room for humor in his daily adventures. One day, the Pratt & Whitney 420-horsepower engine of his Vega quit on takeoff from Petersburg. By the time a mechanic had repaired it several days later, rain and wind were lashing the area. To advise his employer, Alaska Southern Airways, that he was going to resume the flight, he sent the following telegram to company headquarters in Juneau: "WAVES HIGH. SHOULD ENGINE DIE, GOODBYE. I ARE READY. ELLIS."

The humor wasn't always of his making. He laughs as he talks about losing a job three times with Pacific Alaska Airways, which purchased the assets of Alaska Southern Airways in 1934. He was laid off the first time when PAA failed to get a mail contract it sought in Southeast. But Ellis talked the management into rehiring him as a radio operator to relay messages from Juneau to PAA's office in Fairbanks. For brevity, PAA officials sent the messages in code, which Ellis easily broke. One day he read, "FIRE ELLIS." He persuaded PAA to take him back on as a pilot, but competition from Shell Simmons in Juneau soon forced the company to let him go again. Not long afterward, he went into business for himself in Ketchikan.

A modest man like most of his contemporaries, Ellis tends to play down the sensationalism often associated with the pioneer era. Even as a participant, he declined to dramatize his profession. He threw away his helmet and goggles way back in the mid-1930s to protest claims by diehard open-cockpit traditionalists that you had to be in the windstream to fly effectively by the seat of the pants. And disapproving of pilots boasting about their megahours aloft, he discarded his logbooks during World War II (though he admits wistfully, "Now I wish I had them [the helmet, goggles, and logbooks] as mementos"). He states his own flight time as "over 8,000 hours." Only he knows whether that means 8,050 or 20,000.

For Ellis, romance in bush flying meant exploration and new experiences rather than danger. He pauses as a 185 begins a takeoff run too close to the waterfront, sending a window-rattling reverberation across the porch. Then he chats about long, spontaneous charters he made from Southeast into unfamiliar territory up north. In July 1933 he flew all the way to Nome to join in the search for pilot Jimmy Mattern, missing in Siberia on an attempted around-the-world flight. Ellis's passengers were a group of New Yorkers who had organized the "Mattern Relief Expedition," buying a Bellanca for the effort. They had gotten as far as Terrace, British Columbia, when low clouds forced them to land in a farmer's field. Unwilling to push on into the North Country themselves, they decided to charter an Alaskan bush pilot to take them the rest of the way. Unknown to them, Ellis, whom Alaska Southern Airways assigned to the flight, knew almost as little about the route as they.

This Cabin Waco, at Juneau in the mid-1930s, was the airplane Bob Ellis used to start his Ellis Air Transport in Ketchikan. *Courtesy of the Lund Family*

Bad weather in mountain passes and inadequate charts caused many detours, but finally they reached Nome. There they learned that Mattern had been found by Siberian Eskimos after making a forced landing in his Vega because of engine trouble.

While waiting for Russian permission to enter Siberia to pick up Mattern, Ellis agreed to make a couple of local charters in his Vega floatplane for Nome pilots, who had only wheelplanes. "One trip went to St. Michael on the other side of Norton Sound," he says. "The weather was pretty low, and when I hit land I wasn't sure where I was. So I landed by a riverboat coming out of what turned out to be an entrance to the Yukon River, asked directions, and went on my way."

The other charter took Ellis to an Eskimo camp near Kotzebue with a Chinese man wishing to buy reindeer antlers. It was Ellis's first direct contact with the Eskimos, and he watched in fascination as they methodically rounded up the animals the visitor had selected. The antlers were to be shipped to China for use as aphrodisiacs.

Back in Nome, Ellis heard that the Russians themselves had decided to fly Mattern to Alaska. When the Russian flying boat arrived with the American on board, the language difference prevented Ellis from chatting with them. But he shook hands with the flight leader, Sigizmund Levanevsky, one of Russia's most famous fliers. Levanevsky himself would disappear in the Arctic four years later on an exploratory flight from Moscow to New York. No trace of his four-engine airplane has ever been found.

Ellis flew Mattern and the New Yorkers back to British Columbia, then returned home to Ketchikan.

The next year, after a fire destroyed much of Nome, he headed back to that old gold-mining community with relief workers. Ellis had to pick up his passengers in Seattle, and on the leg from there to Tanana, where they spent the night, he logged the longest day of his career in the air: thirteen hours, thirty minutes.

"We'd go on for days flying all over hell into areas that weren't even on the map," Ellis says of those and other long charters. After a moment he adds, "Every flight then was a grand adventure."

But he collected his fondest memories right in his own backyard in Ketchikan. In 1936, after working in succession for Alaska-Washington Airways, Alaska Southern Airways, and Pacific Alaska Airways, he started his own air service (initially called Ellis Air Transport) there with a YKS-6 Cabin Waco floatplane. Competition from Munter's Aircraft Charter Service forced him to concentrate on the local market, and soon a special relationship developed.

Over at Temsco Airlines, passengers file down a ramp and climb into an Otter. "They're probably all going to the West Coast," Ellis says, as we watch. (In Ketchikan, "West Coast" means the west side of Prince of Wales Island, location of three important fishing villages.) "Well over seventy-five percent of our business was over there, in Craig, Klawock, and Hydaburg, so I knew everybody. Everybody knew me. I took quite an interest in the people we carried and would sometimes spend hours at a town waiting for passengers." He also took shopping orders and wheeled from store to store on his bicycle in Ketchikan to fill them. When he delivered the items, he would report on the progress of villagers in the Ketchikan hospital and other news he had gathered.

Every Christmas, Ellis donned a Santa Claus costume and walked through the village streets, dispensing candy from a sack to delighted kids. So much did he gain the villagers' trust that they often gave him their paychecks to cash at the end of the fishing season. Ellis would place the cash in separate envelopes, writing the name of the recipient on the outside.

Photos from the mid-thirties show a smiling, clean-cut young man anyone would automatically trust. Ellis's thick, dark hair is slightly tousled. Usually he's wearing a tie, and often he's standing in a military "at ease" stance, ready to serve. It's an image that would make a good first impression on a prospective employer or the father of a date.

But war interrupted Ellis's warm association with his West Coast customers in April 1941, when the Navy called him to active duty. While his wife, Peg, pilot Norm Gerde, and mechanic Jack Sherman kept his air service going, he spent the next four years in command positions at naval air stations in Sitka, Kodiak, and Attu. After V-J Day he returned to Ketchikan to expand the company in the postwar boom.

The war also marked a transition between the glamour years and the business years, between the pioneer bush pilot and the airline executive. With a growing fleet of war-surplus Grumman Gooses and scheduled flights to many Southeast communities, Ellis Air Lines needed the boss in the office rather than the cockpit. The airline eventually became part of Alaska Airlines through mergers that began in 1962, the year Ellis retired. Before moving to the condominium, he and Peg lived for years aboard their yacht *Chilton* north of Ketchikan by Ellis Island.

Ellis has a scrapbook and photos, and sometimes he reminisces with his peers. But as long as seaplanes operate from Tongass Narrows, his favorite route to nostalgia will continue to be from his porch. "We sure could have used one of those back then," he says as a Beaver taxis out. He nods slightly. "Still, I'm very content with the era I lived in. Few people have had a more interesting life than I have."

TONY SCHULTZ

— *Maverick* —

REPUTATION CAN sketch a bush pilot's personality for you long before you meet him. It may seem exaggerated or a bit distorted, but if you hear the same assessment from at least a couple of independent sources, you can be sure there's some truth in it.

Several pilots had described Tony Schultz as a maverick, a non-conformist who did things his way. I'm not surprised, then, to find him wearing only jeans when we meet at his home in Fairbanks. It is late evening, and as he talks about his flying career in the semi-darkness of his fairly cluttered living room, he slouches in an arm-chair bare-chested and bare-footed, his fingers locked behind his head, oblivious to the mosquitoes that keep my hands constantly on the defense.

With a weathered, craggy face beneath light-brown hair, Schultz *looks* like a bush pilot. Many of his contemporaries, most of whom also appear hardy and fit, could now pass for retired engineers, pharmacists, teachers, or other ground-based city professionals; you'd have to be told that they once flew the bush for a living. One glance at Schultz, however, and somehow you know that he's spent a lifetime battling nature and usually winning. Along the coast he might have just stepped from the bridge of a fishing boat. Here in the Interior, he could be a prospector, trapper, construction worker, game warden—or a bush pilot. He has the right face, the right agility, the right confident, steely blue eyes.

Schultz acknowledges that he was "controversial" from time to time, although his background sounds perfectly conventional. Like many Alaskan pilots, he was born in the Midwest, in his case Bristol, South Dakota, in 1909. An air show up in Minot, North Dakota, hooked him on aviation as a teenager. "Everything else was secondary after that," he says. Pretty normal. His father had hunted for gold in Nome from 1900 to 1906 and brought back tales of adventure. To escape the Depression, Schultz headed north himself in 1938 and gradually worked his way into a flying career. Again, routine.

Perhaps his first unconventional move was turning down an offer in February 1942 to fly for a major airline. While Outside in Yakima, Washington, training for a commercial license and an instrument rating, he had shown so much natural talent that the Civil Aeronautics Authority encouraged him with two $500, no-obligation grants. Pan American Airways apparently took notice and later tried to woo him away from Star Airways in Anchorage. But by then Schultz had become too emotionally attached to bush flying.

"I told them I know all these old-timers in the sticks and what they need," he pleads, gesturing like a lawyer in a courtroom. "John Vogter has to have groceries and beans, and John Olson wants a case of rum every other month or so. I know the little places to land and when not to land because the ice is too thin. And too many other pilots here are being siphoned off elsewhere in the United States. So I told them I can't just go and leave these old-timers."

Schultz flew long, hard hours serving bush customers, especially when they required medical evacuation. "I never, shall we say, cared what the weather was doing, or whether it was night or day, or how tired I was. When someone needed me, I went."

It seemed every time an emergency arose, conditions conspired against him. He was asleep in Fairbanks one winter night in 1945 when the station manager at Ruby radioed his employer, Dodson Air Service, that a trader in the village had collapsed from a heart attack.

"Get help out here fast!" the station manager urged. A Fairbanks physician provided a nurse and a tank of oxygen, but the two pilots at the airport at that hour declined to make the flight because darkness and fog had reduced visibility to a few feet. So, at 4:00 A.M., Schultz's phone rang.

"I needed twenty minutes to dress for the forty-five-degree-below weather," he recalls. "At the airport, I taxied onto the runway on skis and turned for takeoff, but I could see only two lights on one side of the runway. That will give you some idea of the density of the fog. After takeoff, I climbed over the hills and landed on the Yukon River ice at Ruby about six-thirty, in the dark, with no lights."

To make sure the Gullwing Stinson would be ready to fly the trader to Fairbanks, he immediately wrapped the 220-horsepower Lycoming in its engine cover to retain heat. The dog team that picked up the nurse and oxygen had no extra room for Schultz, forcing him to snowshoe a mile and a half into the village. When the nurse reported that the trader would not have to be evacuated, Schultz made the best of his presence anyway. "I moved passengers, mail, and freight between four villages, and after gassing up twice and adding three gallons of oil, I again landed at Ruby in the evening dark. This time there was a firepot to mark the end of the ice runway. At 6:00 P.M. I took off again with the nurse and two other passengers and returned to Fairbanks in the dark." He then, presumably, went back to bed.

On another frigid winter evening early in 1963, Schultz, stationed in Fort Yukon for Wien Airlines, had retired for the day—or so he thought. A nonstop flight schedule had deprived him of lunch, but now he smiled as he prepared to cook the steak that had been thawing on the drainboard since seven in the morning. The frying pan began to sizzle, then someone knocked sharply on the door of his log cabin. A young village boy had just been run over by a car, the caller announced.

"It had been a long day, and I could tell it was about to get longer," Schultz says grimly. "I dreaded the flight; the temperature in Fairbanks was minus-fifty-three degrees and the ice fog was thick enough to slice with a knife." But the injured boy could not wait. Like a gladiator draping his body in armor, Schultz pulled his heavy clothing back on and hurried out to warm up the Cessna 180, which was equipped with wheels/skis to allow for operation on either hard surfaces or snow. With the boy and the village nurse on board, he took off.

"The sky was inky black until we reached 7,000 feet and saw the stars," he continues. "Forty-five minutes later, I called Fairbanks. Air Traffic Control told me the temperature had dropped to fifty-six below and the visibility was a quarter-mile in ice fog. But they gave us priority over Pan Am's 707, which also wanted to land and was using over a thousand gallons of fuel per hour, compared to my sixteen."

In daylight, a quarter-mile slips by awfully fast when you're approaching a runway in an airplane at 65 or 70 knots an hour. It seems to pass even quicker at night in a bush plane that lacks an airliner's sophisticated instruments. All Schultz had to guide him to the runway other than his eyes was an Automatic Direction Finder, a navigational radio with a needle that points to a low- or medium-frequency station. It's an imprecise system, and when used for airport instrument approaches the official visibility minimum is a mile or more.

As he groped for the runway that night in the quarter-mile fog, Schultz was probably literally on the edge of his seat, or at least as far forward as his seat belt allowed. He may have also been gritting his teeth, or chewing his lip, or gripping the yoke in his concentration. (The 707 crew decided a quarter-mile was too paltry and diverted to Eielson Air Force Base 25 miles southeast.)

Year after year, National Transportation Safety Board investigations pin many small-airplane accidents on landing attempts in bad weather. But airborne mavericks seem to have an extra measure of ability, which is no doubt why they get away with being mavericks. The 180's wheels thumped safely onto the runway, and Schultz taxied rapidly to the ramp. After waiting medics whisked the young victim into an ambulance, Schultz scrambled in and rode along to the hospital. The boy was still conscious, and in the emergency room a doctor asked him his name and age. "Jimmy," he whispered. "Six."

The next day, after he had returned to Fort Yukon, Schultz learned that little Jimmy had died. Nearly thirty years after Jimmy became Fort Yukon's first automobile fatality, I hear Schultz's voice quiver slightly at this point in the story.

Without his concern for the people of the bush, Schultz never would have pushed the weather as hard as he did, or made airplanes perform maneuvers that would have wrung curses from their manufacturers. Schultz was no company man; mavericks seldom are. Bush people motivated him, not a desire to follow the crowd.

April 1950. Twenty-four men from Mountain Village desperately wanted transportation to Anchorage for jobs as laborers on the Alaska Railroad, but it was breakup time and the regular strip at Mountain Village had turned into a quagmire. The only alternative, a 450- to 500-foot-long gravel bar on a bank of the adjacent Yukon River, was so short that other pilots had rejected the flight. Schultz's Gullwing Stinson normally needed a third more length to take off with any load. Yet, if the men failed to show up in Anchorage, they'd lose precious income; you don't find many cash-paying jobs along the Yukon.

Schultz, based at McGrath in that period, somehow squeezed extra performance from his Stinson and made seven shuttles in twenty hours to deliver all the men sixty miles to Fortuna Ledge, which had a long, still-usable strip. From Fortuna Ledge, the passengers boarded other airplanes for Anchorage. "They [fellow pilots] were all twiddling their thumbs saying it can't be done, while I'm out there doing it," he proclaims with a note of defiance.

On his fifth stop at Fortuna Ledge, Schultz was refueling when two nuns in mud-splattered skirts walked up and asked him to fly them to St. Marys, forty miles along the way to Mountain Village. At first Shultz shook his head. His Stinson was on wheels, and skis

Tony Schultz, on a mail stop by Fortuna Ledge in 1953, with a straight-wing Stinson leased by Alaska Airlines. *Courtesy of Orville Tosch*

were necessary for the snow-and-mud-covered strip at St. Marys. Like Mountain Village, St. Marys had a single, lousy option: a short, slick grassy bank five miles away with a gully at one end. "It's too tight," he admitted. "You'll have to wait until the regular strip is usable."

But the nuns said they had been stranded at Fortuna Ledge for two weeks trying to get to the mission at St. Marys and had hiked a mile through the mud to see him. Looking up at the pilot with anguished faces, oblivious to the laws of aeronautics, they implored him to reconsider.

"I felt so sorry for them," Schultz says. "I agreed to at least go look." Circling the bank with the nuns a half hour later, he frowned. It appeared prohibitively short, and the gully at the end gaped like the mouth of a monster. Realizing he had no margin for the slightest misjudgment, he lined up into the wind, touched down at the edge of the bank and braked hard. The Stinson skidded across the slippery grass toward the gully. They were going to crash! In a frantic gamble, Schultz stamped his foot on the left rudder pedal and ground-looped the airplane on one wheel 180 degrees so that it was now moving backward. He then opened the throttle, and the Stinson stopped just short of the gully. The maneuver was tantamount to reversing direction in a car by spinning it on the highway and avoiding a roll-over. Schultz refused payment for the flight.

After takeoff, he circled once before heading back to Mountain Village. Both nuns were kneeling on the grass, with hands clasped and heads bowed.

Such tactics ingratiated Schultz with passengers and made him a legend in the bush. Authorities and managers were sometimes less impressed. In fact, unfairly or not, controversy dogged him almost from the start of his career. When he was a fledgling in 1940, he picked up a small bag of gold from a bush customer one day and, after landing back in Anchorage, took it to the bank as instructed. The institution was closed for the day, but he knocked on the window and handed the bag to a worker inside who had not yet left. Schultz neglected to ask for a receipt. Later, the bank could find no record of the deposit. For months the customer, the bank, and Star Airways eyed Schultz with suspicion, despite his indignant insistence that he had delivered the gold.

After the attack on Pearl Harbor, the government ordered banks to inventory their assets. There in a dark corner lay the bag, with the customer's tag attached and all the gold still inside.

In the cockpit, it was Schultz's disdain for rules and policies that got him into trouble. One drizzly, foggy summer day in 1942 a mud slide pinned a road-construction worker against his tractor at the old mining camp of Tokotna near McGrath. Fellow workers notified McGrath shortly before Schultz landed there in a Stinson on a flight from Anchorage, the nearest community with adequate medical services. He had just weaved his way through Rainy Pass, a major route across the Alaska Range that is aptly named for its prodigious clouds and precipitation. Pilots used to joke that you could find your way from one end of the pass to the other by the wrecks on the hillsides.

"The gas man at McGrath told me they just got a message that McDonald got crushed at Tokotna, but he said, 'I guess you can't go because the weather's so bad.' I said, 'Well, I'm going.' The Tokotna airport was on a hill, and I had to circle waiting for a break in the clouds so I could land. I picked him up and came back to McGrath to refuel. Then I flew back through Rainy Pass again, and I mean I followed the dog-team trail, right through that S-turn; sometimes the trail was above me, but I wanted to be sure I was in contact all the time." (Schultz says he negotiated Rainy Pass more times in 1942 than all other Alaskan pilots put together.)

Finally on the other side, Schultz tried to radio the tower at Merrill Field in Anchorage for landing authorization. No answer. A periodic wartime military alert had closed the airport to all traffic, and inbound aircraft were required to proceed elsewhere. The continuing silence in his headphones quickly alerted Schultz to the situation. Nonetheless, he went straight in and landed.

"On both sides of me as the airplane was rolling down the runway, there was a jeep with GIs and pistols drawn." The furious airport manager joined the military police in his station wagon. But when the pilot explained that a passenger on board needed immediate hospitalization, the manager, a friend of Schultz's, persuaded the MPs not to arrest him.

Another unauthorized flight led to an encounter with Civil Aeronautics Authority inspectors at McGrath. Schultz had picked up a badly burned miner at Ophir and landed at McGrath for fuel before going on to Fairbanks. "The weather was right down on the ground," he says. "The birds were walking and the parking area was filled with airplanes awaiting better weather. The separation between the clouds and the trees was about zero, but I knew the country and was able to follow the creeks and turns." At McGrath, the two inspectors glanced at the Stinson and the weather. "The CAA guys were ready, shall we say, to tie me up. I pointed at poor Pete in there—eighty percent of Pete's body was burned—and told them, 'I'd do the same for you,' and took off for Fairbanks. I thought I was going to be written up, but I never heard a thing about it."

In addition to instinct and a gritty determination, an instrument rating helped Schultz work his way through weather that often forced other pilots to turn around, or stay on the ground. Few pilots had that rating in the 1940s; few airplanes, airways, and airports were equipped for instrument flight. As late as the 1970s, many old-timers with 20,000 or 30,000 hours were still flying without one—who needs a darn instrument rating when you fly by the seat of your pants and navigate by following the passes and the rivers? (In fact, after the FAA mandated the rating for air taxi pilots, some veteran pilots retired prematurely in protest rather than go to the trouble and expense of acquiring it.)

It was a wise Pan American Airways pilot who persuaded Schultz to get an instrument rating early in his career. "That was the best investment I've ever made," Schultz proclaims. "It's saved my life a hundred times." The government never intended the instrument rating to save lives per se, but rather to provide a means of traveling from one point to another without visual terrain contact, usually in a highly structured environment. Schultz's use of his instrument training would have shocked federal inspectors like the ones at McGrath: making timed turns to follow winding mountain passes in the fog, climbing out through the overcast rather than landing after becoming trapped in a snow squall, punching through clouds here and there while scud-running, and so on. Ordinary pilots who try to fly close to the terrain on the gauges often contribute to the accident statistics.

But even mavericks cannot avoid the law of averages. "I've had, shall we say, quite a few cases where I had problems in flying," Schultz admits, emphasizing that even in the most dire of emergencies, he never panicked. An in-flight fire is serious enough without complications. When smoke and flames erupted from the heater duct shortly after takeoff from Fairbanks one day in the early 1940s, Schultz faced the additional distractions of a snow shower and a distraught fur buyer who began pummeling him in terror. Schultz managed to get the Stinson back to the runway, but a landing gear broke on touchdown and the airplane "rolled up in a ball." No one was seriously hurt.

Another broken landing gear, this time on a Bellanca, caused a 1942 takeoff crash at McGrath, and "they hauled it away in a wheelbarrow." A pint of whiskey one of the passengers was carrying in a coat pocket smacked another passenger on the head, causing a cut that constituted "the most serious injury anyone ever had with me."

There were also minor injuries the time Schultz hit the ocean ice during a bad-weather instrument approach to Moses Point in the early 1960s. The Wien Airlines Beech 18 twin flipped over and caught fire, but Schultz kicked out the windshield and evacuated his passengers. He notes that the local weather observer had reported better conditions than existed ("They wanted to see their people get in") and that according to an investigation, an ajar cabin door had caused an erroneous altimeter reading, making him think he was 350 feet higher on the approach than he actually was.

Regardless of cause, an accident naturally mars any pilot's career, both in terms of personal satisfaction and opportunities. The Moses Point crash hurt Schultz's chances to move into the left seat of Wien's airliners. So did his expertise in the bush. When Schultz joined Wien in 1954, he was already a veteran bush pilot (he had been chief bush pilot for Alaska Airlines before switching), and the company was reluctant to lose such experience by putting him on the line. He did fly as first officer on DC-3s and C-46s for a while, but he and the captains, many of whom were years younger, often disagreed on decisions in the field. One day he infuriated both his captain and the operations manager by grounding a DC-3 at Fairbanks because of a missing bolt in the rudder. They insisted the airplane was airworthy and Schultz insisted it wasn't. When the DC-3 finally took off for Fort Yukon, a bolt had been installed.

"I wasn't in very good graces with them on some things, but they didn't hesitate to send me out on tough assignments when they had something real sticky to do or you had to stay overnight," he comments.

By the 1960s the bush had changed—modern technology, better communication facilities, new faces—and bush residents enjoyed more options. Schultz no longer needed to make sacrifices for them. Many customers continued to request him as their pilot, including Standard Oil, which used him for seven consecutive summers to support North Slope oil exploration.

After retiring from Wien in late 1966, he flew a Beech 18 for Interior Airways for a year, then operated his own air service with a Cessna 180 until competition forced him out in 1976.

In the latter part of his career, Schultz developed some misgivings about having devoted his flying to the bush instead of climbing up the seniority ladder on a major airline. Turning down Pan Am in early 1942 "is hurting me at this late date because I could have been, shall we say, drawing a much, much better retirement program than the near-zero one I have now. I'm one of the poorest pilots in town."

Yet, financial security is not the only compensation in a flying career. Schultz cannot walk very far in downtown Fairbanks without hearing his name called: "Hey, Tony!" An old-timer walks up, shakes his hand vigorously, and reminds him of the day he flew through a gauntlet of nasty weather or made an "impossible" takeoff to provide vital transportation.

"When I see the thanks in their eyes, I know it was all worthwhile," Schultz says.

Jack Wilson

— *Glacier Expert* —

RETIRED *GLENNALLEN* bush pilot Jack Wilson knows what's first, in between, and last about operating on glaciers. From the early 1950s to the late 1970s, he made hundreds—maybe thousands—of landings on glaciers in the mountains of the Alaska, Wrangell, Chugach, and St. Elias ranges, hauling climbers and scientists and their gear in and out. He's given lectures on the subject, and his experiences literally fill a book (*Glacier Wings and Tales*, 1988).

> The first thing you have to do is read the glacier from the air to see what you're getting into before you commit yourself to land.

Valdez's Bob Reeve may have pioneered glacier work,* and Talkeetna's Don Sheldon certainly got more publicity for it, but the unofficial title "Dean of the Glacier Pilots" fits Wilson well. He even resembles a dean, the scholarly type, as he sits in a storeroom office adjacent to Basin Liquor, a store his wife, Bonnie, runs at Mile 182 on the Glenn Highway. Wearing large-frame glasses and a cap of

*Joe Crosson of Alaskan Airways made the first recorded glacier landing in Alaska in April 1932, on Mount McKinley's Muldrow Glacier. Five scientists had chartered Alaskan Airways for transportation to the glacier. Neither Crosson nor Jerry Jones, who participated in the mission, pursued glacier operations after that (see "Jerry Jones: Old and Bold" for the full story of this project). Bob Reeve was the first Alaskan pilot to develop glacier operations into an art.

Jack Wilson spent part of his World War II Army Air Forces assignment flying P-40 fighters in Great Britain, where this photo was taken. When he earned his wings he was an enlisted man and often flew multiengine planes. Most of his copilots were officers. "I saluted them on the ground and gave them orders after takeoff," he says.
Courtesy of Jack Wilson

forest-color camouflage, he puffs thoughtfully on his pipe. He has just driven four hours from a trading post he's building for his oldest son on the McCarthy Road, and fatigue deepens both his voice and the craggy lines in his face.

On the surrounding walls hang photos of proud hunters and the mounted heads of moose, sheep, and other big game. All eyes seem to be upon Wilson, as if he were a teacher in a lecture hall.

> You won't have trouble landing on a damn glacier. Landing is very easily done. The problem is taking off again, and that can be a son of a bitch. You got to get that figured out before you land. You need enough room, and you have to take off downhill, regardless of the wind. Above 6,000 feet you don't land a damn skiplane on level snow; you just

> might not take off again. You have to find a slope, even if it's off to a side somewhere.

Wilson got a head start in learning the art of glacier flying. After four years at the controls of Army Air Forces C-47s in Europe during World War II, he returned to his native Colorado and became a civilian charter pilot. Many sportsmen wanted rides into the Rocky Mountains to hunt or fish. With the sixty-five-horsepower engine practically gasping in the thin air and the rate-of-climb needle barely above zero, he'd coax little Taylorcrafts and J-3 Cubs to alpine meadows as high as 11,000 feet. To get airborne again, he'd have to take off down the slope.

Thus, after he moved to Alaska in 1952 as a thirty-one-year-old adventurer, glacier flying brought a certain feeling of deja vu. Even so, the first landing taught him a lesson.

While based at Chitina, working for Cordova Airlines under the famous Mudhole Smith, Wilson got a charter to take four climbers to the Nabesna Glacier in the Wrangells. Excited, he placed the first passenger in the rear of the Super Cub's two tandem seats, flew to the glacier, and touched down at the 6,000-foot level. Both men lurched against their seatbelts as the airplane decelerated like a fly hitting glue. As soon as the Cub stopped, the skis sank into two feet of mush. The snow was as unsuitable for a campsite as for a skiplane, but Wilson could not take off with any load. So he told the man to climb to a higher elevation, and he would bring the other three there.

After a long, faltering takeoff run, Wilson managed to unstick the Cub. At 7,500 feet, he found the snow firm and slick.

> You have to know what kind of snow it is, and you got to know the temperature. Avoid glaciers during the summer, because the snow's so damn rotten the airplane can bury itself to the belly. And stay away from old avalanche tracks at any time of the year.

Of course, sometimes a glacier pilot assesses the snow condition inaccurately, just as a floatplane pilot can find the water deceptively rough. Wilson, who started his own air service out of Chitina in 1956 (later he based his operation at the Gulkana Airport), estimates he's been stuck a couple of dozen times—once overnight—waiting for colder temperatures to convert slush into usable runway. Even with the 300-horsepower, six-place Cessna 185, he occasionally had to restrict his takeoff load to one passenger because of especially sticky snow.

> Drifted snow is fine to land on; it gives you a tiny shadow so you can tell how far off it you are. On nice smooth snow, you can't see where the hell you are and you're landing blind just as if you were on instruments. Watch out for crevasses, too. You can see them from the air, but you can't from the ground.

It was a crevasse that wrecked the only airplane Wilson lost during his over 20,000-hour career. Attempting a takeoff from the Kaskawulsh Glacier in the Yukon Territory in October 1967, he ran into a snow ridge that tossed the Cessna 180 into the air prematurely, causing a momentary loss of control. The plane plopped back down, and Wilson yanked back the throttle to abort. The 180 began slowing down.

Suddenly he saw a crevasse ahead. Unable to stop in time, he jammed the throttle to the firewall, pulled back the yoke, and tried jumping it. But the 180 had already slowed too much. It plowed into the snow on the opposite side of the crevasse, stopping with the tail perched on one side and the engine on the other.

Unhurt, Wilson and his passenger gingerly climbed out. The mountain undoubtedly echoed for several minutes with Wilson's expletives. He probably redistributed a bit of snow with some forceful kicks, as well.

Deciding that the plane was in no immediate danger of plunging into the chasm, Wilson reentered the cockpit and radioed for help. The two camped for the night nearby, and in the morning a Canadian helicopter pilot evacuated them. The 180, Wilson notes as he relights his pipe, is now a permanent part of the glacier.

> As soon as you land, give it full throttle and make yourself some tracks to take off in. Then turn the goddamn airplane around before you stop; point it back downhill if it's not too steep, or sideways otherwise. Let it inch down till it stops. Keep some snowshoes in the airplane in case you have to tramp out an area in front to take off in. Snowshoes work as well as a shovel, if you have to dig yourself out, and you can use them for other purposes.

A glacier pilot can get a real workout with snowshoes. Wilson flew a geologist to a glacier in the Chugach Mountains one day, added power after landing, and skied uphill for takeoff room. But the slope was steeper than it had looked from the air, and when he kicked left rudder at the top of the run, the Cub slid sideways . . . and slid and slid. As the left ski dug into the snow, gravity and momentum began to pull the plane toward the vertical. Inside, helpless, Wilson and the geologist gripped the sides of the cabin.

Just as the Cub was about to flip over on its back, the left wing jammed into the snow like an ice ax arresting a climber's fall. The airplane stopped with the right wing pointing almost straight up and the right ski suspended in the air. Shaken, the men jumped out.

After informing that part of Alaska of his attitude toward the situation and exercising his kicking muscles, Wilson sighed deeply and pulled out the snowshoes. For an hour they dug, Wilson freeing the buried left ski and the geologist fashioning a trench beneath the right ski. To keep the plane from suddenly sliding away as they removed the snow, they buried the geologist's sleeping bag upslope to serve as an anchor (the weight of the snow held it in place), with one end of a rope tied around the bag and the other end wrapped around one of the struts.

Next, they pulled the right wing down, and the ski on that side dropped into the trench. Slowly, inch by inch, shoveling more snow as needed, they manhandled the Cub ninety degrees around until it pointed downhill. Then they climbed back in.

With the engine warmed up, the geologist reached out and cut the rope, and Wilson shoved the throttle all the way forward. Like a sled on a steep hill, the Cub shot forward. In seconds the men were airborne.

Wilson calls the place "Sleeping Bag Glacier."

> You can get a 180 or a Cub up to 14,000 feet and they'll start right up. But watch out for the 185, with that damn fuel-injection system. You got to get the mixture just right for the engine to catch. If you take that thing above 12,000, carry an extra battery along.

Although Wilson can't even estimate his total number of glacier landings, he kept track over the years of the ones he made at extremely high altitudes: sixty-nine, for example, at 14,000 feet in 180s and Cubs at the summit of Mount Wrangell. The Geophysical Institute of the University of Alaska gave him a plaque to thank him for his aerial support there.

He landed even higher, at 14,300 feet, on Mount McKinley in a Cub while participating in a 1960 rescue operation with the legendary Don Sheldon. Wilson and Sheldon worked together on more routine projects, too. One hundred fifty miles separated their respective bases, and one man or the other often hopped over the Talkeetna Mountains to provide an extra airplane when there was more flying than a single pilot could handle. "Don was a really good pilot," Wilson says. "He took an awful lot of chances, and of course he cracked up an awful lot of airplanes doing it, but he was good. I enjoyed working with him." Sheldon's death from cancer in 1975 left Wilson as Alaska's premier glacier pilot.

Two Wilson Air Service Cessna 185s bracket a company Piper Super Cub on a glacier in southern Alaska. *Courtesy of Jack Wilson*

> If you're going to leave people on a glacier, rent them a damn radio so they can call you in case they need to be rescued. That way, they'll get help quicker. And you'll have a little extra income from the rental.

Like Sheldon and other glacier pilots, Wilson also flew floatplanes to lakes and rivers and wheelplanes to runways, strips, meadows, and gravel bars. Glacier pilots are bush pilots, and bush pilots have to be versatile. In fact, Dean of the Glacier Pilots wasn't his only distinction. "I was kind of the head bush pilot in this part of Alaska for years," he says. "I had a little more experience than most men, and I became pretty safety-minded and took care of a lot of other pilots. They kept getting out there and cracking up and busting up airplanes. It was mostly damn foolishness. So I began having safety seminars to tell them how to fly an airplane properly. I think maybe I might have saved a life or two."

He saved a life or two more directly on dozens of nonglacier rescue missions. Many victims were hunters who had suffered broken bones or gunshot wounds in the Wrangell Mountains. One winter night, he received an emergency call about an area resident who was in excruciating pain from appendicitis. Just as television sets, plumbing systems, and furnaces seem to break down more often on weekends than when repair services are open, bush people seem to choose nighttime or stormy weather for their emergencies. Wilson wanted to wait until morning to evacuate the resident, but he realized that the man's appendix might rupture by then.

"The only place to land was a frozen lake near the guy's home," he says. "I flew out there with the 185 and just eased her down and down until the landing lights picked up snow, and went on and landed." The patient survived.

Bush people without telephones in their isolated homes usually have radios with which to call for help, he notes.

Some calls concerned victims for whom help was too late. "Ever try to cram a dead body into a Super Cub?" Wilson asks, gestering with his hands. "It's a hell of a job. I've had to do that a few times." He puffs on his pipe for a moment. "Getting a body into a 185 can be a little difficult, too." When word arrived that an elderly trapper had died in a trapline cabin near the Copper River below Chitina late one November, Wilson agreed to pick up the corpse. "He had been dead for about a month. One knee was bent ninety degrees and his right arm was sticking out, and he was frozen harder than hell. There was no way he was going to go into my 185. Well, I had a state trooper with me. I also had a damn good ax. I said to the trooper, 'Now, if you don't object, I'll fix him so he'll go into that airplane.' The trooper helped a little, and we got him all straightened out and put him into the airplane. We never heard a word about it."

Other nonglacier flying took Wilson into the Interior on forest fire patrols and up to the Arctic to deliver supplies to Distant Early Warning stations. In the Arctic he also engaged in aerial wolf hunting for fifty-dollar bounties (the practice is no longer allowed). He points to a photo on the wall that shows him and a buddy standing by twenty-five wolves they had bagged from a Super Cub. "I got sick of shooting wolves," he mutters. "Those poor bastards just couldn't get away from us. They weren't doing all that much damage, that I could see."

Construction of the trans-Alaska pipeline in the early 1970s lured thousands of job hunters north from the Lower 48. At one point, Wilson Flying Service employed six pilots to handle the frenetic demand for pipeline-related charters. Extra pilots meant more airplanes to buy, an accountant to hire, and other business responsibilities. "I made more goddamn money by myself than when I had all those pilots flying for me," he admits.

By the late '70s, Wilson was daydreaming about a more relaxed lifestyle, about time for fishing and mining gold. Also, his hearing was deteriorating from more than 20,000 hours behind roaring airplane engines. In 1978 he sold his outfit.

But, like most retired pilots, he still spends many hours hangar-flying—reminiscing with other flyers. For Wilson, the fondest memories linger in the glacier country, although flying elsewhere involved fewer problems and risks. Sticky snow, crevasses, avalanches, diminished aircraft performance, lifeless desolation—what was there about glaciers that inspired him to go back again and again?

Wilson draws deeply on his pipe several times without success, then relights it. A cloud of blue smoke rises like a volcanic eruption toward the ceiling.

"I guess I was just a damn fool. I wanted to fly in those glaciers, and so I did."

EMITT SOLDIN

— Government Pilot —

YOU CAN'T HELP feeling compassion for Emitt Soldin on the first meeting. Crippled by arthritis, he sits for hours in his favorite chair at the kitchen table of his home on West 74th Street in Anchorage. Mere sitting doesn't hurt. He chats with visitors, answers one of seven telephones he's placed strategically around the house ("Howdy!" he greets callers), opens his mail, taps on a calculator with fingers that never uncurl.

When he absolutely has to rise—the refrigerator, the garage, the bathroom—he pushes himself up inches at a time, grimacing, then hobbles to the goal hunched over a cane. Because he is unable to stand erect, he seems even shorter than his five feet, six inches.

But you won't hear any griping, and after a while Soldin's enthusiasm for aviation seems to steal the limelight from his ailments. The living room is cluttered with aviation books and videos and airplane models. On the kitchen table lie aviation magazines and newspapers. Framed photos on the walls show various airplanes and pilots, as do unframed ones taped to the refrigerator. A wingless, skinless Super Cruiser fuselage occupies the garage.

Aviation also dominates the conversation. A native-born Alaskan (Skagway, 1924), Soldin has flown all over the state, on land and sea, in big airplanes and small, by instruments and seat of the pants. He has a mechanic's license from his Army Air Forces days, and he's also a certified flight instructor. So he can expound with authority on practically any Alaskan aviation subject.

Don't count on listening to him uninterrupted for long, though. Soldin, who began his flying career as a pilot for Alaska Coastal Airlines in Juneau, is in the middle of a story about making a precautionary landing in a Seabee just south of that community in 1949, when the first of what will be a fairly steady influx of aviation-oriented friends arrives.

"Hey there!" Soldin welcomes him. The visitor is a retired Alaska Airlines captain who has parked his motor home in Soldin's driveway for a few days while getting ready for a journey. He pours himself a cup of coffee, and he and Soldin discuss yesterday's Boeing 737 crash at Unalakleet. Probably not the result of erroneous navaid signals, speculates Soldin, who often checked facilities there as an airways systems flight inspection pilot with the FAA.

When the captain returns to his motor home, Soldin continues the Seabee story. No real emergency, he says. He was heading for a logging camp at the south end of Admiralty Island when suddenly he noticed the oil-pressure needle drop to zero. A leak in the propeller assembly had drained most of the engine oil. He landed in sheltered water by Marmon Island, extended the gear, taxied onto a beach, and radioed Alaska Coastal.

"I've had the Seabee belch on me once or twice over the ocean where I couldn't have landed if it quit," he adds. "That was kind of scary."

Except for the Alaska Coastal stint and a few other short-term civilian flying jobs, Soldin was always a government pilot: Fish and Wildlife Service, Bureau of Land Management, state Department of Fish and Game, FAA. Which of those agencies did he enjoy flying for the most? He pauses and glances blankly out the window at a light rain shower. Then, in the manner of someone making a comparison, he cites aspects of his career with Fish and Wildlife. Two years in Bristol Bay, then three in Ketchikan. Grumman Goose. Scouting for illegal fishing activities, dropping off guards at closed streams, fish-trap patrols, herring surveys. He especially liked the herring surveys. "That was a lot of fun—two or three guys in a Goose, just go out and fly all day long and get a paycheck for it."

Soldin was reassigned to Bristol Bay in 1958, a year before his boss, Clarence Rhode, disappeared on a flight over the Brooks Range to count Dall sheep and deposit caches of fuel. What happened? Was Rhode ever found?

The front door opens—people just walk in—and a burly young man seats himself at the kitchen table. "Hi yuh!" Soldin says. The newcomer is rebuilding his Super Cub and needs advice on covering the frame with fabric skin. Soldin maintains a long-term three-way partnership in a Super Cub himself, although his disability grounded him years ago, and the two spend the next forty-five minutes discussing covering techniques and exchanging anecdotes about the Cub's superb short takeoff and landing ability.

The Super Cruiser in the garage belongs to another rebuilder who is there now tinkering away. Soldin has already announced that he'll have to get up eventually to inspect the man's work. "People need help on these airplanes," he explains. "I've made so many mistakes over the years, I can sometimes keep them from making the same ones. I'm a consultant in aviation, you might say." One side of a business card he hands out identifies him in that capacity. The other side contains some rather bawdy humor.

Returning to his story about Clarence Rhode, Soldin notes that the search for the highly respected Fish and Wildlife commissioner was one of the most extensive in aviation history, alongside the searches for Amelia Earhart in the South Pacific in 1937, World War I ace Eddie Rickenbacker in the same part of the world in 1942, and Congressmen Hale Boggs and Nick Begich in southern Alaska in 1972. Based in Bettles during the Rhode search, Soldin one day scoured an area just a few miles south of the dead-end Brooks Range pass in which hikers would discover the burned wreckage of the orange and black Goose twenty years later.

"Clarence Rhode was a super guy," Soldin says. "Well liked by everyone. He was a workingman's boss." The tribute prompts the same praise for another revered boss, the famous Jack Jefford, under

Emitt Soldin logged some 3,000 hours in Grumman Gooses such as this Fish and Wildlife plane at King Salmon, Alaska, in the late 1950s.
Courtesy of Emitt Soldin

whom he flew in the FAA. Then, once more, the door opens. Soldin obviously is untroubled by loneliness.

"Hi! Coffee's hot," Soldin says. The latest visitors are a father and son who have just returned from a week in Seattle. They own a Grumman Widgeon, and the conversation quickly evolves to a comparison of the Goose and Widgeon. All agree the Widgeon is more of a recreational machine, the Goose a commercial workhorse, and both are fun to fly.

By now you find yourself concluding that Soldin's arthritis is only incidental to his popularity. Friends come not to check on his welfare (a daughter from one of his two marriages drops by regularly for that purpose), but simply to enjoy his company. What pilot could fail to find satisfaction at the table of a cheerful aviation aficionado like this, who speaks with knowledge and humility, a man so selfless he offers his three spare bedrooms and the run of the house to people who need a place to stay, for a day, a week, a couple of months, be they longtime acquaintances or virtual strangers.

For Soldin, the payoff is a constant supply of vicarious copilots. His more exotic house guests have included two Russian women, a nineteen-year-old flight attendant for a TU-154 airliner, and a thirty-one-year-old journalist for a Soviet aviation magazine.

It is well after lunch before he gets another break. After statehood in 1959, he says, Fish and Wildlife, a federal agency, cut back its Alaskan operation and he had to look for another job. During the following two-year assignment with the Bureau of Land Management, he flew firefighters to interior forest fires and made various charters. One flight was to a lake on a coastal island to resupply a group of German naturalists studying sea lions. "They had taken only rice and salt with them, figuring to live off the land," Soldin says, shaking his head. "They had been there two weeks and were pretty hungry."

He faced a problem of his own on that flight. Tree stumps jutted up from the lake, and he had to circle several times to pick out an obstruction-free landing path. He touched down okay, although the Goose "got bumped a few times"—harmlessly—as he taxied through a maze of stumps like a skipper maneuvering a boat through a mine field.

Soldin's prudent, modest personality suggests he approached flying conservatively. In fact, he never crashed or scraped a passenger in his 13,000-hour career. The few incidents that caused minor damage resulted more from bad luck than carelessness. While he was taxiing down an icy dirt road toward the strip at an Arco Oil camp in Wide Bay on the Alaska Peninsula one day, his Goose's right wingtip struck a box that had fallen off a forklift. (The Goose's structure and tail-low angle limit cockpit visibility during a ground taxi.) The impact swung the airplane to the right and it slid into a ditch, damaging its right wing, prop, and landing gear. A camp crane deposited the Goose back on the road.

In another mishap with the Goose, Soldin was marooned all one September night on a beach in Kachemak Bay on the Kenai Peninsula. He had taxied onto the beach to drop off his passengers, and after they putt-putted off in a boat toward a cabin-construction project on the other side of the bay, he restarted the engines. Halfway back down the beach, the Goose's left landing gear dropped into a soft spot, canting the airplane. The more throttle he applied trying to power the airplane free, the deeper the left wheel dug into the gravel and sand.

"So I decided I'd just sit there and wait for the incoming tide to float me free," Soldin says. "But it didn't. I found out that when the left wing dropped, a rock had punctured the wingfloat, and as the tide came in, water filled the float. The weight kept the wing down and the Goose stuck."

He had already notified the Homer Flight Service Station of the situation. Now, with darkness covering the bay and a twenty-five-knot wind blowing onshore, sending help would be impractical until morning. For much of the night he kept the left engine idling, providing forward thrust to prevent the wing from dipping farther under water.

When the tide ebbed, Soldin experimented with differential power, turned the Goose this way and that, and finally popped the wheel out of the hole. A few minutes later he was airborne. "I landed in the slough by Homer and drove the Goose up on some floating muskeg," he continues. "It was about 4:00 A.M. then, and I was exhausted. I told flight service, 'I'm going to sleep; I'll talk to you in the morning.' " Later, local pilots helped him get the Goose off the muskeg, and he flew back to Anchorage.

Since morning, the phones, all seven of them, have rung, jingled, or beeped regularly. Now two callers in a row keep Soldin busy for more than twenty minutes. Hanging up, he smiles as if to apologize. "I had a little problem with a 180 one time, too. I was taking off at Anchorage International for Merrill Field when the seat slid back on me."

Any pilot would immediately sympathize. The sliding seat is one of the most innocuous-sounding yet potentially deadly events that can happen in the cockpit. A pilot adjusts his seat by moving it fore or aft, in most configurations on two metal runners. If the seat is not locked in place, various forces can send it sliding abruptly backward: acceleration on takeoff, a hard push on a rudder pedal in the air, bounding on waves during a floatplane landing. The slide often pulls the pilot's hands off the wheel and throttle, and his feet off the rudder pedals, rendering the airplane out of control.

Soldin's 180 ground-looped instantly to the left and the right gear collapsed, dropping the right wingtip onto the runway.

The greatest damage Soldin ever experienced, in the air or on the ground, actually occurred to an Anchorage house he used to own. The infamous March 1964 earthquake destroyed it. While waiting for things to settle, he moved to Seattle and got a job as a C-46 pilot for Skyvan Airways. In winter, his mission was to haul cargo back up to Alaska. Springtime brought various charters, including transporting bees from Chico, California, to Canada. "Ten million passengers!" he laughs.

Resettled in Anchorage, Soldin got back into Gooses and various single-engine airplanes to fly three years for the state Fish and Game Department, which had assumed responsibility from Fish and Wildlife for management of most of Alaska's nonhuman creatures. Many flights took him to Bristol Bay or Prince William Sound for surveys of salmon-spawning streams. He'd fly as low and slow as possible while an observer estimated fish counts. Not much room for error in that kind of work.

When the conversation moves on to Soldin's eleven-year career with the FAA, his smile reflects a particular pride. At first, joining the agency in 1966 was a matter of security. "I was getting along in years," he says, "and it was time to get on the old shirttail. The FAA was my retirement."

But he quickly found more to appreciate. "That was a good job. Good equipment, real good people to work with." As one of many FAA pilots in the state, Soldin flew DC-3s and a C-123 on cargo and airborne facilities inspection flights. In one six-month period he logged 500 hours in the C-123 alone. "I commissioned the most northerly ILS [instrument landing system] in the state, up at Point Barrow," he boasts. "There will never be another farther north."

When the FAA decided to phase out its piston-powered fleet in favor of turbine-powered aircraft, he attended "jet school" at FAA headquarters in Oklahoma City. Midway through the course, he lost his flight medical because of medication he was taking for his worsening arthritis. At age 53, his flying career was over.

Well, not quite. He remained with the FAA for another year, officially as a nonpilot crewmember. "The guys let me fly anyway," he whispers. Such camaraderie continues today each Thursday at the Elks Club in downtown Anchorage, where retired FAA people gather for lunch. Soldin never misses it.

"Yeah, I wish I could do it again," he says softly, a trace of misting evident in his eyes as he averts his gaze. "Give me another twenty years. Just one more twenty."

George and Virginia Clayton

— *Serenade in the Sky* —

PASSENGERS ON Wien Alaska Airlines' airliners between 1960 and 1980 had no inflight movies to watch, nor a variety of stereo musical programs. If George Clayton was their captain, however, they were entertained nonetheless. At various times on most flights, Clayton would relinquish the controls to his copilot, pull a harmonica from his flight bag, and play a tune over the public-address system.

The passengers and the flight attendants alike would be tapping their toes and clapping in rhythm to "Springtime in the Rockies," "Bicycle Built for Two," or "The Sound of Music." Many would sing along. Even grim-faced passengers who habitually rode gripping the arm rests would relax a little amid the merriment.

Over the years, hundreds of customers requested "that pilot who plays the harmonica" when they booked a reservation with Wien. On May 1, 1973, during a scheduled flight from Fairbanks to Anchorage in a Boeing 737, a harmonica version of the wedding march flowed from the PA system. Then Clayton asked his first officer to take over, walked from the cockpit into the cabin, and united his daughter Nancy in marriage with Wien employee Lars Petersen, while invited guests and ordinary passengers looked on. (A judge had previously encouraged the arrangement.) The airliner covered 170 miles during the 31,000-foot-high ceremony.

In a way, every trip aloft was a celebration to the flamboyant Clayton, for more than most pilots he celebrated flight. He still does.

Chat with him at his home in Fairbanks, and you realize that here is a man truly satisfied with his lifework. Given the chance, he wouldn't change a moment of it, lest that somehow alter the outcome: his flying has honored a paternal family tradition, brought him a family of his own, and involved him in an enjoyable, memorable profession.

A heavy-set, happy-go-lucky sort with gray hair and a smile that livens every facial feature, Clayton has the air of a master of ceremonies. He welcomes the opportunity to talk about his aviation career, even if the audience consists of only one. Like most impassioned people, he's attentive to the details, and in good James Michener style he often digresses to focus on a sidelight.

He'll start with Clayton aviation before he was born, telling you about his balloonist grandfather, Henry H. Clayton, a member of the German team that captured the 1907 International Balloon Race. Then he'll talk about his father, Henry C., a naval pilot in World War I who became a barnstormer after Armistice Day, and about his mother, Augusta, who participated in the barnstorming acts as a wing-walker, until morning sickness grounded her in 1919. She didn't want George to be airborne before his time.

It was Henry C. who in 1928 gave eight-year-old George his first airplane ride, in a Curtiss Flying Boat over Long Island, where the family had moved from Massachusetts. Afterward, Clayton and his parents often went up together on aerial versions of the Sunday drive. One family flight turned into an ordeal when the engine suddenly exploded in flames. "Mother held the plane in a glide while my father put out the fire," Clayton says. Back at the controls, Henry C. maneuvered around buildings and bridges and landed on New York City's East River.

As Clayton discusses such early encounters with aviation, you sense the excitement he felt in an open-cockpit airplane looking down on the busy metropolis, and you share the admiration he still feels for his father (he had planned to join Henry C.'s Naval Reserve squadron as soon as he reached the minimum age of eighteen). The smile fades from his face as he mentions his father's death in a 1937 airplane crash while en route to an air race at Cleveland.

Despite the tragedy, Clayton pressed on with his aviation career. Not yet licensed to fly, he joined Pan American Airways as a mechanic. After stints in Africa and Whitehorse, he was transferred to Fairbanks. A portable instrument panel he built in Pan Am's hangar on Weeks Field helped him learn instrument-flying techniques while he served as a flight mechanic on the line's scheduled runs. But formal lessons were necessary for certification as a pilot. Only one flight instructor then worked regularly at Weeks Field, and even people with no interest in aviation came to gawk at her.

Virginia Merrill Clayton believes she was the first woman flight instructor in Fairbanks; certainly she was one of the first in Alaska. The world of flying in the 1940s largely belonged to men, the accomplishments of Amelia Earhart and other pioneer women aviators notwithstanding. Women were absent from the cockpits of both civilian airliners and military aircraft. Yet, at the instructional level, Virginia says she experienced no prejudice or harassment, either in Alaska or in her native Pacific Northwest.

As a girl in Baker, Oregon, Virginia had watched biplanes pass overhead on their way to or from the local airport. "I'm going to fly one of those someday," she told her mother. Her intention was to join the government's Civilian Pilot Training Program in college, but after initially accepting women, the CPTP administrators then barred them.

"I was going to buy a horse, but then someone knocked on my door and said he had heard I was interested in learning to fly, and he invited me to join a flying club, so I did," says Virginia, whose dark hair and pleasant face look little changed from her 1940s photos. On December 7, 1941, she soloed in Baker in a Piper J-3; she was nineteen. But because authorities had already officially grounded all light aircraft in the region after the attack that day on Pearl Harbor, she had to solo again on December 15 to make it count.

That summer she got a job as a flagman at the Walla Walla, Washington, airport (some fields without control towers used flagmen to direct air traffic), where Whitman College students in a naval flight program were learning to fly. "I had a white flag and a red flag and a little box to sit on at the end of the field," she says. "Sometimes they'd buzz me, maybe because I was a girl."

When she wasn't working at the field, Virginia took lessons. Then, with commercial and instructor certificates in hand, she signed on as the only woman among ten instructors for the cadet program. Any suspicions she had about male chauvinism on the part of her fellow instructors evaporated when she was hospitalized for an emergency appendectomy: all of them chipped in to pay for the operation.

Virginia had hoped to join the Women's Airforce Service Pilots, or WASP, a wartime project in which women pilots ferried aircraft from the manufacturer to military bases in the United States and abroad. Before she could achieve that goal, however, a representative of Top of the World flying school in Fairbanks who'd come to the airport to buy several used J-3s offered her an instructing job at Weeks Field. "He told me I could instruct twenty-four hours a day if I wanted to," she says, laughing. "I thought he was kidding, but I didn't know that there was daylight all night up here in the summer. There was lots of interest in learning to fly in Fairbanks, and it turned out I actually could have instructed all day."

The representative gave her a round-trip ticket in case she became homesick, but she tore it up after arriving in Alaska. The North Country makes a lot of instant converts. In Fairbanks, Virginia found residents friendly and curious. "People wanted to look at this woman flight instructor."

George Clayton wanted instruction as well as a look, and he earned a certificate in both areas. Several months after he became a licensed pilot, he and Virginia were married.

It was a generation before women's lib, and even women adventuresome enough to fly airplanes often deferred to the ethic of home and hearth. "I gave up flying after marrying George because I felt I should be at home raising a family," Virginia says, adding

George Clayton and Virginia Merrill were married in Ketchikan on September 26, 1944. They spent their honeymoon in a cabin on a Prince of Wales Island lake. *Courtesy of the Clayton Family*

that she's never regretted the decision.

Virginia's flying career was over, but her husband's had just begun. Clayton joined Northern Consolidated Airways and was assigned to the southwestern Alaska community of Bethel. In what he terms a "low-grade seniority position," he flew a Gullwing Stinson on scheduled mail runs along the Kuskokwim River, as well as charters to other places.

Low grade position or not, Clayton harbors a special fondness for those early bush years. "That type of flying was new and fascinating to me," he says, in his New England accent. "I'd stop at various places and grab a cup of coffee, throw off a few mail sacks, load on a few others, and maybe pick up a passenger here and there. It was a good thing I was on the river, with skis in winter and floats in summer, because sometimes the plane would be loaded so heavily that it took 4,000 feet to get airborne."

Clayton half-points, as if the relatively flat, isolated wilderness of southwestern Alaska in the mid-1940s lay just across his living room. "It was easy to get lost out there. You got involved in some pretty adventurous flying. You never knew what was going to happen when you flew the bush. Nearly everyone wrecked an airplane sooner or later. I've been overloaded trying to take off, and I couldn't give up because we'd come to the rough ice and if you chopped the throttle you'd wreck the airplane, so you leave everything to the firewall, bouncing from one bad jounce to the next, hoping the skis don't tear off, and then finally, *twang* and no more bouncing and you're gone."

Other than twisting skis on such takeoffs, Clayton never damaged an airplane. But he has endless anecdotes. Arriving over Napamute on a mail flight one mid-spring day, he saw that the Kuskokwim River ice below appeared too unstable to support the Stinson's skis. He'd have to air-drop the two Napamute-bound mail bags he had on board. The first plunged into the snow fairly close to the waiting postmaster. When he shoved the second out the window, however, it flopped over the wing strut like a corpse. The bag was too far away to reach by hand, and every aerobatic maneuver he tried failed to dislodge it.

"It just hung in there," he says. "By this time the postmaster was shaking his fist at me. Finally, it dawned on me that if the sack did come off, there was no telling where it might end up, and the people down there might never get their mail. So, I figured I'd better try to land after all. I got down without breaking anything and threaded my way through the rotten ice right up to the postmaster, with the sack still on the strut. He wasn't in the best of social graces. After a few heated words to each other, I told him I wasn't going to deliver any more mail until the river broke up and I could land on floats."

On another flight, Clayton took Virginia with him "to show her what all this bush flying was like." At Akiak on the homebound leg, the village schoolteacher, who had no reservation, begged for transportation downriver into nearby Bethel. When Clayton told him all seats were filled, he claimed it was an emergency. Clayton wasn't about to leave Virginia behind, although she was traveling non-revenue, so he simply removed cargo and mail from the Stinson's baggage compartment and carried the man there. Each time the Claytons glanced at each other on the flight home, they had to turn quickly away to keep from laughing.

Soon the Claytons began to feel a bit discontented in Bethel. Both longed for the less isolated Fairbanks, and George saw little future for himself in bush flying. "I felt there was only one way a guy's going to get ahead," he says. "He's got to get a job as a copilot and fly the line on tin birds and someday move to the left seat."

After eight months in Bethel, the Claytons went Outside so George could get his airline transport rating. Back in Fairbanks, he signed on with Wien Air Alaska as a first officer. His initial assignment, riding right seat in C-46s on runs from Fairbanks to Whitehorse, Juneau, and Seattle, demonstrated that he hadn't left bush flying as far behind as he thought. "It was winter, and we picked up lots of ice," he says. "Sometimes we'd have to go right down to the water to get rid of it" (that is, descend almost to the surface so warmer air would melt off the ice).

Moisture on the *inside* of a C-46 caused a few tense moments on an early-spring charter several years later. By then a captain, Clayton was flying a cargo of ninety-nine sled dogs that were going home from Fairbanks after racing in late-winter carnivals. The dogs' breath raised the humidity so high that soon all the windows had fogged, and he had to open his side window for visibility during his landing approach at Hughes. "I leaned my head out and partially covered my eyes with my hand so they wouldn't freeze," he says. "When the temperature's thirty-five degrees outside and you're going through the air at ninety miles an hour, it's cold!"

Keeping the runway in sight wasn't the only challenge. After landing, the big twin suddenly veered to the left when the left main

On a mail run, George Clayton stops at Beaver before continuing in the Norseman to his next stop, Stevens Village. *Courtesy of George Clayton*

gear broke through the snow crust. "I had to use almost takeoff power on the left side to keep the plane straight," Clayton continues. "Then the right gear went through, and I yanked off the power on the left engine and added some on the right side." His deft throttle jockeying prevented the C-46 from going off the runway.

With forty dogs unloaded, Clayton and his copilot drove down the runway in a jeep to inspect conditions. "The grooves the wheels cut were so deep it looked as if someone had been digging a couple of ditches for pipes," Clayton says.

The lighter load helped them take off with little trouble. At Kotzebue, where the remaining dogs were bound, Clayton again had to open his side window for the landing, but thanks to colder weather there the runway was firm, and the wheels stayed on the surface.

About 1960, Clayton, then a captain on Fokker F-27s, began his habit of serenading his passengers with a harmonica. He had learned to play the instrument while in Africa, and the F-27 was the first airliner he had flown that had a good public-address system. On an impulse one day he blew a tune into the microphone. Encouraged by the enthusiastic response, he became a regular performer.

On April 18, 1980, Clayton gave a final airborne recital. When he stepped on board the Boeing 737 assigned to the Anchorage-to-Seattle run, he was wearing the musty helmet and goggles his father had worn as a barnstormer. After reaching cruise altitude, he informed his 110 passengers that this would be his last flight, and as the tiny sparkling lights of Victoria, British Columbia, came into view, he played "Harbor Lights" for them.

An airline captain about to retire naturally wants to make the very last landing a smooooooth one, to cap his career with finesse. Seattle-Tacoma International Airport had light rain but good visibility and ceiling that evening—little challenge for a pilot with 24,600 hours.

Clayton notes, "I think I concentrated harder on that approach than I ever did in the nastiest conditions." He greased the twin-engine jet onto Runway 16R as if everyone on board were holding a full glass of champagne, and the cabin erupted in cheering and clapping—applause not only for the gentle touchdown but also for Clayton's having shared a special personal occasion in an age of cockpit aloofness. Dozens of passengers scribbled notes of congratulations and appreciation.

The passengers are gone now, but Clayton's celebration of flight continues. Like many retired professional pilots, he's owned a number of private airplanes over the years—historical ones, in his case. At one point he had seven AT-11s and C-45s, both military versions of the Beech 18 he leased or simply kept for nostalgia's sake. He used to park several in his yard, making the place look like an aviation museum. One he donated to a real museum, the local Alaskaland Pioneer Air Museum. He's considering loaning the museum his prized Stinson Reliant and his "war bird," a Ryan PT-22.

Virginia, "retired" now from raising the couple's three children, says she enjoys George's continuing romance with aviation because it allows her to fly vicariously. Even his serenading goes on, in a sense: anyone who listens to him talk about airplanes and bush flying is bound to be entertained.

KEN EICHNER

— *Always on Call* —

AS IT SO OFTEN DID, the call came during a gale. A boat was foundering by Ratz Harbor, the Coast Guard reported to Temsco Helicopters in Ketchikan. A cutter was in the vicinity but could not locate the vessel because of driving rain and quarter-mile visibility. Would Temsco help?

Temsco president Ken Eichner, then sixty-seven, grabbed an assistant and lifted off in a Hughes 500D. Ratz Harbor lies some fifty miles northwest of Ketchikan on the east side of Prince of Wales Island. Navigation is normally a direct shot up Clarence Strait, but on this October day Eichner had to pick his way carefully along the rocky shoreline beneath a ceiling of just 200 feet as turbulence continually pounded the helicopter.

Finally on scene, he began searching for the boat in what he felt was the most likely direction. "Soon we spotted a gasoline slick in this real rough water," Eichner says. "I said, 'That's it!' So we turned downwind and in two or three miles here's a guy in a survival suit."

The man, the lone occupant of the now-sunken boat, waved his arms frantically in the three-foot waves as the 500D emerged like a buzzing angel from the gloom. Eichner maneuvered upwind, and his assistant dropped a life raft to the castaway.

For the next fifteen minutes Eichner maintained a hovering vigil alongside until a halibut boat, alerted by radio exchanges between the helicopter and the Coast Guard, arrived by radar and hauled the man on board. Eichner then opened the throttle and headed for home.

The boater joined a large club of hunters, pilots, fishermen, and other outdoors people who have welcomed Eichner's helicopter in an emergency. Just try to find an article about a search or rescue operation in a back issue of the *Ketchikan Daily News* that doesn't contain the name Ken Eichner. The director of the Alaska State Troopers called him a "living legend" in a thank-you letter. The Ketchikan Gateway Borough named one of its airport ferries in his honor. Citations have come from the Alaska State Legislature, the Ketchikan Chamber of Commerce, the Alaska Air Carriers Association, and other organizations. Local citizens regard him as a hero.

When you meet Eichner in his comfortable, three-story home overlooking Tongass Narrows in Ketchikan, you might expect the attitudinal swagger of a veteran fighter pilot; here's a man who has been at the forefront of some 200 search and rescue missions. Eichner, in fact, could pass for a retired general. His sparse white hair is cut short, and his strong neck, muscular shoulders, and agile movements indicate a militarylike attention to health. He wears no glasses, and his eyes reflect the confidence and intelligence characteristic of someone accustomed to being in authority.

Yet, the soft-spoken Eichner seems almost self-effacing as he relates his exploits. Whenever he comes to a part in an incident that obviously involved personal courage or skill, he hesitates, apparently wondering how much to include. You often have to prod him for significant details—like the fact that the wind was blowing forty at Ratz Harbor, and that another rescue occurred at night in heavy fog.

No general ever waxed this humble. But Eichner's modesty is relative. He's so dedicated to saving lives that self-aggrandizement and romanticism simply get in the way. On the subject of political interference in search and rescue, he pontificates like a preacher, raising his voice and spitting out a few four-letter words.

When he arrived in Southeast from his native Oregon in 1938 at the age of twenty, his own survival seemed in jeopardy for a while. Two uncles had engaged him to help set up their fish traps on Etolin Island, but afterward they abandoned him in Ketchikan. There he built rock walls, cleaned chicken coops, and bummed halibut on the docks before eventually finding steady work driving for Northern Bus Company. In 1939 he married a woman named Peggy. The next year he and a fellow driver borrowed $5,000 and bought the company.

By 1941, Alaskans were warily watching the horizon for Japanese warships and planes. Although the draft board had declared bus driving an essential service, Eichner, who had joined the Territorial Guard, decided that if he did end up on active duty he wanted to be in an aviator's uniform. So he took flying lessons in an Aeronca Chief from Ketchikan Air Service. His instructor made him fly for miles at wave-top level, perform low-altitude stalls, and follow every bend in a shoreline—maneuvers that later would prove invaluable for developing the concentration that search and rescue demanded, although they're considered too dangerous for modern training.

Once he had his license, Eichner was hooked. In exchange for more flying opportunities, he began making unpaid commercial flights for Ketchikan Air in his spare time, logging about 300 hours a year in a Taylorcraft, a J-3 Cub, the Chief, and later a Republic Seabee.

It was aboard a boat, however, that he first demonstrated his propensity for finding missing objects in the wilderness. In January 1943, famous pioneer bush pilot Harold Gillam crashed on a mountainside near Boca de Quadra Inlet. Studying the shoreline from the deck of a Coast Guard cutter looking for Gillam, Eichner spotted an orange streamer the pilot had hung in a tree during a struggle to hike for help. Beneath it lay his frozen body.

Four years later came Eichner's first aerial search. A Pan American Airways DC-4 had disappeared following an aborted instrument approach at the Annette Island airport, and, flying

Ketchikan Air's Chief, he joined other local pilots in scouring the island's forested slopes for the airliner. After five days, clouds finally dissipated to reveal the scattered wreckage on Tamgass Mountain. The Gillam and Pan Am searches convinced Eichner of the need for a formal rescue service, so he and fellow Ketchikan resident Dick Borch organized the Ketchikan Volunteer Rescue Service. The KVRS—air taxi pilots, firemen, police, and other citizens—would form the backbone of virtually every future search and rescue case in the Ketchikan area.

Eichner gradually discovered that responding to emergencies in the bush often demanded sacrifices. Like the fireman, the search-and-rescue pilot is always on call. When the phone rings, you go. If you were about to sit down to dinner, too bad.

One late-September evening in 1951, a pilot friend called him to report that a hunting partner had gotten lost by Little Goat Lake in the Coast Mountains. An avid hunter himself, Eichner knew that the temperature plummeted at night in the mountains. He was also aware of a bad-weather forecast for the area. "I thought, geez, if somebody doesn't get there and he is alive, he won't live. He was in a T-shirt; that's all he had."

He took off with his friend in a Piper J-5, landing on blackened Little Goat some forty minutes later. Flint sparks from the missing hunter's lighter—the lighter would not ignite—led the men to him.

"He was so cold he could hardly walk," Eichner continues. "We got him in the airplane and just did a squeeze job on him until he could talk again and got circulation back." From a previous trip Eichner knew about a local cave where they could build a fire to keep warm, and there the men spent the night. In the morning low clouds surrounded the lake, trapping them for three days before they could fly back to Ketchikan.

With a helicopter, Eichner might have been able to sneak home the first night; negotiating mountain passes in the dark is less risky if you can slow down and hover. But helicopters had yet to make their appearance in the Ketchikan area. And when the early ones arrived for a federal mapping project, they were underpowered lemons. The float-equipped Bell 47s "were always getting in trouble," says Eichner, who by then owned a Piper Super Cruiser. "The first one they dumped in Bradfield Canal, and I helped them get out. From then on I became the helper for all the helicopters that came to town. It was a pretty small circle. I'd air-drop parts from my Cruiser or land in small lakes and rivers to deliver them. It was a good learning experience."

Despite the initial breakdowns and limitations, Eichner recognized the potential of the helicopter for commercial work and rescue services in Southeast's isolated, rugged terrain. In 1958 he and several investors founded Temsco Helicopters. Temsco, an acronym for timber, exploration, mining, survey, cargo, and operations, eventually became the largest helicopter company in Alaska, with forty machines and several branches around the state.

From the start, Eichner, who served as Temsco's president, placed his helicopters on standby for local emergencies. Although other Temsco pilots occasionally performed search and rescue while the boss attended to business, Eichner typically assigned himself to the more difficult, dangerous missions. When pagers became available, he carried one wherever he went. Whether a call came from a government agency or a private citizen, he would quickly evaluate the situation and, if a life seemed threatened, dispatch a chopper. Never mind a guarantee of reimbursement for fuel and other expenses; he'd try to collect from the appropriate agency later. (One year Temsco counted $30,000 in unpaid medivac bills.)

Nor was Eichner particularly concerned about personal safety. He accepted the inherent risks in search-and-rescue operations as part of the price of saving lives. Airplanes usually don't crash into mountains in good visibility; boats usually don't sink in calm winds; hikers usually don't fall off gradual slopes. If you're a fair-weather pilot, stay away from search and rescue.

Dusk had already darkened the Coast Mountains to the east one gusty October evening when word came that a Cessna 185

Ken Eichner, Southeast's most famous helicopter rescue pilot, loading supplies into a Hiller at Ketchikan. *Courtesy of Ken Eichner*

floatplane had crashed by Lake Leduc. A fellow pilot, concerned when the 185 became overdue, had discovered the wreckage and hurried back to Ketchikan to report the crash. Minutes after the call, Eichner and another pilot lifted off for Leduc in two Hughes 500D helicopters with three emergency medical technicians.

Eichner hoped to evacuate any survivors out of the stormy mountains at least as far as a cabin down on the Chickamin River for the night. But low clouds forced them to detour on the way, and by the time they reached the mouth of the lake, darkness and heavy rain had dropped a curtain in front of them. Reaching the crash scene at all seemed impossible. "The lake was just an ink bowl," says Eichner. "There was no definition; I couldn't penetrate."

To orient himself, he descended foot by foot until the landing light picked out a waterfall against a cliff a few yards away. The lake, he knew, was its source. Squinting to keep the cascading water in sight, he inched back up the cliff to the top of the waterfall and slowly flew into the bowl, the 500D's runners practically nicking the rocks below. The second helicopter followed closely behind with its landing light on the leader.

"It was just pouring rain," Eichner goes on. "But I could see enough terrain to fudge my way to the head of the lake and land on flat ground. Then I said over the radio to the other pilot, 'Bill, I think we can move up a little farther.' He said, 'I don't want to move. We're on the ground and I want to stay there.' "

Hunching against the storm, the pilots and emergency medical technicians flicked on flashlights and stumbled across the slippery rocks to the wreckage several hundred yards away. One passenger was dead. Another had hurt his back and was lying in a nearby creek. The pilot had a broken forearm. After erecting a tent, the men moved the injured passenger inside, and the EMTs tended to him. Eichner and the pilot crawled into the broken 185's fuselage for shelter. By dawn, the rain had slackened, and the helicopters evacuated the survivors to Ketchikan.

To reach the wreckage of another 185 floatplane, Eichner and several rescuers once had to struggle up a steep, rocky mountainside for four hours. They had had to leave the helicopter a quarter-mile away on the nearest reasonably level ground. After extracting the body of the pilot, the only occupant, they needed the rope they had brought to get back down. "It was a mountain climbing situation and we didn't have mountain climbing equipment," Eichner notes.

In addition to the inherent dangers, he accepted the humanitarian responsibilities of search and rescue: comforting the injured, consoling the distraught, calming the hysterical.

Eichner's growing reputation occasionally thwarted other rescuers. When an old man living in a cabin by the Chickamin River became ill and radioed for help, the Coast Guard directed one of its helicopters that was already in the vicinity on a search to pick him up. The man shooed the crew away. "Send Kenny Eichner out," he told them. "I won't fly with you guys."

On the way to the Chickamin, Eichner located the two missing boats the Coast Guard had been trying to find. The occupants told him the big Sikorsky helicopter had flown overhead several times without spotting them. Eichner notes that while the Coast Guard has saved hundreds of lives in Southeast, it rotates its personnel before they can acquire local savvy.

But he admits having a knack for "being at the right place at the right time" for rescues. Returning from a routine flight one day, he overheard a radio call from the Ketchikan Flight Service Station: smoke was rising from a thickly wooded hillside above Ward Cove just west of Ketchikan. Would any pilot in the area take a look and report the source?

His 500D was just around the corner, and seconds later he spotted the ominous black plume, intruding into a clear sky. As he circled the site, he saw through the smoke the burning wreckage of an amphibious Beaver sprawled in the trees below. He radioed for help, then landed in a small muskeg meadow just above the crash and tore through the forest.

"I had recently looked into two other Beavers that had crashed and burned everybody up." Eichner slowly shakes his head. "You have to look hard to see that there were people in the airplane. Generally, all you can find are skulls, and that's what you're looking for. So I knew it was another horrible mess."

But the occupants of this Beaver were luckier. When he reached the plane, Eichner saw them lying and huddling among nearby trees. Only one of the five passengers had suffered serious injuries. The pilot had pulled them out of the wreckage before the fire spread, although he burned his hands in the process. Apparently, the Beaver had crashed after the pilot flew by a cloud close to the hill and became disoriented.

While Eichner attended to them, another helicopter arrived. He directed the evacuation, and soon the survivors were being hustled into Ketchikan General Hospital.

Eichner was also first to respond to the region's worst land disaster. Six feet of snow had fallen in the Coast Mountains around the Granduc copper mine, some eighty miles northeast of Ketchikan, in the first part of February 1965. By the eighteenth, the snowpack was dangerously unstable. Suddenly, at 10:16 A.M., it let loose. The avalanche wiped out most of the mining camp, killing twenty-six men and injuring many others. One survivor rigged a battery from a vehicle to power a radio and screamed for help.

When Eichner arrived with a doctor in a Hiller helicopter at the base of the glacier that led up to the camp, heavy snow driven by a thirty-five-knot wind seemed determined to keep them away. "It was just solid snow," he says. "I managed to set it down and stepped off the helicopter and went in so deep I had to have help getting back up. We stamped out a landing area with snowshoes. Then I turned on a lantern and left it in the snow so I could come back to this one spot."

Again and again Eichner tried to "crawl up the glacier" with the doctor to the camp at the 2,500-foot level, but the Hiller's landing lights did little to improve the near-zero visibility in the whiteout. Finally, with dusk closing in around them, Eichner inched back to the makeshift helipad for the night. The two men were unloading their camping gear from the helicopter when a deep rumble turned their heads. Avalanche!

"We got back into the helicopter and I fired it up and lifted off," Eichner relates. "But I couldn't see to go anywhere. I set it back down. There was nothing we could do. The avalanche rolled out about a hundred feet from us onto the flat. The avalanches went on until about midnight. We'd hear them start and they'd come, and we finally had to accept the fact that there's somebody bigger than we are and we're either going to be lucky or we're not."

A cold but clear morning allowed them entry to the camp—after they laboriously chipped off the helicopter's coat of ice. One survivor "ran up to me and grabbed me and hugged me," Eichner recalls.

The improved weather also brought two Canadian helicopters from Stewart, British Columbia, thirty miles south. But menacing clouds soon began reconverging on the surrounding ridges. Although Stewart offered the closest hospital, the pilots needed to climb over 5,000-foot terrain to get there. With new snow showers threatening to close off that route, they decided instead to ferry the survivors down the glacier to the mouth of the Chickamin River and utilize Ketchikan's facilities.

Eichner, who by tacit agreement had become operations leader, picked up the camp radio's microphone. " 'We need all the help we can get,' I told Ketchikan. 'We've got a hundred men to move to salt water and it's an hour round-trip and three helicopters just aren't going to do it.' "

He also arranged for the KVRS to deliver fuel to the Chickamin. Meanwhile, he and the Canadian pilots would have to make do with what was in their tanks—and by the time they touched down on the beach after the first shuttle, all three were glancing at the fuel gauges. Eichner took off alone and flew down Behm Canal toward Grace Lake, where he had previously cached several barrels of fuel for a U.S. Army Corps of Engineers project. On the way the needle moved against the "E." "I got there and found the fuel," he says, frowning, "but that was the closest I ever came to running out."

The two barrels he hauled back put the three helicopters into the air again. By afternoon seven other choppers from Alaska and Canada had joined the effort, and the Coast Guard cutter *Bittersweet* and the Royal Canadian Mounted Police cutter *Nanaimo* were plowing up Behm Canal toward the Chickamin for a mass evacuation.

Alaska governor William Egan sent a third vessel, the state ferry *Taku,* up Portland Canal on the other side of the mountains on the assumption that Stewart was the drop-off point. Many journalists from both countries also guessed wrong. Once in Stewart, they begged every local air service for a charter to the Chickamin, learned there wasn't an unused aircraft in town, and begrudgingly went out on the *Taku*.

The Granduc evacuation taught Eichner much about operating on snow. Every mission, in fact, contributed to his search-and-rescue acumen. "You develop a lot of little techniques, like your one-skid landings and things you could do and couldn't do and how to do them safely, and they all came from experience doing them the hard way first," he comments.

After a youth fell off a cliff at Port Malmesbury on Kuiu Island one day, a Coast Guard helicopter delivered the KVRS rock-climbing crew to recover the body. But the pilots could not maneuver the cumbersome Sikorsky close enough to the cliffs to pick the men up, so the Coast Guard called Eichner.

Even with the much smaller Hiller he was flying, Eichner could get only one skid on the ledge where the crew was waiting. The whirling rotor blades flung off a steady shower of spray from an adjacent waterfall as he hovered delicately with the outer skid suspended in air. Crouching, the first rescuer stepped forward and yanked on the door. And yanked. And yanked. Unable to release his hands from the controls, Eichner motioned frantically with his head that the door had to be slid open. The engine drowned his shouts. "The guy finally got enough bend and twist in the door that it popped open," he says with a grimace. "I don't know why manufacturers make every door handle different. That just taught me that when you go to do those things, you take the damn door off first."

Problems in rescuing people from the water with a helicopter inspired him in the early 1960s to design the "people-netter," a large, foldable device fashioned from a fire ring. Before a rescue, the pilot lands on the nearest beach, opens the people-netter with two flips, lifts off with it trailing on a line, and scoops up the victim. Since no action on the part of the victim is required, it works whether or not he's conscious. The one disadvantage: unless the victim is protected in a survival suit, he risks exposure during the open-air ride from the water to a beach or boat.

As a public service, the KVRS donated several people-netters to the Alaska State Troopers but decided against patenting, marketing, or publicizing the device. "You don't blow your own horn," Eichner says.

The KVRS fine-tuned its emergency-response system so well that just five minutes after an Alaska Airlines 727 crashed at the Ketchikan airport on a foggy, snowy morning in early April 1976, the service had five helicopers on scene. Fortunately, only one person died, but KVRS members had to smash into the cockpit with axes to pull the flight crew out before flames reached them.

Ironically, it was often a government decision rather than Mother Nature that got in the way of a rescue. When a satellite detected an emergency locator transmitter (ELT) signal by Wilson Lake in Misty Fiords National Monument late one summer afternoon, the state troopers chose not to notify the KVRS. This was probably just another accidental activation, Troopers officials agreed. That night, a private citizen picked up the signal and called the squad.

At 4:00 A.M. a KVRS pilot took off to investigate, found the wreckage of a Beaver floatplane on a mountainside, and called for assistance.

"Kenny, I knew you'd come!" declared one passenger after she was hoisted into Eichner's hovering helicopter. Another passenger, apparently suffering more from exposure than injuries, died shortly after Eichner shuttled her to a Coast Guard helicopter at Wilson Arm. "We never got her to town," Eichner says bitterly. "It was just hypothermia, all because of the time delay."

The KVRS blasted the Troopers for assuming the ELT signal was accidental. "The false alarms you get in a remote area are going to be mighty few," Eichner told them. He also chided the Coast Guard in general for trying to do too much itself. "My contention was that the Coast Guard shouldn't be sending their aircraft out looking for people. They should notify the local air taxis; we have airplanes all over the region. They'll come tooling down here for 200 miles [from the Sitka Air Station] looking for someone in our backyard that we could find in a minute if they told us. And the air taxis should get paid for it."

But the KVRS will have to find another advocate. Eichner, now in his early seventies, sold Temsco late in 1989. While he remains ready to help in any mission, he no longer is on twenty-four-hour call. "Every time I went fishing on my boat I'd get a call. Some emergency. Back I'd come. I don't know how many times I'd go out to the cabin and a helicopter would come out and get me. I'm not going to chain myself to that anymore. I also realize that younger people are better than I am now. There comes a time when everyone gets replaced."

Then he smiles and adds, "So far I'm not completely on the shelf."

Randy Acord

— *Still Infatuated* —

MANY PROFESSIONAL Alaskan pilots fly the bush for decades; others get out after just a few years. Randy Acord, a bright, jovial, heavy-set man, belongs in the latter category. He joined Wien Alaska Airways in 1946 upon his discharge from the Army Air Forces at Ladd Field near Fairbanks. Within a decade he had quit bush flying.

A bush pilot might change careers for any of several reasons. No one would have blamed Acord for resigning after his very first flight with Wien. It was July 8, 1946, a date he'd never forget even if he didn't have a superb memory for numbers. In the left seat of the Boeing 247D sat veteran Bob Rice, who had the task that day of introducing copilot Acord to the run. It was a long one: from Weeks Field in Fairbanks to Bettles, to Kotzebue, to Nome, to Gambell on Saint Lawrence Island, back to Nome, and then a return to Fairbanks.

The 247D had already logged more than ten hours when it passed over Manley Hot Springs at 7,000 feet on the homebound leg. For a tired Acord and Rice, Weeks Field and a shower and dinner were just 90 miles away.

Suddenly, the left engine started smoking and running rough. Cockpit hands moved quickly to shut it off and feather the prop. Even today, few piston-powered twins can maintain altitude on one engine with a heavy load; hauling nine passengers, mail, and cargo, the 247D began losing 200 feet a minute, although the men had pushed the right engine's controls forward to takeoff power.

"About halfway between Nenana and Fairbanks, we discovered we weren't going to make it," Acord says, a trace of his native Texas Panhandle accent still evident. As he talks, he fires off specific figures, including aircraft serial numbers, as if he has been up all night cramming for an exam. "But we had a few options to think about: Are we going to put it on the railroad? Are we going to put it in the trees? And our third option was, crank up the other engine and let it smoke."

Crash-landing threatened injuries to the passengers and guaranteed damage to the airplane. So, poised to flip its fire-extinguisher lever if a fire erupted, Acord and Rice restarted the left engine. Blue smoke again began trailing from the cowling, but they held just enough power on that engine to clear the upcoming terrain. After the 247D slipped past the community of Ester, Weeks Field was downhill, and again they shut off the defective engine.

Following an uneventful single-engine landing, the pilots turned the airplane over to Wien mechanics, who found that the supercharger-impeller shaft had broken, causing oil to be sucked from the crankcase into the induction system.

A tough beginning. For some, it would have been an ominous one. But Acord was neither intimidated nor superstitious, and he came back the next day, and the next, and the next.

Several years later, while he was taking off from the arctic village of Umiat, another emergency developed. In the fuselage of the C-46 cargo plane lay twenty-eight barrels of diesel fuel bound for Barrow, fourteen on either side. Loaders had secured each row with a rope running from barrel to barrel, but they had neglected the further precaution of knotting the rope between barrels.

The distribution of passengers, baggage, cargo, and fuel is just as important to the safety of an airplane as their total weight. That's why aircraft manufacturers establish balance as well as weight limitations. If the load's center of gravity shifts outside the allowable range, the resulting imbalance can render the plane hard to control,

Captain Randy Acord, an Army Air Forces engineer flight test officer in World War II, holds the prop of a twin-engine P-38 fighter at Ladd Field near Fairbanks in 1944. *Courtesy of Randy Acord*

like a seesaw with a skinny kid on one end and his chubby buddy on the other. A load too far forward or rearward is especially hazardous at takeoff, when the airplane is low, slow, and sluggish.

As the C-46 roared down the strip over potholes and bumps, jostling the barrels, the rope along the right side snapped. All fourteen barrels rolled into the "orchestra pit," a step-down area behind the cargo bay, suddenly shifting more than 5,500 pounds into the extreme aft portion of the tail.

"I almost lost it," Acord says. "The trim was all the way forward and I was pushing forward on the stick. I left takeoff power on until I got up to 170 miles an hour, then sent the copilot back to roll the barrels forward."

Gradually, as the center of gravity moved toward its proper envelope, Acord regained control. His heart needed a little longer to slow down.

Almost losing it has scared many bush pilots out of the cockpit forever, or prompted them to move into a less adventurous area of aviation. Yet neither of these incidents, nor the specter of others, had much influence on Acord's decision in 1949 to resign from Wien. "I had hundreds of things like that happen while I was a test pilot at Ladd Field," he points out. "But we *were* playing a few games at that time, like taking a C-46 with a 1,400-pound overload into an 1,800-foot strip. There are really only two laws affecting flying: the law of averages and the law of gravity. If you keep pushing it, one of them is going to catch you. All these things do add up a little in the final consideration."

If close calls don't end a bush pilot's career, burnout frequently does. Despite the occasional roller-coaster thriller, most flights in the North Country, as elsewhere, are about as adventurous as a ride on a merry-go-round. Back and forth flies the pilot to the same places over the same routes, day after day. In summer, when the days are long and the charter demand high, routine conspires with fatigue to tug at the eyelids; sometimes you have to open a vent and blast yourself with cool air to stay awake. Pilot Bob Rice, who died in 1983 from injuries suffered in a mugging in Fairbanks, reportedly logged a herculean 320 hours in a single month during a strike in the early 1950s. Wien policy grounded pilots when they reached 120 hours in a month, a limit the FAA imposes on air taxi pilots today. Nonetheless, even that's a grueling regimen, especially in operations requiring the pilot to make multiple stops and handle the fueling, loading, and unloading himself. Every season in Alaska, a few pilots hired in April have shuffled away by July, afflicted with premature burnout.

But Acord flew his 120 hours a month with only an occasional sigh over the lack of free time for trout fishing or other hobbies. Long hours were part of the job. He tolerated the fifty-five-below-zero days and the eighteen-hour winter nights, the sirens of big-city civilization failed to lure him, no family crisis compelled a relocation, no latent desire to hunt for lost Inca temples in the jungle or to teach philosophy at Princeton distracted him.

For Acord, the incentive was simple economic angst, on a couple of fronts. "Wien was always working close to the line financially," he says. "We often carried three or four paychecks at a time in our pockets until someone said, 'Okay, you can cash them now.' " After a fire destroyed much of Wien's hangar in 1948, Acord started his own air service on the side, leasing his Beechcraft Bonanza to Wien when it needed an extra airplane. He still flew full time for that company, but now he had an alternative source of income to support his wife, Marion, if Wien folded.

Then a meeting of company pilots made that extra insurance seem a little thin. "There were forty-two pilots there, and a third of them said they were concerned about passing their physicals year after year. I had always had high blood pressure. Not real bad, but marginal. Still do. Here were men forty, forty-five years old, wondering if they were going to continue passing their physicals. Well, they didn't know anything but flying. I thought, what if it happened to me? What if I failed my physical? I decided to get into something nonflying I could do when I'm seventy-five, if I was lucky enough to live that long, and make it a secondary job."*

Building a sideline business as a hedge against involuntary grounding has helped thousands of professional pilots in Alaska and the Lower 48 sleep more easily. Take a poll of any group of pilots and you'll find that this one owns a small deli, that one just got a real estate license, a third is taking a night teacher-certification course at the local university. If their eyesight goes bad, or they develop diabetes, or the doctor finds some other disqualifying ailment, the pilots will have a head start on another career.

In 1949 (April 15, 1949, Acord specifies—with his memory he could probably tell you what time it was, too), he left Wien to enter the food-brokerage business. For several years he continued to operate Acord's Charter Service during the summers, taking winters off to concentrate on his sideline enterprise. By 1956, however, the "secondary" job had become primary, and he closed his air service. He kept the Bonanza for calling on outlying customers and hauling food.

Acord sought economic security and found it. "He was smart," said many of his more career-minded bush pilot peers.

Perhaps he was unwittingly smart in another way. By retiring from professional bush flying after just ten years (the last few as a part-time pilot), he left a bit of his psyche unfulfilled. Like a single pancake for breakfast, one decade of bush flying merely whets the appetite. In ten years, you can taste but a sampling of detouring around snow squalls, chatting with passengers, evacuating the injured and ill, gazing at wildlife, exploring valleys, overnighting in

---

*Although modern bush flying—air taxi flying, the FAA calls it now—is physically safer than in earlier years, thanks to more reliable airplanes and engines and the proliferation of airport, navigation, and communication facilities, the economic risks lurk just as perniciously. Competition, insurance premiums, taxes, fuel prices, salaries, and overhead still create fog banks for operators. All four of the southeastern Alaska air services I flew for in the 1970s and '80s have folded their wings. Bill English, a Wien pilot who elected to remain in the cockpit for his career (see "Bill English: Cherishing Two Cultures"), submits that commercial flying in Alaska today "is an economic hazard because of all the mergers and changes in the aviation industry. I've told young people that if you're going to fly, you'd better really like it." Not long after English reached the mandatory airline retirement age of sixty, Wien ceased operations.

villages, surviving close calls, pointing out sights to tourists, taking photos of rainbows, searching for missing hunters, snacking in a mining camp mess hall, watching the sun rise, delivering Christmas packages, landing on frozen rivers, fishing off pontoons, sighting an avalanche, buzzing a grizzly bear, gawking at the northern lights, transporting a state trooper with an accused murderer. . . . Private or military flying produces only a few such memories, and without the same intensity.

Pilots who've flown the bush for thirty or forty years tend to be contented with the variety and depth of their experiences. Although most would turn back the clock if they could, the excitement they once felt has mellowed to a warm glow, like a long-term marriage maturing from passion to love. But part of Acord is still the day-dreaming youngster pausing in his chores on a Texas farm to watch a DC-3 rumble by overhead en route from Dallas to Denver.

Now retired from the food business, he continues to fly privately in a Bonanza (the first one was run over by a C-46 at Fairbanks International in 1969—May 2, to be precise), and on September 11, 1991, he will commemorate fifty years of active flying in a gala celebration with aviation buddies. Aviation-related plaques, certificates, and pictures cover the walls of his office at his home in Fairbanks. He recently won a ten-year campaign to persuade the National Park Service to designate the original portion of Ladd Field a historic site. And he's a founding father and the curator of Fairbanks's Alaskaland Pioneer Air Museum, which was scheduled to open in 1991 displaying many items he had stored in his garage.

Yes, Acord is still infatuated.

Jim Hutchison

— The Interior's Mechanic —

LIKE THE UNSUNG but indispensable linemen on a football team, aviation mechanics have always labored in the shadows of recognition. Especially in the early days, when flying was more art than science, more romance than routine, cockpit quarter-backs in scarf and goggles or spiffy, gold-braided uniforms received an unfair share of the glory.

The overall-clad "grease monkey" may have been invisible to the writer, the Hollywood producer, and the armchair adventurer, but let a bush pilot with one empty seat find all four awaiting rescue and it would be the mechanic who'd go home first. Cruising above endless miles of wilderness, pilots listened to the reassuring drone of the engine and knew who deserved their loyalty.

What pilot, for example, would have hesitated to hold open a door for Jim Hutchison?

Talk to anyone who flew Alaska's Interior for the half century beginning in the 1920s, and the name "Hutch" will inevitably arise. Usually no identification will follow; the pilot will mention Hutch as casually as he would "Nome" or "Mount McKinley." He'll say, "Hutch put it back together and I flew it out." Or, "I had Hutch take a look and he found a cracked cylinder."

If you ask, "Who's Hutch?" the pilot will stare in silence for a moment, as if you had asked, "Where is Fairbanks?"

Noel Wien, Carl Ben Eielson, Frank Dorbandt, Jerry Jones, Joe Crosson, Herman Lerdahl, Sam White—Hutchison knew them all, the legendary pioneer bush pilots of the Interior. He flew with them, fixed their airplanes, and socialized with them (Eielson, who in 1924 made Alaska's first airmail flight, accidentally broke Hutchison's nose in a basketball game). He participated in Alaska's most famous search operation, the one for Eielson and a mechanic in Siberia. He repaired the right landing gear and helped install a new propeller on the *Winnie Mae* for one-eyed pilot Wiley Post after the Lockheed Vega ran into a ditch on his attempted solo round-the-world flight. He mended a Waco floatplane being used to support the filming of the classic silent movie *The Eskimo* in the Arctic. Interior aviation history seems to ooze from this rugged individualist.

The general public in Fairbanks has also acknowledged Hutchison's contributions: on University Avenue sits a building officially named the James T. Hutchison Adult Career Development Center.

Who's Hutch, indeed.

Born in 1900 in Williamsport, Pennsylvania—where Lycoming aircraft engines are manufactured, he'll point out—Hutchison came to Alaska three years before the first commercial flight in the Territory. As a U.S. Army bugler at Fort Liscomb at Valdez in 1919, he had never ridden in an airplane, much less planned a career in aircraft maintenance. And Fairbanks had yet to become the aviation hub of the Interior when he moved there as a civilian in 1922. A baseball buff, he had heard that the Fairbanks city team needed several players. A promoter sent him $100 in travel funds when he touted himself as an experienced shortstop.

Skilled with tools as well as with glove and bat, Hutchison was doing maintenance for a local mining company in 1925 when Noel Wien, the first pilot to fly north of the Arctic Circle, asked him to repair a Standard that had been damaged in a forced landing on a Toklat River sandbar. In gratitude, Wien took him up for his first flight.

"That was a thrill, I'll tell you!" Bright and feisty, lean and hardy, Hutchison laughs often as he talks to me in the living room of his barn-red 1906 log cabin home near the Chena River in Fairbanks. He bought it for $75 in 1922 and over the years built additions to accommodate his wife and eight children. (He has forty-three great-grandchildren and six great-great-grandchildren.) Like Hutchison himself, the house retains a historical flavor, with aviation memorabilia on the walls and shelves and traditional furnishings throughout. The atmosphere adds even more color to Hutchison's stories.

"That flight with Noel was in a biplane," he says, slapping his hands together. "You can't believe all this damn stuff they got shooting around now. Pretty soon you'll get on board a rocket and be in London in twenty minutes. It's amazing the way things have leaped and bounded ahead."

Only some of his laughter seems intended to emphasize a particular point. The rest erupts as general gusto, in the way a mountain climber might yell with joy upon reaching the summit. It's nostalgic zest for having experienced practically the entire span of aviation development in the Interior, for having lived a rich life and being able to share it with a visitor. Behind his black-framed glasses his eyes, alert and sparkling, laugh too. You can't help laughing with him.

Hutchison's formal aviation maintenance career began in 1929 when he joined Alaskan Airways. That November Carl Ben Eielson, part owner of the company, and a mechanic, Earl Borland, disappeared in a Hamilton en route to pick up furs from the icebound schooner *Nanuk* on the Siberian side of the Bering Strait. Pilots throughout Alaska, some from the Lower 48, and even two from Russia joined in the search for the pair in bitter subzero weather.

When Fairbanks received a telegram in January 1930 that searcher Harold Gillam had broken his Fairchild 71's landing gear, Hutchison and fellow mechanic Bill Hughes took off with pilot Pat Reid in another 71 to do the repairs. The three got as far as the hills west of Nulato, where they ran into heavy snowfall. As Reid was making a precautionary landing on a frozen creek, terrain knocked off five feet of a wing.

Jim Hutchison, right, and fellow mechanic Herb Larison weld a tail ski bracket for Pat Reid's Fairchild 71 while Siberian Natives watch, aboard the vessel *Nanuk* on the the Bering Strait in 1930. *Courtesy of Jim Hutchison*

"So there we are," Hutchison says. "I had my welding gear but no tanks. I did have three wooden gas cases full of airplane supplies. You're not supposed to use nails in the wing, but we didn't have much choice. I took those boxes apart and very carefully took all the nails out. When we finished that thing, you looked at the wing and saw the words 'Standard Oil, 80 Octane' on the end of a gas case nailed on the spar."

He tilts his head, closes his eyes, and laughs.

The unorthodox wing splice took a week to fashion, in the middle of the Alaskan winter miles from civilization and communications facilities. Meanwhile, families and friends of the trio were worried.

A Fairbanks official wired Hutchison's mother in Pennsylvania:

HAVE DISCUSSED WITH HONORABLE DAN SUTHERLAND, ALASKAN DELEGATE TO CONGRESS, MATTER OF RELIEF EXPEDITION TO SEARCH FOR MISSING PLANE ON WHICH

JIM HUTCHISON WAS MECHANIC. AM ASSURED THAT PLANES ARE WAITING AT FAIRBANKS TO MAKE SEARCH AT THE FIRST MOMENT WEATHER CONDITIONS WILL PERMIT AND VISIBILITY WARRANTS. DOG TEAMS ARE ALSO BEING EMPLOYED IN SEARCH. AS FAR AS POSSIBLE EVERYTHING POSSIBLE IS BEING DONE FOR THEIR RESCUE.

But thanks to her son's ingenuity, Mrs. Hutchison soon received another telegram informing her that his Fairchild had emerged from the wilderness. At the *Nanuk,* searchers had one less missing airplane on their list.

By January 25, the Hamilton was also accounted for. Pilot Joe Crosson, accompanied by Gillam with his rebuilt landing gear, finally sighted the wreckage buried in the snow in Siberia. Eielson and Borland were dead.

Spending days or weeks in the wilderness to repair a damaged airplane became a regular part of the $225-a-month job for Hutchison. Since a limited amount of maintenance equipment could be flown or hauled in, field work usually required lots of creativity, improvisation, and use of local resources. To install a new engine, he typically built an A-frame hoist from saplings. To gain working room for replacing landing gear, he might dig a hole or ditch beneath the gear.

On one three-week field job near the settlement of Chicken, west of the Yukon Territory border, he made new wing ribs from seventy-five lengths of quarter-inch tubing for a wood-and-fabric Stinson.

"Frank Pollack, the pilot, was afraid the wing would be too heavy with all that metal," Hutchison recalls with a note of pride. "But he said that when he got in the air he took his hands off the stick and it flew perfect."

Unless a village lay nearby, the first on-scene chore was to build a shelter in which to sleep and keep parts and extra clothing dry. Sometimes it was also possible to construct a makeshift hangar.

Jim Hutchison, right, and fellow Alaskan Airways mechanic Eddie Moore at Weeks Field in the late 1920s. Behind them in the hangar is part of a Standard. One of Interior Alaska's most skilled mechanics, "Hutch" had no formal training. He learned on the job.
Courtesy of Jim Hutchison

Except for whatever fire they built, Hutchison and any helpers had only their clothes to ward off winter cold and summer mosquitoes.

They had to work wherever a mishap had occurred; pilots weren't always considerate enough to come down on firm, level ground that was sheltered from the wind and adjacent to a stream for drinking and washing. Once a damaged airplane was ready to fly again, Hutchison often had to help clear a takeoff strip—cut trees, clear brush, remove rocks.

And throughout a project, he usually had to do more than his share of the work: "Pilots in those days were fancy pants."

A field job occasionally exacted a physical toll. After a month and a half at the old mining camp at Kantishna mending a broken Stinson, Hutchison came home with blood poisoning. Another job gave him a slipped disk in his back.

As the wing-damage incident en route to the *Nanuk* demonstrated, the flight in or out could be as much of an adventure as the job itself. On a trip to old McGrath to repair a landing gear and a bent prop, Hutchison noticed his pilot was intoxicated. Fortunately, the pilot managed to find his way and land safely.

Hutchison also remembers the time he got his feet wet returning from a repair job at Teller. Snow and fog had forced pilot S. E. "Robbie" Robbins lower and lower as he worked his way eastward toward Fairbanks in their Waco floatplane. Suddenly they flew into a whiteout. Robbins yanked back the throttle and plopped down on the Tanana River below. The Waco slowed, then, *wham!* The floats slammed onto a sandbar, ripping the left float's keel.

The sandbar offered no shelter; the two men had to get to shore. While Robbins gunned the engine and rocked the airplane with the stick, Hutchison darted from side to side, pushing on the tail this way and that, grimacing from the prop blast on his face. At times he was up to his knees in water. "Ice cold," he says, simulating a shiver.

Like a ponderous sea mammal, the floatplane inched across the sand. When it finally slipped into the river, water gushed into the damaged left float and the plane began to list. Hutch scrambled onto the right float for balance, clinging to the wing strut as Robbins powered the Waco across the river and ran it up on the bank.

Hutchison built a fire and spent the night thawing out. In the morning, he patched the ruptured float as best he could. Realizing water would still flood the float as soon as they launched the Waco, he agreed to stay behind to shorten Robbins' takeoff run. To further lighten the load, Hutchison stripped the plane of everything removable, including the seat cushions.

Then they warmed the engine and pushed the Waco into the river. Robbins jumped in and slammed the throttle forward. Moments later he was airborne.

"You ought to have seen the water coming out of that float!" Hutchison says, with a chuckle. Robbins made it to Fairbanks, and pilot Ed Young hustled out in a Travel Air to evacuate the mechanic.

Did Hutchison ever learn to fly himself? In 1930 he took a lesson from Ralph Wien, brother of Noel. "I had forty-five minutes and I was doing real good," he proclaims. "Ralph said, 'Geez, it'll be no time at all before you'll be flying, Hutch.' Then he went and got himself killed, and right away quick my mind started working. I had a bunch of kids, and I just backed off of it for that reason, not because I didn't like it. I gave it up." Riding as a passenger several times a month to and from repair sites was less risky than daily flying in the left seat, he points out.

Typical of a man who condemns the government's practice of subsidizing airlines ("I like to see a job pay for itself"), Hutchison remained fiercely independent professionally during his career. "I never belonged to a union. I made my own decisions. No union was going to tell me when I could work or when I couldn't."

He was eighty-two when he retired. "I just didn't want to get cold anymore," he quips, adding quickly, "but I could still do it!"

There's no doubt of that. Hutchison keeps his car and other machines in tip-top condition, and he operates them himself—all of them. Stored near his lawnmower out back is a snowmobile.

Alden Williams

— Master Teacher —

Alden Williams knew early on that he wanted to fly. As a farm boy in Smith Center, Kansas, he'd watch chicken hawks glide above the hayfields, then swoop down to catch rabbits. How graceful and free the birds seemed, he thought. What Williams didn't know was which flying niche would suit him best. It took him half a century to find out.

Today he reveals his preference even before telling you that he's spent the last 4,000 hours aloft instructing. Sit awhile with him on the porch of his house in Anchorage to discuss his career, and every few minutes he'll throw in an instructional tip, often with a wagging finger. "You got to have some kind of a checklist," he admonishes, after mentioning a fatal accident in which a pilot landed a Cessna 206 amphibian in the water with its wheels extended. "Under some conditions you can get sidetracked. Unless you have a checklist you can get in trouble."

No matter that he knows his guest is an experienced commercial pilot long familiar with checklists and amphibians. Instructing has become habit; he can't get away from it. And he's good. His delivery is simple, straightforward, and effective, with interest and dedication coloring every bit of advice.

Actually, Williams is in the second of two stints as an instructor that bracket his overall career. When he moved to Bend, Oregon, in 1936 to work for an uncle's construction business, he brought with him 460 hours of flight time and faced a paradox common to low-time aspiring professional pilots: inexperience means no flying job, no flying job means trouble building experience. Since soloing in 1929 at age nineteen, he had averaged fewer than sixty-six hours a year putt-putting around the farm country in various biplanes.

Meager in pay, fraught with stress and tedium, instructing has seldom attracted aviation's elite. Perversely, it's the low-time pilots who resort to instructing to finance their own training, to earn advanced ratings and accumulate enough hours for more interesting, higher-paying jobs with charter or scheduled outfits. (Flight lessons count toward overall hours for both instructors and students.) Of course, young, new instructors have demonstrated the ability to pass on their learning of the basics. But they have had little time to hone skills, to develop finesse and acquire wisdom. Aviation textbooks don't discuss landing an airplane so tail-heavy that you run out of elevator control; young, new instructors *can't* discuss it.

So, besides barnstorming in his free time, Williams instructed. In 1940, after soloing thirty students (including his wife, Dorothy), he took his savings to Los Angeles and earned an instrument rating. He also applied for flying positions with United and Pan American. Neither airline felt he had enough experience, but the Lockheed Aircraft Corporation gave him a job, sitting in the copilot's seat on flights ferrying Hudsons from Burbank to the East Coast. Although the flights required a copilot, the airplanes lacked dual controls. At least he was aloft.

Three months before Pearl Harbor, Williams met the famous Alaska pilot Bob Reeve, who was picking up a Trimotor in California to use for supply flights to airport-construction sites in the Territory. Reeve offered him a copilot job (the Trimotor had dual controls), and Williams has been in Alaska ever since.

"You've got to know how to hold a heading," he says while talking about flying in low visibility, his hands raised for emphasis. He looks remarkably trim and robust for a man born in 1909. "When you're going across the flat in a whiteout, there's nothing to see till you come to a river. So you have to hold your heading."

Alden Williams and his wife, Dorothy, with his first airplane, an OX-5-powered Swallow, which he bought in 1934. *Courtesy of Alden Williams*

After the job with Reeve ended, Williams joined Dodson Air Service's flight department in Fairbanks. He stayed on with the company as it expanded through mergers into Northern Consolidated Airlines and later Wien Consolidated Airlines.

Steady bush flying over the years brought a great variety of experiences that would eventually coalesce into the background and savvy a master instructor needs. He hauled sportsmen, government workers, scientists, villagers, mail, food, booze. Twice, pregnant women gave birth on board. There were corpses, too ("I've gotten both the beginning and the ending of life"). Snow squalls, fog, and high wind caused close calls and unscheduled nights in the bush. He evacuated injured trappers and searched for missing pilots.

"If you've got to pick up someone in a floatplane off a beach and the tide's going out fast and it's a rocky beach, you better have a boat bring the passenger out to you. Floats can be damaged quite easily. It takes just one odd-sized rock sharp on one spot to rip a float open."

Inevitably, Williams' experiences included some mistakes. Once, he misjudged the amount of snow on the ground at a mining camp, landed, and cringed as the Gullwing Stinson scraped across patches of rough, frozen ground covered by only a light dusting. Before he could take off, he had to do makeshift repairs to the badly damaged skis. Another time, he forgot to extend the gear in a Bamboo Bomber and nicked the props on the runway before realizing his mistake and firewalling the throttles. In the early 1960s, he crash-landed a Stinson SR-5 into a stand of spruce trees after the engine quit, injuring his only passenger. He had had an inadequate checkout in the operation of the airplane's fuel system and had left the fuel-selector valve in the wrong position. All lesson material for future student pilots.

When Wien began acquiring Boeing 737s in the mid-1960s, Williams underwent copilot training in them. Getting from Point A to Point B in a jet involves heavy reliance on computers and fairly rigid adherence to altitudes, airspeeds, courses, and other "numbers," as the aviation industry calls such parameters. But Williams didn't quite think of all that as flying. In addition, he noticed a lack of common sense in some of the much younger, recently hired captains already schooled in jet techniques. So, after six months he was back in Wien's bush airplanes.

"I tell students, 'I don't care if you're a hundred feet high. I don't want you fifty feet low. That gives you a built-in safety margin in case the altimeter is wrong.' "

In 1969, Williams reached the mandatory airline retirement age of sixty and had to leave the company's cockpits. (The FAA allows a pilot to fly small aircraft commercially after sixty, as long as his company operates no aircraft he would be ineligible to fly because of age—that is, large planes assigned to scheduled routes. Since Wien's fleet included the latter, Williams could no longer legally fly its bush planes, either.) Not ready to quit flying, he went to work for Anchorage-based charter outfits and began instructing again.

Putting in 120 hours a month during the summer for air taxis strained his body far more than did his career with Wien, during which he usually logged about 105 hours a month. In an air taxi Cessna, Williams was an overworked hired hand who flew where he was told and got yelled at if he took too long returning for the next flight. As an instructor, however, he could control the hours, the pace, and the program. He was a mentor who "enjoyed trying to keep the boys right-side up." Not surprisingly, Williams concentrated more and more on instructing.

Teaching proved to be his most satisfying aviation role, representing the ideal instructor-student relationship: the old veteran imparting the lore, the wisdom, the tips that only many hours in the cockpit—37,500 in Williams' case—can produce.

"If you get vertigo and there's no copilot to take over, put your ear over on your shoulder and look at your instruments. Bring your head back slowly after about a minute and you'll get over the vertigo." Try to find that one in a textbook. "When you have vertigo in a mountain pass, you can look at the trees on the mountain. They should be straight up. If you see trees at a forty-five-degree angle in the fog, you're not exactly right-side up." Williams laughs. "Of course, in mountain passes above the timberline, you don't have trees to look at. They should put up vertical poles for pilots there."

How *do* you land that hypothetical tail-heavy airplane mentioned earlier when you run out of elevator control? Williams had faced such a problem one day in a Wien Twin Otter. He and his copilot had placed heavy mail sacks in the tail along a multistop village run. No problem as long as the cabin contained passengers to balance the load.

But at one destination, everyone disembarked except a 300-pound man sitting in the rear, creating a dangerous imbalance. The two pilots neglected to readjust the load before takeoff.

When Williams reduced airspeed in preparation for the next landing, at Bethel, the nose went up as if pulled by a giant magnet. The elevator-trim wheel was already rolled full forward, and he had to hold the yoke against the stop just to keep the nose level. Experience warned that if he throttled back farther to touch down at the normal sixty knots, the airplane would certainly stall.

So he increased power. The extra airflow over the tail restored enough elevator control to land safely, albeit at 100 knots, stressing the tires and landing gear.

Unless an old pro had advised him on what action to take in such a predicament, a twenty-two-year-old, 350-hour pilot might crash struggling to reach the prescribed sixty knots.

Williams also teaches spins to students, although the government eliminated them from the formal training curriculum decades ago. "Knowing how to get out of spins saved my life twice," he explains. "Spins are something you want to stay away from, so you've got to nibble over into what you shouldn't be doing to recognize when you do get into them."

The FAA probably will never require prospective instructors to first serve a long flying career. Too bad.

Mike Hunt

— *Bushing in the Big Ones* —

MENTION BUSH FLYING and most people think of Beavers, 206s, Super Cubs, and other light single-engine aircraft. Large twins like C-46 transports are for airports and long, paved runways. Aren't they?

Anchorage's Howard "Mike" Hunt smiles at such nonsense. He took C-46s into places in the wilderness that many pilots of those singles wouldn't go. With a gross weight of 48,000 pounds, a wingspan of 108 feet, and a pair of 2,000-horsepower Pratt & Whitney engines, the C-46 (it resembles a large DC-3) is no docile Super Cub.

"The C-46 was built as an assault transport and was almost a natural to use for big-ship bushing," Hunt says. "It could carry a 14,000-pound load off of a pretty short strip. We sort of pioneered bushing with big planes." "We" refers to a coterie of Army Air Forces buddies. Some pilots might dispute the pioneering claim, on grounds that Alaskans were landing Ford Trimotors on gravel bars when Hunt was still a farm kid in Polk City, Iowa. But everything's relative: a Trimotor might be big by Super Cub standards, but place it alongside a C-46 and it looks pretty puny.

Certainly no one made more of a business of big-plane bushing than Hunt, rebuilding, chartering, leasing, and salvaging as well as flying C-46s and even larger aircraft. "You call, we haul" was his motto. Bad weather, high mountains, no landing strip, bitter cold—regardless of the obstacles, Hunt found a way. A handsome man

Army Air Forces cadet Mike Hunt, age twenty, just after graduating from advanced multi-engine flight training school in Victorville, California, in 1942. The airplane is a Curtiss AT-9 trainer.
Courtesy of Howard Hunt

with a trim figure and a thin mustache, he emanates a "can do" attitude in his relaxed, confident demeanor. His intelligent eyes seem to notice all details. He wears a Confederate Air Force cap everywhere he goes, a habit that supports the impression that he and his commandos would be the ones to call on for a hostage rescue in a faraway place.

Hunt seemed destined for a career with large aircraft right from the beginning. Assigned to the Air Force's Air Transport Command in 1942, he became an aircraft commander on four-engine B-17 bombers out of Gore Field in Great Falls, Montana, with less than 200 hours in his logbook.

Because some ATC missions involved ferrying P-39 fighters to Fairbanks for pickup by Russian pilots, he also got an early introduction to Alaska. Wartime exigencies allowed as little margin for weather as for experience, so he quickly learned about flying long distances on instruments over rough terrain through clouds, icing, and turbulence. On his very first P-39 flight, the engine suddenly quit above the Canadian Rockies. Even over the Midwest, with its flat farm fields and straight country roads, an engine failure pumps up the pulse. Over mountains, it brings the same feeling you'd get if the brakes of your car went out going down a steep, winding hill.

Hunt lost several thousand feet before he figured out how to restart the engine (there hadn't been much time for instruction in the airplane's fuel system). But at least he got to Fairbanks that day—three of the five P-39s in his squadron did not.

After the war, Hunt and four fellow veterans decided to create a nonscheduled airline to compete in the hot Seattle-to-Alaska market. Their first venture went bankrupt after a typhoon damaged three surplus military C-46s they had purchased on Guam. Their second company, Seattle-based Air Transport Associates, began in 1949 and became the largest and busiest of twenty-four nonscheduled airlines serving Alaska, pulling in two million dollars a year.

"I had a Buick station wagon with wood paneling on the sides, and I was smoking a cigar now and then, trying to maintain an airline image," Hunt says. Although he served as the Anchorage-based Alaskan manager, he regularly made flights, too. "Any time a pilot balked at the weather, I took it." Weather along the North Pacific coast could cause so much ice accumulation that the company had to install reinforcing plates on the fuselages to prevent chunks flung off the props from punching holes in the aluminum skin.

When ATA's business began to outgrow its fleet of six C-46s and a DC-3, the company bought a DC-4 that had been converted into a hamburger stand in Louisville, Kentucky, and sent it on a railroad car to California. A born scrounger, Hunt traveled around the world scavenging parts from wrecked DC-4s and shipping them to California. The company ended up with enough pieces to build a second DC-4.

Not all schemes worked, however. Since most revenue derived

from northbound flights, Hunt wondered how to make the often sparsely filled southbound flights more profitable. Then it came to him: clams! Seattleites would pay for all the big, fresh Alaskan razor clams he could fly down. A food consultant from Bellingham, Washington, concurred with the idea.

So he bought an old military landing craft, hired diggers, and invaded beaches in Anchorage's Cook Inlet.

Laughing, he says, "By the time we hauled the clams to Anchorage, put them in the airplane and flew them to Seattle, the only thing we had was sacks full of shells—plus a lot of stink." A month and $10,000 after it began, the venture folded.

By 1953 the company faced liquidation. "The CAB [Civil Aeronautics Board] decided we were flying too often," says Hunt, who has a scrapbook of newspaper clippings about his legal battles with the agency. "We were becoming competition for the scheduled airlines, which were subsidized. We were showing them up."

When the CAB squeezed ATA out of business by imposing restrictions on its operations, the company kept several C-46s and became a charter outfit. Two major assignments took a C-46 to the high Arctic on support flights for construction of radar stations on the DEW (Distant Early Warning) line, first in Canada and then in Alaska.

Landing on short strips or sea ice with loads of heavy equipment was the easy part. It was getting from point A to point B in the Far North, in those years before high-tech navigation systems, that challenged every airman. The extreme difference between true north and magnetic north made the magnetic compass difficult to use, and the frozen, desolate terrain provided few landmarks. While the stations did have nondirectional beacons, crews had to dead-reckon for hundreds of miles before their automatic direction finders began to home in on the signals.

"We never got lost, but sometimes we didn't know where we were," Hunt acknowledges with a smile.

On one flight out of their base on Baffin Island in the Northwest

Many North Country air services have used the C-46. This Alaska Airlines C-46 sits at Paine Field in Everett, Washington, in the early 1940s.

Photo by Lloyd Jarman

Territories, Hunt's C-46 rumbled on and on through the clouds without finding a beacon signal. Dead-reckoning on instruments, he began to frown. Obviously either the aircraft radio or the station beacon had failed. When he estimated he was near the destination, he began descending.

"All of a sudden rocks started moving right under the belly of the airplane," Hunt says, grimacing. "Man, that really frightened us. We put the power on, climbed back to 11,000 feet and sat there for another half-hour before we had the nerve to start down again."

This time the C-46 popped out safely over the frozen ocean. After making a 180-degree turn and flying for thirty minutes back to the coastline, Hunt found the station by a fjord. Loaders there had shut off the beacon because it interfered with a radio program they wanted to hear.

"That DEW line job was pretty primitive flying," he says.

To encourage cooperation from the loaders and other ground workers, he provided them with "a little bounty"—the drinkable kind. And because the stations were hundreds of miles from the nearest maintenance facility, Hunt carried spare parts and tools with which to make repairs on the spot.

Such foresight enabled the company to squeeze 300 hours a month out of the airplane. But that meant little rest for the crews. Noticing his copilot's eyes drooping one night, Hunt told him to nap while he handled the flying. Shortly afterward he nodded off himself.

"When I woke up, we were in a deadman's spiral and the altimeter was unwinding like mad," he says, his face grim. "I was terrified. I didn't know what was happening, whether the airplane was right-side up or what. By the time I got it level again, we had lost 5,000 feet. Now, anytime I get sleepy on an airplane, all I have to do is think about that night and I'm wide awake again."

Between charters back in Anchorage, Hunt resumed his wheeler-dealing. When an Alaska Airlines C-46 crashed at Cape Lisburne, he decided he could salvage it for a profit. He submitted a bid to the insurance company, then had two of his partners pose as prospective independent buyers and bid different amounts. One of the three came in low.

After installing a new right wing and making temporary repairs, Hunt flew the C-46 down the coast to Nome for fuel, then it was off to Anchorage for a thorough revamping. A C-46 has three fuel tanks in each wing. Well into the flight, he switched to the right engine's front tank. (Multiengine pilots change tanks one engine at a time to make sure each keeps running.) A moment later that engine quit. The selector-cable for the front tank, he would later discover, had become disconnected from the cable drum. The Pratt & Whitney R-2800 filled the silence on the right side with a welcome roar when he quickly returned the selector to its previous position on the center tank.

But the unavailability of the front tank's precious liquid placed the whole flight in jeopardy. It was November and nighttime, and a fierce storm had rendered Anchorage International the only available port. Over at Merrill Field, Anchorage's general aviation airport, controllers had abandoned the tower because of high wind.

Hunt announced a fuel emergency, battled severe turbulence, and forced the big twin onto the runway. The right engine quit as he taxied beneath the tower. "Whew!" he exclaims, reliving both the lack of margin he had that night and the relief he felt at being back on the ground.

That wasn't the only time the fuel-gauge needles brought perspiration to his forehead. After that postwar typhoon on Guam, Hunt and his buddies salvaged two of the damaged C-46s and sold them to an airline in California. The deal called for delivery to Burbank. Following the hop from Guam to Honolulu and a fourteen-hour flight to San Francisco, Hunt decided not to "give fuel to the airline." He took on just enough gas in his C-46 for the final leg to Burbank, no more. His less confident buddy flying the other C-46 opted for a reserve.

During the flight, evening sea fog rolled in to the California coast. The resulting air traffic delays made Hunt squirm. "I sent my copilot back to see how much fuel was left in the long-range tank we had rigged. He held it up till the engines burped, and then I went to the other tanks."

In low visibility, an airport tower typically clears inbound aircraft to land on a first-come, first-served basis. Hunt couldn't afford to wait for his turn. "I declared an emergency and went straight in. We made it okay, but when the airline pulled the wings off [in preparation for renovation] and went to drain the tanks, there was no fuel in them."

He's silent for a moment. "I realize now that it wasn't all skill and daring, the flying we did. There was some luck involved, as I look back on it. Some guys didn't make it. But we did know our stuff."

One indication Hunt knew his stuff is that throughout his career he managed to avoid a crash—at least as a pilot. He did experience one as a passenger. During the abortive clam scheme, a pilot friend flew him out to the digging area. Hunt advised him to land on the miles-long beach, but the pilot looked askance at the beach's angle and lined up instead on an adjacent 800-foot strip. Worried about overshooting, the pilot let his Gullwing Stinson slow down a little too much. The airplane stalled seventy-five feet in the air, slammed onto the ground, and cartwheeled, tearing off the wings. Both men crawled out shaken and bruised.

"That was my only real crash," says Hunt, "and I wasn't at the controls. After that, I didn't allow my life to be in the hands of just anyone."

In addition to the Alaska Airlines C-46 at Cape Lisburne, the company salvaged a four-engine C-54 that had crashed on frozen Hudson Bay in Canada and bought a four-engine PB2Y flying boat to use as an airborne fish tender. Yet few deals made much money. In 1956, Hunt agreed to go on someone else's payroll, when Cordova Airlines sought a consultant and veteran C-46 pilot for a bush contract in the Far North. Later, Interior Airways and Alaska Freight Lines also hired him for contract stints in large aircraft.

At Yakutat one day, he saw the famed FAA pilot Jack Jefford and several coworkers loading moose onto the agency's big C-123 after an off-duty hunt. "I said to myself, 'That's the airline I want to work for,' " Hunt chuckles. So for the next twenty-six years he flew DC-3s, a DC-4, a Convair 580, a Sabreliner NA-265, and the C-123 as an FAA cargo and airways inspection pilot. After bush flying and worrying about business deals for ten years, working for the FAA was "like being on vacation."

Hunt is retired from the FAA now, but not from various other enterprises. Although he's busy developing real estate and prospecting for gold in his own helicopter, he'd probably listen to anyone needing a soldier-of-fortune C-46 pilot for a profitable project in the bush.

BUD HELMERICKS

— *Arctic Philosopher* —

"*YOU AND YOUR FAMILY* probably feel like the Swiss Family Robinson in the Arctic after all these years," I say to Harmon R. "Bud" Helmericks as we climb into his white Toyota. Helmericks, a tall, husky man with a firm chin and penetrating eyes, wants to show me Fairbanks's Phillips Field, a small airport the state plans to close for a highway project. "I'd guess that anyone who has lived up there as long as you have has learned to be resourceful. After all, the Arctic is so far from civilization."

Helmericks smiles patiently, as if he's heard such comments before. "I think *this* is the center of civilization," he answers in a midwestern accent, gesturing to the north with his hand. "It gets worse as you go into the more congested parts of the world. Now, if you want to talk of smog, car wrecks, robbery, rape—if that's civilization, then we don't have it. But if love for one another, a family, a home, and a beautiful land are civilization, then that's what we have."

I clear my throat. "Good point. Well, don't you miss the trees, though? I mean, the Arctic certainly has its own beauty, but without trees it seems pretty barren."

For a moment Helmericks drives in silence, like a deft country lawyer savoring his rebuttal. He pulls onto Airport Way. "Sailors all love the Arctic, because their life is the sky and the distance and the vast panorama. I'm always lonesome when I'm in trees, because I can't see, and I feel shut in. New York City is what I think of as barren. Not even grass can live there. You can't get more barren than that."

"I, uh, never thought of it that way."

Stretching some 700 miles from the Chukchi Sea to the Yukon Territory and about 200 miles from the Brooks Range to the Arctic Ocean, Alaska's Arctic has always presented a remote, forbidding image to people who live elsewhere. In Helmericks, the Arctic has its most eloquent spokesman and ardent defender. It's been his home for five decades. There he's explored, hunted, trapped, guided sportsmen, raised children, and flown most of his 34,000 hours. All of the eight books and numerous magazine articles he's written have concerned it. During trips to the Lower 48, he's lectured on it. Members of his audiences no doubt go home realizing that in some ways the Arctic is a little less cold than they thought.

Helmericks may have developed his need for wide-open spaces in the farmlands of Illinois, where he was born on January 18, 1917, or in the deserts of the Southwest, where he studied mechanical engineering at the University of Arizona. Perhaps he associated elbow room with the freedom and adventure suggested in stories his uncle Fred told about laying the first telephone lines to Nome.

When he discusses flying, though, I suspect that being aloft has inspired him as much as anything. His tone reflects the same poetic reverence he reserves for the Arctic. "You'll never know your world unless you fly around and look at it. Otherwise, you'll always have kind of a mole's-eye view. When you look down on the world, it gives you a fair perspective of yourself. You feel that all of your struggles and your hassles and what they were trying to sell you for breakfast cereal on the TV don't matter."

Yet, Helmericks points out that he has had no flying career. "It's just been my method of transportation. You wouldn't say you've had a taxi driver's career, although you've driven cars all over." An avid explorer, he realized the value of flying soon after moving to Alaska in 1940. "When you walk across Alaska, you soon learn to fly if you want to get anyplace."

Bud Helmericks fuels his Cessna 170B skiplane with a jerry jug at Point Barrow in 1962. *Courtesy of Harmon Helmericks*

He flew the first airplane he owned, a tiny two-seat Cessna 140 on floats, across the continent from the pickup point in Connecticut to northern Alaska with his wife and as much gear as they could stuff in. His 1952 book, *The Flight of the Arctic Tern,* describes that journey. He had Alaska's first Cessna 170 floatplane, and he's gotten himself around in four-place Cessnas ever since. Son Jeff and he now share ownership of the 170. His own airplane is a 180, currently on floats at Fairbanks International Airport's float pond. There are three other airplanes in the family.

Helmericks is the quintessential bush pilot: a seat-of-the-pants airman who knows whether an extra forty pounds of moose meat would keep him from out-climbing the trees at the end of the strip; a jack-of-all-trades mechanic who can mend a busted landing gear 100 miles from the nearest maintenance facility; a self-reliant outdoorsman who coaxes flames from kindling in the rain. He's a self-taught naturalist who can tell from the air whether tracks in the snow belong to a fox or a wolf, an amateur anthropologist who passes cold winter evenings reading about the cultures of the Athapaskans and the Eskimos, and a romantic who loves it all so much he's kept a daily diary that now fills seventy-nine book-length volumes.

You can't imagine Bud Helmericks wearing an airline uniform.

Helmericks and his family maintain two homes north of the Arctic Circle, one of them almost at the very top of the state on the Colville River Delta, near the Arctic Ocean, the other on Walker Lake in the Brooks Range. Which home they occupy at any given time depends on the season and their activities. For accommodations on visits to the Interior, they also have a house in Fairbanks. It's there that Helmericks keeps the Toyota.

Like his speech and personality, his driving is relaxed, assured. He slows as we pass a row of apartment buildings sitting on what used to be historic Weeks Field. Carved out of the bush in 1923, Weeks Field became the North Country's most famous airport, the center of aviation in Alaska until the jet age transferred that role to Anchorage.

"I have a bit of a hard spot in my heart for that apartment complex because it did in Weeks Field," Helmericks says, pointing. He sounds unruffled, but the lines in his face tense. "To stop the people flying they put a power line across the field, and then they built that. In a land where we've got nothing but space it seems rather ironic that they would take the one link to that land away. The International Airport is a link to the outside world, but this was the link to Alaska. You say they did the same thing in the lower states, but of course they didn't, because they had roads and horses and railways and everything else to go where they wanted to. But you stopped here. There weren't any more roads."

We turn onto Peger Road and, then, a few blocks later, onto Phillips Field Road. Phillips Field lies several miles west of downtown Fairbanks between the Chena River and the Alaska Railroad. Only a handful of airplanes are parked on the grass. Most of the runway is still unpaved.

"Pretty soon this airport will be gone, too," Helmericks continues. "It's being closed to put a road through so they can save two minutes crossing town with cars." I follow him into the hangar office, where he introduces me to airport lease co-owner Ann Bachner. She and her husband, Jess, who is off fishing, began operating an aircraft maintenance and service facility on Weeks Field in 1948. They built Phillips Field in 1950 after the city decided to close Weeks, and have been here ever since. Like the Bachners themselves, Bachner's Aircraft Service is familiar to all long-term Interior pilots.

"We built every bit of it," Bachner says, sweeping her arm in a semicircle as we stroll outside. A grandmotherly woman, she speaks with the same nostalgic sadness as Helmericks. "We cleared the trees, hauled in the gravel, planted the grass, everything. Now the state seems to think it's a big joke. It'll cost five million dollars to replace us out in the bush, and they don't even own the land we're on. They aren't very fair. People don't realize how much money aviation brings in to this city. They really don't. Everything changes. Not always for the better."

Answering my questions, Bachner talks about growing up in the Valdez area and meeting Bob Reeve, Harold Gillam, and other pioneer pilots who flew there. But her mind is on the imminent closure of Phillips Field (the state Department of Transportation planned to begin plowing up the field in the fall of 1991), and after a few minutes she returns to that subject.

"They told us fifteen years ago they were going to take it, so people gradually moved out. We used to have about 200 airplanes here. Fifteen years ago Jess and I were going to move to someplace else, too, but you know, you get older. . . . I don't know what we're going to do when we're shut down."

She pauses to glance around. "I'll miss it—all my friends, everybody we knew over the years. I've picked mushrooms here, and berries. They say that's progress."

On the road again, Helmericks notes that while the airplane serves as the automobile of the sky for him, it has brought home a few incidental dollars over the years, too. He's hauled fish to market in Barrow for local villagers, shuttled Lower 48 hunters between big-game camps (he holds a master guide's license), and conducted aerial surveys for several oil companies.

Supporting the petroleum industry seems paradoxical because of the changes oil has wrought in the Arctic, changes seemingly inharmonious with a man who cherishes the wilderness so much he once spent a year in the Brooks Range without seeing another human except his wife. (That experience resulted in another book, *We Live in the Arctic,* 1947.) The 800-mile-long trans-Alaska oil pipeline now snakes from Prudhoe Bay down to Valdez, and the associated Dalton Highway introduced cars into the Arctic; Helmericks and his wife, Martha, can actually drive to their home on the Colville Delta, although they usually fly. Whereas their only neighbors once were Eskimos, they now share the Arctic with pipeline maintenance and oil rig workers as well. To appease conservationists, the federal government, which owns two-thirds of Alaska, has set aside for wildlife preserves and national parks vast arctic tracts Helmericks once used for guiding.

Grassroots arctic aviation is not quite the same anymore, either. As in other parts of the country, such adverse economics as exorbitant insurance premiums have "changed the face of interior Alaska," he says, his voice rising slightly. "If you had to do the same thing with automobiles you have to do with airplanes, you would clear up the highway congestion in one fell swoop. Make common automobiles cost $250,000 and require them to be licensed and maintained yearly to aviation standards, and you wouldn't find our cars on the road at all. Private aviation is becoming extinct." Helmericks acknowledged the evolving personality of North Country aviation in his 1969 book, *The Last of the Bush Pilots.*

Perhaps no one could have foreseen these changes, nor perhaps could anyone have prevented them. Nonetheless, Helmericks contends that much about the Arctic remains undiluted, including the challenge of flying in it. "The cold's still there in the winter, and the fog's still there in the summer, and you still only have one life to lose," he says. "I guess the modern pilots are just as scared as we bush pilots were. If they aren't, they aren't as smart as we were."

He insists that crashes in the Arctic result not from a single factor, but from several of them, and that bush pilots who survived "did so because the combination never did happen to us."

Helmericks may owe part of his survival to his willingness to pay whatever toll the Arctic demanded for the privilege of operating there. When the Helmericks family spent winters trapping from their Walker Lake home, the monthly flight to the trading post at Hughes for supplies involved more than just stepping in and firing up the 170. First, they'd tramp out a runway in the snow a day or two before, so it would have time to freeze and provide a solid base for the airplane's skis. Before the flight, they cleaned snow and ice off the machine, preheated the engine and instruments, and poured hot oil into the crankcase—all in the predawn darkness, because the short daylight hours had to be reserved for flying. Upon returning, they immediately drained the oil from the engine before it could congeal in the extreme cold.

Helmericks still looks after his airplane as diligently as he would a team of sled dogs. We approach the International Airport's float pond, and he parks, pulls on a pair of hip boots, and wades into the water to check his 180's tiedown lines. "The Helmericks" is inscribed in script lettering on the left-hand door of N5208E. This airplane, a 1958 model in black, gray, and white, has logged so many hours that it's on its sixth engine. As he tests this line and resecures that one, I find myself wishing he were untying the lines in preparation for a two-week guided tour of the Arctic.

Helmericks still uses elbow grease and an A-frame to switch among skis, wheels, and floats in the Arctic. He still spends an occasional night alone in the bush when the weather closes in, camping alongside the airplane in benign conditions, or stretching out his six-foot, two-inch frame inside to avoid the elements.

"In flying we have to feel our way as we go, and when the birds are walking it's good to wait," he says as we head back toward the city. "You just fit in. If you don't live *with* something, you're going to be in trouble all your life."

He passed that philosophy on to the three sons he and Martha raised in the Arctic. The trio learned to fly, to skin muskrat, to back away from a female grizzly with cubs. They mastered much of their academic education through correspondence courses under the tutelage of their mother. One son never saw the inside of a traditional classroom until he left for college, another not until high school. All three have college degrees. Mark graduated cum laude from Harvard and went on to become Alaska's first native-born Rhodes Scholar.

"That shows the power of the individual," Helmericks comments, "both of my wife to teach them at home not only to compete but to excel, and also of the children themselves. It shows that if you have the love of yourself and your fellowman, you can do lots of things, and if you don't have them you can't."

Other youngsters, the children of friends or clients, have spent summers with the Helmericks family to experience the Arctic. One wealthy businessman asked Helmericks to take his wayward son for a year. "I told the man his son can lose his life here," Helmericks says. "He can step outside in a storm and we might never see him again. He can walk into that airplane propeller, he can drown running the fishing boat, or one of the dogs can kill him out there. The man said, 'That's what he has to have to grow up.' " The boy came, survived, and gained a new perspective on life.

Adult guests have also gone home richer. "Many people have spent time with me in the Arctic, including some of America's and Europe's industrial leaders. And the thing they've found without exception is themselves. The Arctic changes a person forever. You can never go back to the way you were before. Life's kind of a one-way trip, anyway; we have to be able to relax and enjoy ourselves so we're not always trying to go back."

"Your visitors didn't mind the isolation in the Arctic, Bud?" I ask.

Helmericks purses his lips. "Isolation is between your ears; you take it everywhere you go."

For Helmericks, real isolation is being away from his family. "I couldn't have made it without them," he admits. "I still think the prettiest sight in the Arctic is the lights of home after a long flight in the dark, with Martha waiting."

Cliff Everts

— *Bush Pilot Entrepreneur* —

TOO BAD Horatio Alger died in 1899, when the Nome and Klondike gold strikes had just begun luring thousands of penniless dreamers to Alaska and the Yukon. Had the prolific American author been able to visit the North Country a few decades later, he would have had to search no farther for subjects for his rags-to-riches novels. From the gold fields, the salmon canneries, the logging camps, and the construction yards have come dozens of intriguing people who started with little and found success in opportunity.

North Country aviation has produced Algeresque characters, too. Fairbanks's Cliff Everts, for instance. "When I came to Alaska I had seventy-eight dollars in my pocket," says Everts, a modest, amiable man who still speaks with his native Yonkers, New York, accent despite almost fifty years in Alaska. "Today I own twenty-one airplanes." He isn't referring to single-engine Cessnas or Grumman Gooses, either, although twenty-one of either would be impressive enough. Everts Air Fuel, based at Fairbanks International Airport, carries fuel and other large freight to villages in multiengine transports worth hundreds of thousands of dollars apiece. The fleet includes ten four-engine DC-6s, once a staple of many major airlines, and seven big, twin-engine C-46s.

Everts is quick to point out that only six of the aircraft currently are flyable: three DC-6s and three C-46s. The others await renovation and licensing for eventual use or sale. The airworthy members of the fleet transport about five million pounds of cargo and two million gallons of fuel a year to destinations throughout Alaska. In recent years, Everts has also leased his airplanes to outfits in the Lower 48, salvaged derelict aircraft, and stockpiled enough surplus aircraft parts to open a commercial warehouse, if he wanted to.

For business and personal use, he has several small planes, among them a rare, restored 1929 Travel Air floatplane. Forty people work for him, including C-46 captain Robert Everts, one of his six children. His operations are located in the old Wien Air Alaska hangar, which he bought in the mid-1980s. It's one of Alaska's most historic aviation structures.

As he props his feet on his hangar office desk cluttered with reports, letters, and file folders, Everts' success at first gives the impression that he's always been an entrepreneur. But business actually was a sideline for most of his career. A former bush pilot, he retired from Wien in 1980 in the number-one seniority position after thirty-five years with the company and 30,000 hours in his logbook.

Everts began combining flying, business, and hard work long before he moved to Alaska. He caught the flying fever when he was "just a young punk" in Yonkers in the mid-1930s. Since Kitty Hawk, kids have been scrambling at odd jobs to scrape together enough money for lessons. Everts financed his training by hawking newspapers. He took his first lesson at age fourteen and soloed at sixteen, before he had learned to drive; he rode his bicycle to the old Valhalla airport near Westchester, New York, whenever he had enough funds to go aloft. With a driver's license in his wallet, he earned extra flying money by chauffeuring for a man who had lost his license for drunken driving.

Once he had his pilot's certificate, he looked for more ways to build flight hours. One proposition took him from Westchester all the way to Cuba on a ferry flight in a single-engine Luscombe. The owner paid his expenses. "That was quite a thrilling flight," he says. Returning to Valhalla in a Taylorcraft on another flight after visiting relatives on Long Island, he had to land in a meadow because of low clouds. The meadow turned out to be on the grounds of La Salle Military Academy. Everts showed the Taylorcraft to the fascinated cadets and spent the night at the school as their guest.

When he had enough experience for a commercial job, he flew briefly for both American Airlines and Pennsylvania Central Airlines. One day he met a representative from Alaska's Star Airways who was on an East Coast business trip. In need of pilots, the representative offered him a flying job and $700 in travel funds—enough to return to the States if he found Alaska too foreign. But to the ambitious twenty-one-year-old Everts, the word Alaska brought visions of other thrilling flights, of adventure and opportunity.

A few weeks later, in the spring of 1943, he was sitting in the copilot's seat of Star's Trimotors. From the start, he loved Alaska's rugged beauty and warmed to its homey, frontier atmosphere. "When you move to Alaska, it's like a little town and you get to know people right away," he says.

Almost as quickly, Everts discovered that flying in the Territory provided all the thrills a pilot could want. "It was tough, real tough," he says. Along with the photos of aircraft on his office walls hangs a huge map of Alaska. He rises and with his finger traces labyrinthine, weather-related detours the flights often had to make on nonstop runs from Anchorage to Juneau. "We tried to go by way of Whittier, and if we couldn't get through, we'd circle around there and come up here, and go down here, around, and down through the Copper River, and down to Cordova and then down the beach. And if we didn't go that way we'd go by way of Northway, down this way, down to Kluane Lake, over Haines, and down into Juneau." Like many people from the New York City area Everts speaks loudly, especially on the phone, as if to resolve a particular situation with volume. Otherwise, he's all Alaskan—casual, friendly, sincere.

In early 1945, after a trip Outside to invest in an instrument rating, he began his long career with Wien. To become familiar with the company's routes and destinations, he often rode with senior

Cliff Everts and a Luscombe 8A he flew for Wien Air Alaska. This photo was damaged in a fire in Wien's hangar in 1948. *Courtesy of Cliff Everts*

Wien pilots. One outing, with Wien president Sig Wien, illustrated just how bizarre the culture clash that was invading the bush could be. "We were on the way to Umiat in a Bellanca," Everts says. "It was thirty or forty below zero and getting dark, so we stopped overnight at an Eskimo village by Chandler Lake. We stayed in a hut covered with caribou skins. There were twelve people in there, along with babies and dogs. The villagers gave Sig and me some caribou meat, which we had to eat with our hands. Someone had a battery-powered radio, and the Hit Parade from Los Angeles came on. As the songs played, I thought how strange it was to listen to the Hit Parade so far out in the sticks."

Everts found that practically every flight left him with a rich memory. He talks about hauling several dozen pigs in a C-46 from Ohio to Big Delta for a farm project, about shuttling a Roman Catholic bishop from village to village on the arctic coast through thick fog and snow ("The weather was lousy, but at least I had religion on board for protection!"), about spending a winter week at the village of Christian in the Brooks Range after damaging the landing gear on a ski-equipped Gullwing Stinson.

While bush flying filled Everts' days with endless color and excitement, entrepreneurial challenges attracted him, too. In 1950, he and a partner, Robert Sholton, successfully bid on surplus military heaters, forklifts, and other items and offered them to the public under the business name "Sholton and Everts." It was the first of many sideline ventures for Everts as he continued to fly the bush. Soon he bought Sholton's interests and renamed the outfit "Alaska Rental and Sales."

Opportunities abounded. He bought ice cream from famous bush pilot Archie Ferguson, who had an ice-cream machine at Kotzebue, and sold it to villagers on his mail runs. He picked up a rare pair of skis for the de Havilland Buffalo for $350 and resold them for $12,000. He purchased the boat *Yukon Health* in Nenana, had it towed up the Tanana River to Fairbanks, and converted it into a restaurant and hotel.

Many deals involved the C-46, which in the postwar years the military had declared surplus. Alaskan air service operators loved the big twin for its ability to carry a 14,000-pound cargo payload, and the market for the airplane steadily increased. Everts acquired his first C-46 from Wien and began leasing it. Another C-46 opportunity took him to Japan to bid on a fifteen-strong fleet of the airplanes the General Services Administration was selling. He eventually bought three, fitted one with extra fuel tanks, and flew it back to Alaska at night up the desolate, 1,200-mile-long Aleutian Island chain, chatting with unseen military pilots for company.

Not all C-46 ventures evolved smoothly. One time Everts flew to remote Banks Island in the Northwest Territories to inspect a C-46 that had crashed, liked what he saw, and bought the wreck. But later when he returned with a mechanic to get it ready to fly out, he found that local Eskimos had since used the airplane for target practice. He salvaged what was still serviceable.

Then there's the saga of N1419Z, a C-46 Everts and Sholton bought from the Air Force in New York State in 1960. The Air

Force had intended the airplane to be used only for spare parts, and when the Alaskans announced they wanted to make it airworthy, several restrictions resulted: the airplane could make only one ferry flight, it had to be dismantled in five sections, and only two of the sections could remain together to form a flyable airplane afterward. Everts and Sholton complied, and for years the wings and fuselage sat forlorn on Seattle's Boeing Field while the men tried to find the time and resources to put the airplane back together.

Sholton, despairing of ever salvaging his investment, eventually pulled out, but Everts clung to his faith in the project. In 1980, the airport operator, King County, finally ordered him to get the eyesore off the field. From various sources, he scavenged landing gear, engines, a tail, and other necessary replacement parts. After weeks of work, he and a crew of helpers ferried the C-46 to Alaska.

"The airport manager was convinced we couldn't get it into the air, and some of the operators at the airport gave him a cake with a candy crow on it to eat after we flew the plane home," Everts says, laughing. But the story isn't quite over; so far, the FAA has refused to license N1419Z because of paperwork technicalities. "I'm going to take care of it," he vows. "I've got too many years in this airplane to give up now."

That problem and other business keep Everts at work into the evening on most days. But he enjoys the challenges. "Aviation has been my life," he says as he folds his hands behind his head and gazes reflectively at the airplane photos on one wall. "I'm in it every day and there's no way I can get out of it. I can't see any joy in doing anything else."

Lloyd Jarman

— *Riding Shotgun* —

As a young man in Juneau in the mid-1930s, Lloyd Jarman liked to phone Shell Simmons' Alaska Air Transport, where he worked in winters, and pretend to be an obnoxious drunk demanding immediate transportation to Hoonah village or some other local destination. After the flustered Shirley Simmons, Shell's first wife, quoted the fare, Jarman would triumphantly assume his normal voice.

Dispatchers dealt with enough real-life drunks as it was. "Damn you, Lloyd!" she would bark.

When you talk with Jarman today in his Bellevue, Washington, office, his sense of humor is still evident. Somehow suggesting a teddy bear, he'll periodically interrupt the discussion to hand you a cartoon or printed witticism. He'll also show you a photo of a Pacific Alaska Airways Stearman that appears to be fitted with a gigantic pontoon on a Juneau dock. "It took me a long time to pump that float out," he says, his voice innocently deadpan but his large blue eyes hinting at mischief. Once you've had a moment to stare incredulously, wondering how such an arrangement ever got off the water, Jarman reveals that the photo is staged. The big float is lying next to the Stearman, unattached to it but blocking a view of the much smaller floats that actually support the airplane.

And he'll probably give you a copy of one of his *Bush Pilot's Log* cartoon books, which show bush planes in preposterously exaggerated scenarios (a floatplane sits underwater on the bottom of a lake;

one of the passengers, looking out, observes, "I think we are overloaded"). Any pilot with Alaskan experience who thumbs through the two books in the series, first published in 1971, knows they could have been created only by someone who was there.

As you glance around his office, you note that Jarman is also an accomplished aviation photographer. Besides the prints of airplanes and pilots on the walls, there are photos in five albums and various files. At home he has five more photo albums and thousands of negatives. His pictures, many taken with a simple box camera, have appeared in several books on Alaskan aviation history, and his is the world's largest collection of photos of the early southeastern Alaska floatplane scene. "I got a picture of that," he'll often comment after describing an incident.

Humor and photography were secondary to Jarman's main interest, however; he wanted to fly. From his parents' house on Second Street he could reach the Juneau waterfront in less than five minutes, and there he spent many of his after-school hours, watching floatplanes land and take off, asking questions, helping with this or that when someone allowed it. Alaska-Washington Airways rewarded him for chores with used crankcase oil, which he sold to local truckers.

As usually happens when a wistful kid hangs around a flight operation, pilots began offering him rides. The first came in April 1930, when he was thirteen. Someone had reported a fire atop Mount Juneau, and before taking off in a Lockheed Vega to investigate, Bob Ellis invited him along.

Of course, a boy in his early teens was a bit young to fly the Vegas, Bellancas, Wacos, and other seaplanes that operated in Southeast then—but not too young to work on them. In 1932, Juneau's Alaska Southern Airways put Jarman on the payroll as a mechanic's helper, and soon he was going aloft daily as one of Alaska's youngest flight mechanics. Photos of him then show a friendly-looking, clean-cut kid with a shy smile and a tie. (Ties were part of the standard attire in the pre-war Alaskan aviation world.)

Actually, "flight mechanic" was somewhat of a misnomer, for seldom did Jarman or his fellow airborne mechanics have to use a toolbox out in the bush. By the early 1930s, manufacturers had weeded out many of the engine and airframe problems that plagued earlier airplanes.

Instead, mechanics served as all-purpose crewmen. Floatplanes in the early days of Southeast aviation lacked water rudders, and pilots liked to have an assistant climb out on the float as the brakeless airplane approached the dock, especially if the wind or current was affecting the already limited maneuverability. (Even today, with a water rudder on the heel of each float, floats and wings inevitably acquire dents and dings because a pilot can't scramble out fast enough to protect the plane from such obstacles as a bolt protruding from the dock or the mast of a boat moored too close. After the mid-1930s, air services stopped assigning mechanics to flights; pilots then were on their own.) Also, there was freight and baggage to load and unload, and the myriad, unpredictable incidents that required an extra pair of helping hands.

In addition to teaching him the country and the floatplane routine, riding along gave Jarman a chance to observe pilot techniques and pick up tips against the day when he would be in the left seat. Pilots regarded him as a likable kid brother to be tutored. Many let him handle the controls.

Each pilot, Jarman discovered, had one or more distinct characteristics. Bob Ellis was "a nice guy, a real gentleman, but he used to become really preoccupied on landings." Simmons was "rough on equipment; it was always wide-open throttle with Shell. He flew with the right wing down a little, and I used to get out of the airplane and walk like this [Jarman extends his arms, with the right one low], but he never once asked me what the matter was." Gene Meyring "didn't have bad days; he flew well every day, even if I did get to crash with him." Alex Holden "sometimes had a little trouble navigating."

Whatever a pilot's idosyncrasies, Jarman found that riding

Adventure was a daily experience for ride-along mechanic Lloyd Jarman, shown here by Alaska Air Transport's "Patco" Stinson in Juneau, 1935. Two in-flight fires, eleven forced landings, and two in-flight cracked fuselages are a few of the incidents on his list. *Photo by Shell Simmons*

shotgun along Alaska's coast thrust him into one adventure after another.

Returning from fish patrolling with Gene Meyring up in Bristol Bay one day, Jarman had to round up sixteen other people to help push a Vega floatplane back into the water after Meyring misjudged the wind on an approach to Severson's Landing on Lake Iliamna and shot fifty feet up onto the beach. On another flight, this time in their native Southeast, a snowstorm forced Jarman and Meyring to spend a night at a fox ranch on Shaw Island in Idaho Inlet. Snow continued to fall throughout the night, and every three hours they had to get up to sweep it off their Vega. Unchecked, the weight of accumulated snow could sink the floatplane at the dock.

On one nighttime flight from Burwash Landing in the Yukon Territory to Juneau with Alex Holden, Jarman struck matches repeatedly to illuminate the magnetic compass in the unlit cockpit so Holden could navigate. Bad weather finally forced them to turn around and overnight back at Burwash.

Sometimes a flight mechanic would be powerless to help out in a predicament. On October 10, 1934, Jarman overslept and almost missed his flight with Meyring. Another mechanic had been assigned in his place, but at the last minute Jarman hurried onto the dock and took his place in the Vega. Also aboard were two young men on their first airplane ride, hoping to connect with a hunting party on the outside coast of Chichagof Island. After a mail stop at Hoonah, Meyring flew down Chichagof beneath an overcast sky and entered a bay, looking for the hunting party's boat. Perhaps because of scud partially blocking his vision, he flew deep into the bay before realizing it offered less maneuvering room than he had assumed.

"It was rougher than hell," Jarman recalls. "At the end of the bay he turned to get out, stalled, and went straight into the trees from a thousand feet. I remember the wings coming off and the floats going by the windows, then nothing." Broken watches indicated high noon.

One of the passengers died in the crash. The other one and

Meyring had broken legs. Jarman suffered seven cracks in his pelvic bone and twenty-three cuts on his face ("I used to get glass out of my face until 1940"). For the rest of the day the stunned survivors ministered to their injuries, tried to stay warm, and slept. The aircraft's batteries dripped acid on Meyring all night long.

Late the next day, Shell Simmons and two observers spotted the wreckage, landed in the bay, and evacuated the three. Unlike Meyring and the surviving passenger, Jarman was ambulatory, although he had to support himself on trees as he staggered toward the beach behind the others.

The eighteen-year-old Jarman spent the next several months in the Juneau hospital. Then came a few weeks on crutches before his doctor allowed him to return to his winter work with Simmons, who at the time was the only Juneau pilot operating in the off-season. Despite the gumption he displayed in promptly resuming an airborne job, Jarman hoped for nice, quiet, uneventful flights.

That was a lot to expect in late winter in southeastern Alaska. Especially with the ambitious Simmons. One March day, the two took off from Juneau with two miners bound for camp at Kimshan Cove on the outside coast of Chichagof Island. Near Elfin Cove they encountered thick snow. Soon Simmons was flying just feet above the water, past barely visible islets and bights. The gray-white curtain drew closer and closer around them, eventually forcing Simmons to land. He had to taxi—sometimes on the step, sometimes at idle—the last ten miles into Kimshan Cove, but he reached his destination, once again upholding his never-turn-back reputation.

Jarman must have squirmed with déjà vu as he sat silently in his seat, squinting out the windows. Here he was again, one of four occupants on board a floatplane in nasty weather on Chichagof's outer shore. Would the repetition include another crash?

After dropping off the two passengers, who by then looked as white as the swirling snow, Simmons motioned to Jarman to get back into the Stinson. Jarman shook his head. "I wasn't ready to be a hero," he says. "I talked him into waiting for an improvement."

When the snow finally slackened, it was too dark to take off, and a gale-force wind had begun battering the coast. Jarman and Simmons secured the Stinson with extra lines, but during the night it blew away anyhow.

Walking down the rocky beach in the morning looking for the airplane, they found fragments scattered among the boulders near the tide line. Simmons muttered just six words: "Goddamn you, Jarman, you're a jinx!"

The mangled bulk of the airplane lay upside down in the water a little over a mile from the camp. A mail boat hauled the wreckage back to Juneau a week later, along with Jarman and the still-fuming Simmons.

Simmons was understandably upset: the loss of his employer's only airplane meant the loss of his job as well. But the incident took a fortuitous turn. Deciding aviation was too risky, the owners of the Panhandle Air Transport Company sold what was left of the Stinson, nicknamed "Patco," to their ex-pilot for a dollar. Simmons then found half a dozen Juneau investors to finance a restoration, and with the rejuvenated floatplane he launched his own company, Alaska Air Transport. Jarman no longer seemed to be so much of a jinx. Simmons even let the young mechanic choose the new colors—yellow and blue—for the Stinson, which retained the name Patco and flew on for years as one of the most familiar airplanes in Southeast.

Like Patco, Jarman recovered from his injuries, at least enough to earn a private pilot's license in a thirty-six-horsepower Aeronca C-3 operated by Juneau's Gastineau Flying Club. But when he went to Santa Monica, California, in 1940 to train for advanced ratings, recurring paralysis from his injuries grounded him. There would be no bush pilot career for Jarman.

(As if it had released a spiteful evil spirit, the Chichagof crash seemed determined to haunt Jarman. A scavenger brought him the overhead cockpit hatch from the wreckage, and he hung it on a wall in his shop. One day it suddenly slipped off its hook and smashed onto the workbench, missing his head by inches.)

A shadow glazes Jarman's eyes for a moment as he talks about the death of a boyhood dream. Then he smiles and shrugs. "So I took a job with Douglas Aircraft and went to Africa." That assignment entailed assembling fighter planes. By the time he returned from the desert at the end of World War II, fate had put him in two more crashes—one in an overloaded PBY that couldn't get airborne, the other in a B-24 that had to land with its nosewheel stuck in the retracted position. He may have jammed his feet against imaginary brakes, as passengers are wont to do in such situations, but he walked away unhurt both times.

Back in Juneau in 1946, he worked for Shell Simmons again, this time as a shop mechanic. But the Southeast aviation scene had changed. Or maybe Jarman had. After six months, he moved his family to Seattle, where he got involved in a number of maintenance and aircraft-parts enterprises.

Today Jarman stays in regular telephone touch with Simmons, Ellis, and other cronies from the old days. Like him, they've come to see nostalgic humor in the storms, the risks, the poverty, the competition, and other aspects of life back then. They laugh a lot as they visit.

Bud Seltenreich

— *Working Man* —

BUD SELTENREICH seems awfully busy for someone who supposedly retired in 1980 at the age of sixty-five. The long-time pilot, mechanic, air service operator, and FAA executive rises early at his house in Anchorage every morning to confront a schedule that would tax the stamina of a much younger man. Since the mid-1980s he's been maintenance director for an Anchorage-based air service, a job that involves inspecting and supervising repairs on aircraft both in town and at a company lodge on the Alaska Peninsula. He also performs inspections and maintenance on many private aircraft at Anchorage-area airports.

Try to reach him during the day, and his wife, Marge, will tell you, "Oh, he's off running around somewhere." During the months when daylight lingers well into the evening, you might catch him examining a weld or filling out paperwork at 10:00 P.M.

Working from dawn to dusk and beyond is a habit Seltenreich picked up long before "retirement." Born in the mining town of McCarthy, Alaska, in 1915, he developed a Tom Edison-like curiosity about gadgets as a kid. He and his older brothers, Fred and Ted, often tinkered until midnight on cars, refrigerators, radios, compressors, even light bulbs, taking them apart to see how they ran or trying to figure out why they didn't. The Seltenreiches built rockets, a motorized bicycle, and one of the first snowmobiles in Alaska. The latter consisted of an ordinary snow sled rigged with a motor.

"None of that stuff worked real well," Seltenreich says with a smile, "but we built it anyway." Although fatigue lines his face—we're talking at 10:30 P.M.—his eyes twinkle with both the satisfaction of a productive day and the pleasure of fond memories. He's a stocky man with a pleasant, happy face that makes him look much younger than his years.

Flying machines fascinated the Seltenreich brothers. They tried to design a helicopter before aeronautical engineer Igor Sikorsky succeeded in the rotor-wing field, but were stumped when it came to figuring out how to change the angle of the blades. While they had no helicopter to examine and experiment with, they periodically saw an airplane fly by. "We've got to have one of those things," they agreed.

To finance their dream, the brothers launched various money-making schemes in the late 1920s. In one winter enterprise, Bud operated a dog team as a taxi between McCarthy and Kennicott four and a half miles away, where the world's richest copper mine was located. By 1930, the coffer held $3,500, enough for a brand-new Swallow biplane with a water-cooled OX-5 engine. They had it shipped from Seattle to Valdez, and a local pilot flew it from there to McCarthy. Ted had already gained some flying experience, so he imparted what he knew to Bud and Fred.

Today's engines are so reliable they need little maintenance. In 1930, however, engines had to be babied. Before every flight, the Seltenreich boys found it necessary to check the valve action, grease the valve rocker arms' pivot pins, check the water-pump shaft packing for leaks, check the radiator and interconnecting hoses for leaks, and oil the valve stems.

To make sure the single magneto was functioning properly (modern aircraft engines have dual, independent magnetos), they checked the breaker points every two or three hours of use. The engine had no carburetor heat system, so the brothers designed and built one. On the airplane itself, the wings' wire bracing needed checking and adjustment for tensions. So did the landing gear shock

An American Pilgrim with wing and engine covers that are standard winter protection for parked aircraft in Alaska. *Peter Bowers Collection*

cords. Ten hours of maintenance for each hour of flight was the rule of thumb for the early 1930s aircraft.

In winter, they had to drain the oil and water after each flight (no antifreeze was available) and preheat them before the next one.

Such experiences helped Seltenreich get his aircraft mechanic's license without attending a formal maintenance school. "A lot of people didn't go to school in those days in order to learn something," he notes. "You learned as an apprentice; you worked at it." Finding an aviation job was only one of his motivations in becoming a mechanic. He planned to operate his own flying service someday and also wanted the license so he could legally maintain his aircraft. "If you have to depend on someone else when you're running a business, you sometimes lose your hind end."

In 1932, he went to work as a mechanic for Harold Gillam's Gillam Airways in Copper Center. The company operated a mail run from Cordova to McCarthy, Chitina, and other communities in the Copper River Valley, and Seltenreich frequently rode along—as much to help turn the airplane around on the narrow strips as to repair whatever broke.

One February, rain melted the snow at Cordova, forcing the company to remove the skis from the American Pilgrim used for the mail runs and install wheels. Since all points along the route were covered with snow, Gillam decided to fly first to Anchorage, which had plowed strips, reinstall the skis, and start the run from there. It was a Sunday. Gillam Airways' own fuel supply was out, and public fuel facilities in town were closed. But clear skies smiled on the Gulf of Alaska, and the plucky Gillam figured the Pilgrim had enough fuel to make the 150-mile flight to Anchorage. They could get more gas there.

He was right—the Pilgrim arrived over Anchorage with the engine still running. Unfortunately, thick fog had formed in the subzero air there, blanketing much of the area. Too little fuel remained to return to Cordova, or detour anywhere else. For precious minutes Gillam circled above the fog, looking for a hole. At last he found one, slipped underneath, and touched down on a farm where Elmendorf Air Force Base now sits.

Suddenly, he spotted a deep ditch looming ahead. With too little room to stop, Gillam pushed the throttle forward and took off again. The engine sucked the last drops of fuel from the tank and quit while he was banking for another approach.

Unable to glide to land, the pilot landed on Cook Inlet. For a few minutes the big airplane stayed afloat, then slowly began to sink. Seltenreich shivered at the prospect of having to swim to shore, so he hitched a ride on a passing iceberg. Gillam and the two passengers on board quickly joined him.

Meanwhile, witnesses to the ditching had alerted the Anchorage Voluntary Fire Department, and soon a member rowed out in a skiff to rescue the marooned foursome.

Seltenreich stayed in Anchorage to help rebuild the salvaged Pilgrim, which was flying again by that summer. (Ironically, brother Ted was killed in 1943 while serving as a mechanic on a Pilgrim that encountered a whiteout and crashed into a hilltop near Nome.)

Afterward, rather than returning to Gillam, Seltenreich, brother Fred, and a partner started their own maintenance facility at Merrill Field in Anchorage. They worked far into the evening day after day, struggling to make Independent Repair Service a success. Some jobs took them into the field. On one outside assignment, Bud again endured a crash—actually two crashes.

When Woodley Airways bought a Cabin Waco on wheels in Anchorage in the spring of 1937, owner Art Woodley hired Seltenreich to ride along to Cordova with a Woodley associate to help put the airplane on floats.

"We got through Portage Pass into Prince William Sound, where we ran into some pretty bad weather," Seltenreich says. "We decided we couldn't make Cordova and turned around to go back. By then the weather had closed Portage Pass. We were on wheels, and there were no airports around there in those days. So we picked out a beach and landed on it, but we hit a log and knocked a gear off."

Because they had expected an uneventful flight to Cordova, the group had brought no emergency supplies. They did have a rifle, however, and a goose they shot helped curb their hunger while they worked on the broken landing gear.

With the job completed the next afternoon, the three climbed in and took off. "This time the weather was worse than before. It was the kind of rain that falls sideways. We turned around again, but we couldn't find the beach because of the clouds. Then we saw a frozen lake on an island and decided we'd better land there. As soon as we touched down we broke through the crust and went up on our nose."

The men waded ashore through ice-cold, knee-deep mush and built a fire beneath a rock overhang. For the moment they had warmth and shelter. But no flight service stations existed then to file flight plans with, and they hadn't bothered to notify anyone at either Anchorage or Cordova of their proposed route or estimated time of arrival. Eventually people would look for them; could they survive until rescue with only the clothes they were wearing? The Waco had one of the earliest aircraft radios, a Lear T-30, an invention so new to the Territory that few stations had yet set up receivers. Nonetheless, the men realized that broadcasting in the blind was their only hope of avoiding a long, potentially fatal ordeal.

In the morning they waded back out to the Waco, extended the antenna, and began calling for help. "We got real lucky. Some kid on the Coast Guard cutter in Cordova happened to be dialing through different frequencies, just playing around with the radio, and he heard us. We had no receiver and were transmitting blind, but from our description they figured out we were on Esther Island."

The next day a Coast Guard ground party hiked up to the lake and evacuated the three to Cordova on the cutter. The men returned a few days later to salvage the Waco. Fortunately, the weather remained cold enough to put the airplane on skis and fly it off the lake.

Back in Anchorage, Seltenreich soon faced another crisis: a fire burned Independent Repair Service's hangar, putting the fledgling company out of business. Having gotten his pilot's license while at Gillam Airways, he now joined Star Airways as a copilot on a Ford Trimotor, making freight runs out of McGrath to mining camps. Like many Alaskan air services then and now, Star operated close to the financial default line. Sometimes paychecks were a bit tardy, and when Seltenreich saw an opportunity to work for the healthier Pacific Alaska Airways at its Fairbanks branch, he took it.

Benefits there included more than regular paychecks. "We worked eight hours a day five days a week and got two days off," says Seltenreich, his voice rising and falling for emphasis. "That was the greatest thing that had ever happened to me, because I had always worked seven days a week."

But so much idle time soon bored him, and he began searching for a sideline activity. Rebuilding a couple of Aeroncas that had crashed in the bush helped restore his accustomed long hours. By then the United States had entered World War II, and new planes

Bud Seltenreich spray-paints the tail of a Stearman at Cordova in July 1935, while working for Gillam Airways. *Courtesy of Bud Seltenreich*

were unavailable for noncommercial civilian use; almost daily someone asked to rent one of his. What to do but start his own outfit?

Seltenreich's Fairbanks Air Service, the first Civil Aeronautics Authority–approved flight school in Alaska, offered both flight instruction and charters, and over the next several years the fleet expanded to seventeen aircraft—Taylorcrafts, J-3 Cubs, Piper Pacers, Stinsons, Aeroncas, and a surplus Navy North American advanced trainer. The air service also became a Piper dealer, and it had the Taylorcraft and Edo distributorships for Alaska.

The workload would have kept an ordinary manager busy all day, every day, handling paperwork in the office, taking an occasional flight to relieve demand on the full-time pilots, helping the mechanics in the hangar, and dealing with the myriad other problems of a thriving business. Seltenreich did those things and still found time for a forty-hour week at the airline—which Pan American Airways had taken over—now as chief mechanic.

By the late 1940s, however, he was finally wiping his brow. He had quit Pan Am to avoid a transfer to Seattle, and more free time had translated into more time at his business. "I was tired of working sixteen hours a day. I'd been doing it ever since the beginning of the war, because I couldn't get out of it. I was stuck with it. I had a tiger by the tail and I couldn't let go." In 1949 he sold his business to brother Fred and his chief pilot, Holly Evans, telling them to "pay me when you have enough money."

For a while Seltenreich, now in his mid-thirties, did something uncharacteristic: he relaxed. "I learned how to dance and chase girls more." But aviation work had become a psychological need, and after six months he felt restless. The growth of the aviation industry in Alaska had created several new slots for CAA inspectors. He applied for one, mostly out of curiosity, intending to stay no longer than a year or two.

Instead, he found the CAA/FAA an interesting, challenging assignment, one that would become a thirty-two-year career. There were plenty of rungs on the ladder for employees who ignored the time clock, and Seltenreich climbed almost to the top. Starting as an Alaskan air carrier inspector, he progressed to Fairbanks field supervisor, then to regional office chief in Anchorage, and finally to chief of the general aviation maintenance branch for the entire country.

The last position, which he held from 1962 to '64, took him to Washington, D.C., into a political lion's den. Eighty employees worked under him there, hundreds more in the field. Responsible for directing nationwide maintenance policies, he took the ultimate heat for controversial decisions.

Seltenreich also oversaw the FAA's airworthiness directive program. The agency issues airworthiness directives, or ADs, to inspect or correct safety deficiencies on particular aircraft models—cracks in a wing spar, tail corrosion, inferior bolts, and so forth. Often an AD will affect thousands of aircraft and cost owners or the manufacturer hundreds of dollars for each plane.

Thus, Seltenreich faced frequent arm-twisting by manufacturers, pilot organizations, and other special-interest groups wishing to have proposed ADs rescinded or modified. Pressure in the opposite direction came from the National Transportation Safety Board, and in both directions from congressmen. As a representative of the FAA, of course, Seltenreich was primarily concerned with safety. Yet, he could not ignore economic considerations: Is this problem serious enough to justify the mandating of a $500 fix for every model in the country? Should we ground the entire fleet immediately, or give owners twenty flight hours in which to comply?

"I could see that in Washington, D.C., it wasn't a matter of if you're going to have a heart attack and ulcers, but when. There was a crisis or two or three going on every day. It wasn't an eight-hour day, either. You caught all the flak. It was a kind of the-buck-stops-here thing."

Eventually, Seltenreich transferred back to Anchorage as supervisor of the FAA district office at Merrill Field. He was based in that city for the remainder of his career.

Although his responsibilities usually kept him at a desk during his FAA years, he made periodic business flights in rented or agency aircraft, including a Grumman Goose. When FAA officials from Washington, D.C., came to Alaska, it was often Seltenreich who flew them to their local destinations.

In his most interesting FAA position, he served as coordinator of the trans-Alaska pipeline air safety program. Pipeline construction in the 1970s involved what he calls "the largest civil airlift in history." Even during the coldest months, dozens of aircraft flew around the clock delivering personnel, supplies, and mail to construction camps. "The various ground equipment needed a total of 55,000 gallons of fuel a day to operate," he says, "and most of it had to be flown in. A couple of days of bad weather put everyone behind schedule."

Several times a month Seltenreich tightened his seat belt in an agency Cessna 185 and took off for a five-day tour of airports along the 800-mile-long pipeline. On a typical trip, he'd land at twelve camps to inspect runway conditions, communications equipment, navigational aids, fueling stations, and other airlift-related facilities.

Like the airlift crews themselves, he stopped only when conditions became unsafe. "I was grounded at Deadhorse one day when the temperature was forty below and the wind was blowing fifty," he says, whistling softly. "You want to talk about *cold* . . ."

When the job ended in 1978, the FAA flew Seltenreich and his wife to Washington, D.C., to receive a citation of thanks from FAA administrator Langhorne Bond and Transportation Secretary Brock Adams.

Two years later, by then sixty-five, Seltenreich retired from the agency. Never having taken a day off for illness, he had earned credit for 3,350 hours of sick leave. Still, he had no intention of resigning from the working life. Before joining the Anchorage air service, he served for several years as director of maintenance for a Nome-based air service, commuting from Anchorage to Nome for a week or two each month.

With his generous FAA pension and income from investments, Seltenreich certainly doesn't need to continue working. "I ought to be out tramping around through the hills, which I like to do, or flying my PA-12. I have a 500-acre homestead in McCarthy and want to clear the land, develop it a little. But as much as I try to stay out of work, I keep getting into it, deeper and deeper."

So if you want to talk with Seltenreich, you may have to make a reservation.

NORM GERDE AND CARL BLOOMQUIST

— *Weather Routine* —

SO MUCH RAIN falls in Ketchikan that the town's mascot is the "Rainbird." In Juneau the Taku winds sometimes exceed 100 knots, and thick ground fog can blanket the entire 500-mile-long southeastern Alaska archipelago for days.

You'd think any pilot who'd flown Southeast's weather gauntlet for a quarter-century or longer would have dozens of weather-related adventures to relate. Yet when veteran Southeast pilots reminisce, weather emerges as a mere nuisance.

Take Norm Gerde, for instance. Slicked-back thin white hair, and fingers stained from smoking. Born in Washington State in 1915. Flew thirty years for Ketchikan's Ellis Air Lines and its successors. Rejected for military service during the war because childhood polio had left his right leg an inch and a half shorter than his left. Twenty thousand hours. Retired in Ketchikan in 1971.

What was his greatest aerial adventure? Gerde strokes his chin for a moment. The first incident that comes to mind involved a brake failure one day after he landed at Annette Island, causing his Goose to run off the runway down a six-foot enbankment. No injuries, minor damage.

Then there was the time a broken oil pump in the engine of his Bellanca forced him to glide dead-stick (engine off) to a landing in Tamgass Harbor, again on Annette Island.

Or that PBY flight between Petersburg and Sitka on which an engine quit, resulting in a diversion to Juneau. Gerde twists his

Norm Gerde logged thousands of hours in Southeast Alaska in Grumman Gooses like this one. *Courtesy of the Gerde Family*

shoulders for emphasis as he talks about wrestling with the ponderous amphibian. "The PBY was awful heavy on the controls, anyway," he says. "You always had to manhandle that airplane. On one engine it was really a beast." Only after prodding does he add offhandedly that he was on instruments in the clouds that day.

Apparently having exhausted the list of his own incidents, Gerde tells about a fellow pilot whose Bellanca Skyrocket hit a set of dolphins—the mooring type—that were obscured by dusk while he was landing in Ketchikan in 1944. The passenger in the right-hand seat died, but the pilot and the other three passengers struggled out and clung to the floating wreckage. A Coast Guard boat from Base Ketchikan rescued them minutes later. "The police told a reporter that the pilot had hit dolphins, and the next day the paper said he had flown into a school of dolphins!" Gerde shakes his head, laughing, and lights a cigarette.

The subject of marine life reminds him of the time he saw sea lions chasing herring along the waterfront. "We had a big float down in front of the office, and the herring boiled up on it to get away. You could pick up hundreds of pounds of them." After a puff he continues. "At times you could look over a great expanse, eight or ten miles, and you'd see herring flipping all over. You don't see that anymore."

Yes, but we haven't finished with aerial adventures yet, Norm; you've left out all the weather ones. Didn't you ever get lost in the fog over a large body of water, with no landmarks in sight? Didn't you ever fly home in violent turbulence from an unforecast windstorm? Stuff like that.

Gerde makes a face and nods slowly, as if to say, "Yeah, lots of times, so what?"

You'll find the same scant attention to weather in Carl Bloomquist, a husky, friendly man. He hesitates a moment when asked about the worst flights he experienced during the 30,000 hours he flew for Juneau's Alaska Coastal Airlines.

One day a broken pin in the landing gear mechanism of Bloomquist's Seabee caused the gear to dangle, preventing him from either locking the wheels down or retracting them. He touched down on the gravel strip parallel to the runway at Juneau, and the airplane slid harmlessly to a stop on its large hull. The sole passenger called for a taxi to the nearest bar.

Another pause. "Oh, yeah!" the Juneau-born Bloomquist exclaims. He's recalled the time his copilot made a water landing in a PBY at Ketchikan and a throttle literally came off in his hand as he pulled back the power. The flustered copilot handed Bloomquist the throttle, as in that Laurel and Hardy film when Stan passes a loose steering wheel to Ollie while their jalopy races down the road. Bloomquist says, with a smile, "I got us to the dock okay."

One memory triggers another. He tells about taxiing a Goose on

During the winter, Carl Bloomquist made as many as seven trips a day from Juneau to the mining camp at Tulsequah in this Curtiss Kingbird wheelplane, landing on a snow-packed strip. *Courtesy of Carl Bloomquist*

the water from Hawk Inlet on Admiralty Island to Juneau over a circuitous, eighty-mile route around islands and tide flats. Failure of the right engine had forced him to land in the inlet, and after dispatching another airplane to pick up his passengers, Alaska Coastal instructed Bloomquist to taxi the Goose home.

With only the left engine running, asymmetrical thrust constantly twisted the Goose to the right, forcing Bloomquist to keep steady pressure on the left rudder pedal. "I could hold it straight for a little while, but then I'd just have to let it go and catch it on the next turn," he says. "We kind of water-looped all the way." Eventually, a mechanic who had come along to provide assistance walked out on top of the left wing and tied a bucket to the wingfloat. Dragging in the water, the bucket minimized the right-turning tendency.

Meanwhile, another problem had developed. Bloomquist had been taxiing as fast as possible, and the engine's thrust had forced the bow lower in the water—low enough to place a preexisting hole in the forward baggage compartment below the waterline. As the compartment filled, water began seeping into the cockpit. Bloomquist asked the mechanic to make the rest of the trip in the rear baggage compartment to provide counteracting ballast for the nose-heavy Goose.

Around two in the morning, after a nine-hour voyage, the crippled plane reached the dock in Juneau. It may have been the longest water taxi in Southeast history.

But what about being trapped between snow squalls in a mountain pass, or blundering into a downpour that obliterated visibility, or inadvertently flying up a creek while trying to follow a shoreline in heavy rainfog? Surely in thirty years Bloomquist experienced these or similar weather problems?

Of course he did. So did Gerde and all the other career Southeast pilots. Again and again and again, so often that weather-related incidents became routine, like close calls on the highway to a truck driver. That's why Gerde says weather is the aspect of Southeast aviation he disliked the most, although he neglects to include weather problems among his tales of emergencies. It's why Bloomquist characterizes his career as "fighting the weather all the time" but deletes weather incidents from his accounts of challenging flights. Engine failures and water-taxi odysseys are memorable because they seldom occur; Southeast weather hurls flak at pilots almost every day.

Which is not to imply that retired Southeast pilots were nonchalant about the weather. Pilots who daydream while flying through fog or snow don't live long enough to retire. Gerde, Bloomquist, and their prudent peers slowed down in low visibility, sought detours often, and turned back when they couldn't get through. But an adversary that regularly appears gradually becomes unremarkable.

So if you want to hear war stories about flying in Southeast weather, talk to the newcomer who has bounced and lurched through only a couple of gales—not the veteran with 150 behind him.

Mary Worthylake

— *History and Perspective* —

In a book about veteran bush pilots, why include someone who logged a total of only twenty-five hours and never even flew the bush?

Historically, Mary Worthylake belongs because she's the first woman pilot trained and licensed in Alaska.

Also, as the widow of a bush pilot, she offers a look at bush flying from a different perspective. A pilot's spouse and family have an important part in any pilot's life, but like the mechanic, they're often forgotten in the excitement and glory of flying. In Worthylake's case, the neglect was literal as well as figurative. She no more represents all bush pilot families than any one pilot exemplifies his or her peers. Yet, her story seems even more interesting than most.

When you first see photos of Worthylake as a twenty-eight-year-old student pilot in Anchorage in 1932, it's pretty easy to feel intrigued. Bright-eyed and attractive, she smiles vivaciously in her leather helmet, commanding your gaze, looking as keen for a stroll in the hills or a philosophical discussion as for a flight in a biplane.

After learning a little about her, you realize that Worthylake would have made a fascinating companion in just about any activity. She was intelligent and articulate enough to teach school, outdoorsy enough to take an eight-day horseback ride as a sixteen-year-old with a girlfriend in rural Oregon (they carried pistols to protect themselves), adventuresome enough to fly as both passenger and

Mary Worthylake found learning to fly easier than many of her fellow students did because of tips she had picked up while riding along with her husband, flyer Joe Barrows.
Courtesy of Mary Worthylake

pilot in open-cockpit airplanes, and traditional enough to bear and raise three children. A man might even start wishing she had been born sixty years later, or himself sixty years earlier.

Longevity has left some characteristics unchanged, however. As we shake hands in her Aloha, Oregon, home, I instantly recognize that 1932 charm radiating from her smile and dark eyes. Telephone conversations have already told me her mind is still sharp. Now I find myself a little on the defensive intellectually. You don't get away with absent-mindedly repeating a question to her. She'll gently chide you in a patient school-teacher tone, "Well, as I mentioned before . . ."

When I peruse her library, which covers an entire wall, I come across seven titles with her byline. The most recent publication date is 1986. She hopes to complete her eighth book, an account of early bush flying in Alaska for juveniles, while her fingers can still tap out the words on a typewriter. Many of the volumes relate to travel, which she did extensively in middle age while teaching in such exotic places as the Marshall Islands, New Zealand, and Afghanistan. Alaska wasn't her only, or even her greatest, adventure.

Although she cites name after date after place after event from the 1920s and 1930s as if they belonged to the 1970s, she apologizes for the few obscure facts that elude her. Her apologies are lighthearted, though, just like the expressions in those 1932 photos. She jokes often, even about her increasing infirmity; her laughter is endearing both for its fragility and the humility that prompts it.

Long before it's time to say goodbye, I realize that Worthylake's affability is just as rewarding today as it must have been when the photographer snapped the shutter in a different era. That's why the longer I chat with her, the more I want to pick Joe Barrows up by the collar and shake him.

Barrows was her first husband, the barnstormer she married in 1924, the adventurer who broke her heart. More than anything, Mary Barrows wanted security and a family life. But Joe's wanderlust apparently blinded him to the rich green grass at home.

They met in his hometown of San Jacinto, California, where Mary (née Moore) was visiting her grandfather on leave from her teaching job in a one-room country school in Oregon. Tall and slim with thick red hair, Joe could play the piano as well as fly. Love at first sight? "Well, second sight, anyway," she says. The day after their introduction, Joe sent over his younger brother with a note asking if Mary would like to go for a ride in his surplus World War I Jenny. She brought a slice of homemade pie. A month later they were engaged.

From the beginning, they planned to build a life in exciting, faraway Alaska, and Mary applied for a teaching job in Anchorage. Like many aspects of their relationship, however, the trip north was delayed. Even their wedding plans stumbled. Mary had to return to her teaching obligations in Oregon, so Joe promised to fly up for the ceremony in several weeks, after soloing some students and assembling another Jenny he had bought.

What was to have been a June wedding finally took place in late September. The couple took off the next day on an eighty-mile flight toward a county fair in Crescent City, California, but three forced landings en route—it took them two days to walk out from the third one—interrupted the honeymoon.

For the next seven years, Joe barnstormed in the West, flew various patrol and survey assignments, gave lessons, ran a Fairchild dealership, and struggled to build his own company, Pacific Coast Air Service. Mary rode with him on some trips, including one ferry flight in a Fairchild 51 from California to New York and back. Despite the risks of traveling in the flimsy, radioless crates of the 1920s and landing as often in farm fields as at what then passed for airports, she felt little fear. "Joe was a very good pilot, and confident," she explains. She did secretarial work to reduce overhead for his various enterprises and occasionally helped him in the maintenance of his planes.

They also moved a lot—Crescent City, San Diego, Oakland, Alameda, San Bruno, Victoria. Joe was often away for weeks at a time, and their limited budget left rooms sparsely furnished and appetites unsatisfied. After their first two children, Margie Lou and Frank, were born, Mary yearned more and more for the comforts of a permanent home, a regular income, and a nightly husband. But she was an aviator's wife in an age when most people viewed flying as a glamorous sport and women as subservient. So each time Joe got a new job or a new scheme, she dutifully packed up and reestablished the household in another town, another rented house.

One move was welcome. When Joe became manager of Alaska's new Pacific International Airways, the Barrowses at last were able to experience the fabled land that had called to them years earlier. They arrived in Anchorage, "at that time like a small town in the Midwest," on July 3, 1931. Prices shocked them ($62.50 a month for a modest apartment!), but the residents were friendly and the scenery spectacular. By the end of the gala Independence Day celebration the next day, Mary was in love with the Northland.

An invitation two weeks later to accompany Joe on a route survey offered her the thrilling prospect of exploring their new environment. The flight, in a floatplane, lasted a month and included stops at more than a dozen villages along the Yukon and Kuskokwim rivers. Joe had to make servicing and agenting arrangements for regular mail runs scheduled to begin that November.

Each community, as yet untouched by electronic technology and commercialism, had its own flavor, and each provided a taste of Alaska. At Tanana, Mary stayed two days in the local orphanage while Joe made a special freight run. At a roadhouse in Ruby, a former gold-mining camp, she watched "a dirty old cook with a dirty dish towel tied around his middle spit on the stove to see if it was hot enough for hotcakes. Then he put the hotcakes right down on the same spot." The cemetery at Nulato fascinated Mary with its Russian tombstones and brightly painted grave shelters. At Unalakleet, where they slept in the infirmary, a gardener offered them a rare luxury along the Yukon: fresh vetetables.

"The schoolteacher at Unalakleet hitched a ride with us to Nome so she could get a permanent," Mary recalls. "But when she got there she found there wasn't any beauty parlor, so she didn't get one." Mary herself found the accommodations crude in that old gold-rush town on Norton Sound, but she and her husband lingered there anyway to meet Charles and Anne Lindbergh, who were passing through on a survey flight to the Orient for Pan American.

After their return to Anchorage, Joe left for the East Coast on airline business, telling his wife and children he would be back in three weeks. Meanwhile, Mary moved the family to a rented house in Fairbanks, where Joe was to be based. When he finally returned three months later, she had struggled for weeks trying to keep the house tolerably warm in the stark Interior winter. Now they moved again, to Nenana so the financially troubled Pacific International Airways aircraft could be a little closer to the mail runs—sixty miles made a difference when the winter days afforded only a few hours of light.

"This is downtown Nenana on a busy day," Worthylake says with a smile, pointing in her photo album to an old shot of a deserted, snow-covered street. Among the quiet buildings sat the Southern Hotel, where the Barrowses rented two rooms for the rest of the long winter.

In the spring, with the company's future still uncertain, Joe went Outside on airline business again—this time for six months—and Mary and the children returned to Anchorage to wait. Mary decided to learn to fly.

"I had no desire to fly commercially," she says. "I was a married woman with no income of my own and two children, and Joe did not think kindly of having a wife with a career. But I wanted to go out and do more things. Flying had always fascinated me; I just wanted to see if I could do it."

Joe had never encouraged her to fly and had let her handle the controls only once, during their courtship in California. So Mary went ahead with her plans without notifying him. She scrounged some extra cash, began taking lessons in Star Air Service's Fleet biplane at Anchorage's Merrill Field, and, after a few early ground loops, learned quickly.

"It was a bit unnerving when I went up on my first solo and suddenly realized there was nobody in that front cockpit," she says. "The plane seemed so much lighter. I came in and made a good landing and got out, and my knees were knocking together. Frank was four then and he said, 'Did you really fly all by yourself, Mama?' I said yes. 'But you're not as good as Daddy yet, are you?' " (Acquainted with her instructor, Steve Mills, the children came to regard their mother's flying as even more daring when Mills died four years later flying a Bellanca floatplane on the Kenai Peninsula.)

To inform Joe that his wife had just soloed, she sent a triumphant wire to him on the East Coast. He later told her he

Mary Worthylake soloed a Star Air Service Fleet at Anchorage in 1932.

Courtesy of Mary Worthylake

avoided newspapers for the next three days, fearing he'd read about a crash.

The next evening another instructor, sensing Mary's self-doubt amid her exhilaration, made her solo again. "Then I figured I really could do it, that it wasn't just a fluke."

During a subsequent solo flight, a bush pilot she had met watched her practicing turns and other maneuvers. "After I landed he approached and told me I had come in and landed just like anybody—which meant, just like a man. I blew up and said, 'What did you expect me to do, crash in the middle of the field?' "

Six weeks after Mary's first lesson, a federal inspector arrived in Anchorage on a periodic visit to the Territory and administered written exams to her and other students. She passed easily. "He said he was going to be there two weeks, and I thought, well, I'll have that much time to practice before the flight test. That morning Steve called and said, 'Mary, I want you out here at the field to take your test.' I said, 'Oh no, I need some more solo,' and he said, 'I'm coming to get you right now.' It happened that the first four fellows had flunked, and he figured that if I knew that, I might chicken out. The first one was a blustering German who had thirty-five hours of solo, and he was very cocky and sure he was going to be good. He was the first up for his license and he had failed it.

"The inspector told me to go up and make I've forgotten how many spirals and come down and land right in front of the McGee [Airways] hangar. When I came down and got out, he started to write a Letter of Authority and I said, 'You mean I passed?' and he said yes. That was when Steve told me about the others. Only four out of twelve passed altogether."

Mary was the only woman among the twelve, and the first woman to be licensed in the Territory. Marvel Crosson, sister of the famous bush pilot Joe Crosson, had flown previously in Alaska but had gotten her certificate Outside. Another woman, Irene Irvine, had soloed before Mary in Alaska but did not become licensed.

Did Mary celebrate? "Oh no, I probably went home and baked

some fresh biscuits for the kids or something."

The next year, while temporarily living in Bellingham, Washington, she became one of the first 120 members of the Ninety-Nines, an organization of licensed women pilots. Charter member Amelia Earhart signed her membership card. To renew her license, she flew ten hours in an OX-5 Waco out of Bellingham's old Graham Airport, logging almost half of them on a 180-mile round-trip cross-country flight to Seattle. She later made one flight in Miami in an Aeronca. "I had to ask Joe for the money; it was not freely given." After her third child arrived in 1935, she decided she could no longer responsibly risk her neck on flying. Her aviation career was over.

The end of her marriage was also at hand. After three more years of moves and separations, the Barrowses were divorced in California in 1938. Mary relocated with the kids to Bellingham, bought a house, and resumed her teaching career. At last she had security and a home of her own.

Joe, who went on to fly Clippers across the Pacific for Pan American, married four more times, the first shortly after his divorce. Mary remarried once, in 1946, when the two eldest children were on their own. That marriage lasted until the death of Harry Worthylake in 1971.

I ask her if she harbors any bitterness toward pilots or commercial flying in general for the disruption in her young married life. Before answering she smiles, a little sadly, I notice. "No, no. I resented that Joe was always jumping from one thing to another, not flying itself. Flying didn't cause it. He simply had no desire to have a home and be settled."

Rodger Elliott

— *Finding Solutions* —

Everyone in the North Country knows what a bush pilot is, of course. In the Lower 48, the term is less common. Mention it there and some people will frown, think for a moment, then ask you for a definition. As long as you can keep a straight face, most of them will nod, convinced, when you state that a bush pilot makes a living by transporting blueberry bushes and other shrubs from the wilderness to greenhouses in various communities.

Ketchikan's Rodger L. Elliott knows I'm not that gullible, so he tells me a true story of how he became a bona fide bush pilot. In the summer of 1946 he was flying several loggers back to camp on the Chickamin River when oil suddenly began spraying onto the windshield. After beaching the Bellanca floatplane on the shore of Carroll Inlet, he opened the cowling and discovered that vibration had broken some tubing at the base of the 420-horsepower engine, allowing oil to escape.

"I jumped off the pontoon and cut off a branch of a blueberry bush," says Elliott, smiling. "Then I whittled it down with my pocket knife, put a rag around it, and tapped it into this hole. I cleaned off the windshield and started up the engine. It worked fine, so I continued the flight, took the loggers to where they wanted to go, and flew all the way back with that bush in there."

Elliott is a heavy-set man with a quiet but self-assured voice. He holds up a hand as I laugh, indicating that he's not through with this subject. "Another time, when I was flying moose hunters in a Goose, the left engine started slowing down, so I landed on a lake to take a look. One of the rods connecting the throttle had broken off. So I cut off a piece of bush and used the safety wire from the emergency kit we always had on board and wired it all together. Yeah, I was a *real* bush pilot."

I get the impression he would have devised some solution in each situation even if he had landed on a glacier miles from the nearest bush. It's not that he's a super mechanic; he doesn't have a mechanic's license. But with his optimism and ingenuity, Rodger Elliott would be a good man to have along in any difficulty. He would be the first to try the implausible, the first to seek the good in an unfortunate development.

After a few minutes of talking with him, I hardly notice that he sits in a wheelchair.

Challenges began confronting Elliott long before he became even a figurative bush pilot. Born in Ketchikan in 1919, he dreamed of a career as a civil engineer. "I think I'd have been a good engineer," he says, a statement easy to agree with because he seems to have the right stuff for anything he tries. But when tuition money ran out during his studies at the University of Southern California, he returned to Ketchikan and accepted a job as a mechanic's helper for Ellis Air Transport.

Working around airplanes inspired him to take flying lessons under the Civilian Pilot Training Program, although he still hoped to return to college when he had saved enough money. "At the time I never visualized being a commercial pilot," he notes. "That wasn't my ambition, but I liked to fly."

Civil engineering was still luring him when World War II arrived. "I caught the first boat south after Pearl Harbor," Elliott declares with the same pride he must have felt as a twenty-two-year-old. "It was December eleventh. I wanted to fly in the Navy because I was born and raised on the waterfront here and had acquired a water rating already, but they were sticking to a two-years-of-college

Alaska Coastal-Ellis Airlines operated its Consolidated PBY amphibians on both land and sea. *Peter Bowers Collection*

requirement and I had only one year."

Elliott doesn't linger on that disappointment. Instead, he launches into a chronology of his stint in the Army Air Corps, which had less stringent requirements for aviators. Like the living room of his Ketchikan home, heaped with papers, books, and other assorted stuff, his mind is crammed with details. He rattles off names, dates, and numbers as if he had taken off his uniform for the last time yesterday rather than almost half a century ago.

Only in passing does Elliott mention that he endured sixteen months in a German prisoner-of-war camp after his B-25 bomber was shot down outside of Rome. Dwelling on the unpleasantness such an ordeal must have involved would be uncharacteristic, and he skips the specifics.

But life behind a barbed wire fence gives a man time to think, to reconsider his priorities. "When I came back from overseas, I had a wife and a two-year-old daughter I had never seen," he says. "I had a job offer here and security, and I wasn't about to go back to college." The job was with his old employer, now called Ellis Air

Lines, which needed pilots for peacetime growth.

Having abandoned his civil engineering dream, Elliott put his heart into his new career. When no passengers were on board his Grumman Goose, he would occasionally practice cruising with one engine shut down and landing with the engines throttled all the way back (you normally land the Goose with some power). On one engine, the Goose handles like an overloaded truck with a flat tire. And with the engines at idle, your timing has to be just right as you prepare to touch down, for a powerless Goose loses flying speed quickly after you flare. Level too high and moments later it'll stall, succumb to gravity, and hit the water hard.

Pilots learn such maneuvers during their checkout in the Goose, but afterward few practice them. Elliott wanted to stay proficient at handling the Goose under those challenging conditions, and his foresight paid off on several occasions when he lost an engine. On one flight in a PBY, both engines failed—fortunately at different times. The second engine quit while he was on final approach to Ketchikan, and he made a smooth, powerless touchdown on the water.

He also made sure he'd be able to find his way around Southeast in the fog. When the sun came out, most of his fellow Ellis pilots climbed a little higher than usual to savor the Southeast scenery so often obscured by clouds. Not Elliott. "The weather here is about the lousiest you can run across in the world. The kind of flying we were doing, you couldn't have a map on the seat and be watching it to see where you were going. You either knew the country or you didn't. You were on your own. It was a challenge. So I was down on the shorelines in good weather, getting familiar with all the points and how long it took to go from here to there and what headings to use from each point." A pilot gets to know the country pretty well with that kind of preparation, and Elliott's boast that he could fly anywhere on 500-yards visibility—less than a third of a mile—probably is no exaggeration.

Even when visibility was measured in feet rather than yards,

Elliott sometimes found a way to keep going. Just out of Juneau one day in the late 1950s, he encountered an extensive barricade of thick fog over Stephens Pass. Civilization and hot coffee were just minutes behind him; most pilots would have turned around. But Elliott landed and step-taxied like a speedboat for almost sixty miles, following compass headings and dodging driftwood and an occasional troller. The fog finally lifted around the Five Finger Islands, enabling him to convert the Goose to an airplane again.

The tactic was safe and legal, he insists, noting that his only passenger on that flight was an FAA inspector. "Of course, there are different regulations now," he adds.

But Elliott admits he often bent the regs in quest of a solution if the remedy was safe. The morning after spending a snowy winter night on a Coast Guard boat (he didn't always get through), he was unable to start the left engine of his Goose, which he had beached near Holkham Bay. So he borrowed a blowtorch from the boat and heated the frozen cylinders. The engine fired immediately. "I don't think the FAA would have approved of that," he quips.

Elliott also had to call on his ingenuity as a passenger on a 1969 moose-hunting flight near Yakutat after the Piper Aztec's left prop dug into gravel during takeoff from an uneven strip. Already committed to flight, his pilot friend managed to coax the twin into the air. But on landing at another strip nearby to check for damage, they found the blades bent and the tips shattered. Dejected, the pilot, who was also the owner, walked away. Elliott went to work.

"I had a little hacksaw, a little file, and steel tape," he says. "That's all I needed. I measured off the worst blade with the tape, marked it, and measured out the same length on the other blade and marked it. I cut the tips off, then took the file and smoothed up the edges."

To bend the propeller back into shape he summoned a fellow passenger, and together they used a six-by-six-foot railroad tie as a battering ram, with their jackets wrapped around the end. "We flew it all the rest of the trip, and it worked fine."

Rodger Elliott flew the first Grumman Goose to Ketchikan for certification, in 1946, and logged a career total of 15,000 hours in the aircraft.

Courtesy of Robert Pickrell

But throughout that trip another, more ominous problem was haunting him. His knees were stiff, and he felt off balance. He sensed something was seriously wrong. The symptoms gradually worsened over the next several years. Doctors could find no explanation.

Meanwhile, Ellis had become part of Alaska Airlines, and in the summer of 1972 Elliott began training on the line's 707 jets. "What a machine!" He closes his eyes for a moment as he returns to the Boeing flight deck. "You go from a Grumman Goose, which is about 8,000 pounds gross weight, into a machine that's 316,000. All sorts of power. What a thrill!"

Before he could make his first commercial flight in the 707, doctors finally pinpointed his ailment: multiple sclerosis. The diagnosis automatically invalidated his flight medical certificate and ended his 20,000-hour flying career. Searching for the positive, as usual, he observes about the 707, “At least I got to fly it.” And, he adds, “flying around here was one of the best experiences I could go through.”

Soon Elliott could walk only with a pair of canes. Refusing to give up, he tried a special diet recommended for MS sufferers, and the disease gradually went into remission—not enough to requalify him for a flight medical, but after three years, three months, and nine days of depending on canes, he could get around on his own again. He notes that hobbies and emotional support from his children (he’s divorced) helped keep his spirits high.

In 1988, a leg problem forced him into a wheelchair. Doctors are still trying to diagnose the cause, although they say it’s apparently unrelated to multiple sclerosis.

“I’m going to lick it,” Elliott declares. He’s well on his way. He’s using crutches now, and has even made a few hunting and fishing trips.

ORVILLE TOSCH

— The Richest S.O.B. —

IF YOU EVER HAVE A chance to visit Orville Tosch in his Tosch Aircraft Industries hangar at the Tacoma Narrows Airport in Washington, give yourself plenty of time; you'll want to browse in his lounge downstairs and the "Alaska Room" upstairs. Lined with photos (many of them autographed) of early aircraft and pioneer bush pilots, model airplanes, and aviation memorabilia, the two rooms are neat, orderly, and well appointed, with lots of color, literal as well as figurative.

Poke your head into the much smaller accounting office inside the hangar at the bottom of the stairs, and you'll find more photos, plus a large painting of Tosch standing by a Lockheed Vega. Even the hangar has a museum flavor: an immaculate, bright-red Staggerwing Beech sits in one corner, and the polished floor shines like a mirror, as if it were intended for ticket-holding weekend visitors instead of the mechanics working quietly on an engine.

In such a history-evoking atmosphere, you might imagine your host as an ancient aviator with a handlebar mustache, a leather flight helmet, and a cane. Despite the first two parts of his name, however, Orville Wilbur Tosch appears much more modern when he walks in. He's a big, heavy man with glasses and short white hair beneath his cap. Wearing gray-green overalls, he grins and begins joking as soon as he shakes your hand. "Pay no attention to that," he admonishes, pointing to a sign on the downstairs lounge door that reads "Bull Shit." "Everything in here is the real stuff. The sign is what people do when they get together in here."

If the group photos with their affectionate personal notes hadn't already suggested Tosch's likability, talking with him for just a few minutes does. Relaxed and jovial, he laughs and banters as if he's known you for forty-five years. The phone rings often up in the Alaska Room, where he chats with guests, and periodically a mechanic or his granddaughter accountant knocks on the door. But he handles each question or problem with just the right touch of decisive aplomb and easily returns to the conversation.

Tosch seems to have ingratiated himself with people early on. As an aviation-struck teenager in South Dakota, where he was born in 1917, he traveled for two seasons with a troupe of barnstormers, selling tickets, washing airplanes, and performing whatever other services he could. At one stop, the pilots let him make his first parachute jump, to the delight of the crowd that watched him leap from a tethered balloon. He was thirteen. "That violated the child-labor laws, I suppose," he says, "but apprenticeship is the best way to learn. Too many people today think you can read a textbook and know it all."

You readily discover that Tosch's ribald style leaves plenty of room for strong opinions, especially about the work ethic.

The barnstormers also informally taught the eager kid to fly in a Waco. In Scobey, Montana, he probably violated a few other laws by soloing at age fifteen and taking up passengers the next day.

Perhaps because he had had his own carpentry shop under the tutelage of his father, a contractor, Tosch was attracted to the maintenance side of aviation as much as the flying. In 1937 he got a job as a mechanic for Northwest Airlines in Fargo, and long before moving to the North Country, he began designing and testing aircraft skis.

Alaska came into his life in the early 1940s. He was working in a St. Paul, Minnesota, maintenance shop that included the Morrison-Knudsen Company among its customers. A large construction concern, M-K had government contracts to build airports in Alaska, and soon Tosch was flying to the Territory on ferry trips, sometimes as mechanic, sometimes as pilot.

Meanwhile, he met his future wife, Katherine, a cadet in the government's Civilian Pilot Training Program in St. Paul. By the spring of 1942 Alaska had become home for them.

After flying for M-K and Star Airways out of Anchorage for a few months, Tosch "got acquainted with Ray Petersen and his bunch." That began a fifty-year friendship with Petersen, who would become one of Alaska's great airline builders. "It was a good family operation," he says. "We had terrible arguments about business sometimes, but we worked well together."

Katherine helped make Tosch's career a family operation, too. While her husband was flying out in the bush for Petersen Flying Service, she often made flights on company scheduled runs as a DC-2 copilot. "She wasn't worth a damn as a freight handler," Tosch quips, "but she was a pretty darn good pilot." When their children began arriving, Katherine quit flying, but she served as a radio operator for Tosch after Petersen stationed him in Bethel in 1943 to oversee the company's lower Yukon and Kuskokwim River operations. "Sometimes the kids would hear me on the radio in the office," he says, laughing, "and Katherine would have to dash to beat them to the microphone."

Within a couple of years, Tosch had taken most of the Bethel-area business away from his main competitors. "You know how we did that?" he asks, leaning forward in his chair to make a point. "We gave damn good service on that mail run. The other guys used wheels in the summer and skis in winter, but what about breakup? There are times when you can't use either one because of the mud. I added a floatplane so we'd be ready for whatever condition we had, and during breakup we'd follow that ice right on down with the mail."

The subject of giving better service leads to a discussion of pushing the weather. Tosch leans forward again. "I flew it awful tough out there. But you can do that if you know the terrain. Up there in

Orville Tosch and his Lockheed Vega on the Yukon River ice by Fortuna Ledge with Deputy U.S. Marshal Al Ball's son in the winter of 1946. The Vega is one of a handful of metal-fuselage versions built. *Photo by Al Ball*

those deltas you have to pay attention to the drainages, because that's whiteout country. There isn't anything to see except the creeks. In the Arctic they have big rivers, and down in the States there are roads to follow, but in that delta country you have only the creeks. You have to know where they're draining, and whether they're going uphill or downhill."

Tosch admits that, knowing the country or not, pushing hard can lead to mishaps. Most of his were minor, such as inadvertently flying onto the snow in a Gullwing Stinson during a whiteout. In his most embarrassing incident, Tosch carelessly landed a Goose in the Naknek River with the gear still extended from takeoff at the Naknek (now King Salmon) airport. He and his helper squeezed out before the amphibian sank. Although Tosch undoubtedly saw little humor in the situation then, he laughs now about Petersen's reaction: "Ray says, 'Tosch, how in the hell could you do anything so stupid?' I say, 'I wish you were with me; I damn near drowned getting out of there, and that water was cold.' Ray says, 'It's a good thing I wasn't with you 'cause I would have had a hard time explaining my footprints on the top of your head.' "

Later developments would show that Tosch at least picked the right airplane to dump.

Petersen had recently merged his outfit with Dodson Air Service and Gillam Airways to form Northern Consolidated Airlines, and the expanded company reassigned Tosch to Fairbanks as manager of the operation there. In addition to flying and doing maintenance work, he looked for ways to generate more business—some which helped develop Alaska's tourism.

"After the war there were lots of government people up there who had time to see the country," he says. "I'd come in from a trip, it was summer, lots of sunlight left, so I started taking them up to Circle Hot Springs to have a big supper and go for a swim. Then I'd fly them up to Fort Yukon to see the midnight sun. Pretty soon I was hauling them out to Nome and Kotzebue, too." Tosch adds with noticeable pride that he later helped start what became the Alaska Visitors Association.

With expansion, Northern Consolidated Airlines began acquiring more aircraft. Two DC-3s stationed at Fairbanks were too large for the company hangar on Weeks Field, forcing Tosch and his maintenance staff to work on them out in the rain, snow, cold, and wind. Next door sat an adequate hangar that Pan American had recently vacated when it began operating DC-4s out of nearby Ladd Field, a military base; the civilian Weeks Field was too short for the four-engine airliners.

One day a group of Pan Am executives bound for a meeting at McKinley Park Lodge arrived in Fairbanks too late for their connecting train. With no Pan Am aircraft available, they chartered Northern

Consolidated. Pilot Tosch found Pan Am president Juan Trippe in the right-front seat of the Stinson Trimotor and began negotiations that led to a commitment by Tosch to purchase the hangar for $25,000.

While Petersen welcomed the acquisition, he squirmed at the price. Northern Consolidated didn't have the money, he protested. But soon an insurance check arrived for the Goose Tosch had flipped in the Naknek River, and the sale went through. The Goose had been the only insured aircraft in Northern Consolidated's fleet.

The degree of the company's involvement in support flights for radar-station construction led to a more serious squabble. Tosch argued for a heavy emphasis, but Petersen insisted on concentrating instead on fishing charters.

"Turned out he was right," Tosch admits with a self-effacing laugh. "The radar stations are long gone, but the fishing camps are still there. But I was pissed off at the time, so I quit."

He spent the next year setting up a maintenance shop for former bush pilot Art Woodley's Pacific Northern Airlines at Boeing Field in Seattle. Then, perhaps with a bit of retaliation in mind, he rejoined Morrison-Knudsen to make support flights to radar sites the firm was building in far western Alaska. It was a seasonal job that required Tosch to invest in a Goose, but recompense was by payload, and he spent little time on the ground at his base in Nome.

While several sites were on capes jutting into the Bering Sea, one lay on St. Lawrence Island, 150 miles offshore. Tosch added charters for Eskimos on King Island to his schedule. "Did I work," he says. "In the summer of '52 I made 272 round-trip crossings of the Bering Sea and flew more than 900 hours in a little over four months. To this day, as far as I can find out, I've been the only one ever to land at King Island in the Bering Sea in the summertime."

If that sounds a little like boasting, Tosch has earned the right. The open sea has always made bush pilots cringe. Frequent fog and the lack of landmarks complicate navigation, but it's the specter of an emergency landing that really dries the mouth. The problem is surviving not the impact but the aftermath. People usually don't die in controlled rough-water landings, unless they drown after bumping their heads or getting tangled in their shoulder harnesses. But count on the airplane breaking up—the open sea's churning waves and swells are like a runway of rocks at fifty or sixty knots. Having floats or a flying-boat hull makes no difference: aluminum will buckle, struts will snap, structure will bend. The wreckage may float for a few minutes, but soon it will sink or capsize.

Then you're going to get wet. Even in summer, Alaska's ocean water rapidly induces hypothermia. Unless you've come down close to a boat or shore, or radioed for a rescue helicopter, there's no escape. Survival suits are too bulky to wear routinely (they were unavailable to Tosch's generation), and emergencies in cramped bush planes seldom grant enough time to struggle into them. A life jacket protects one from drowning, not from cold.

Naive North Country floatplane passengers think they're safe whenever they're over water, even though they might be looking down on a white, seething maelstrom. Their pilot, meanwhile, is holding his breath until he is once again over nice, dry, survivable land. (The question of exposure aside, floats actually provide more protection than wheels during an emergency landing on rough ground because they absorb much of the impact. Wheeled landing gear, on the other hand, collapses immediately, and the fuselage thus bears the full force of the crash.)

"There was no rescue out there whatsoever then," Tosch says about his Bering Sea flights. "I never even carried a lifeboat; I figured you get wet, you've had it anyway." No wonder he kept track of his crossings, like an aerialist counting tightrope walks. No wonder he's proud of challenging the hostile environment out at rocky King Island, where precious little sheltered water and the absence of beaches left his forehead damp.

Tosch spent three summers flying the Bering Sea in his Goose. Then he headed south again, this time to fly for the Louisiana offshore oil industry. The warmer, relatively benign Gulf of Mexico must have seemed fairly tame after the Bering Sea, although local pilots, ignorant of bush techniques, wondered how this northern boy could find his way out to the rigs in crummy weather when they had to turn around.

While down South, Tosch also served a stint as a fixed-base operator in Fort Lauderdale and flew PBYs in the Bahamas and the Caribbean. One PBY assignment took him on a three-month flight around the world for an oil company. Another involved him with the CIA. "I was out there floating between the Bay of Pigs and an aircraft carrier while Kennedy was pulling support out from under those guys," he comments.

In 1971, two years before relocating permanently in the Northwest, he visited Alaska for the first time in seventeen years. "It was lonesome," he says. "I used to think I knew everybody in Nome, but when I went back I recognized four people."

It'll take more than changing faces in Alaska to keep Tosch lonely, however. Few people in the western Washington aviation industry are still unfamiliar with the name Orville Tosch and all that it implies—friendly socializing, a colorful flying background, and high-quality maintenance and restoration. Tosch is high on the invitation list for practically every regional aviation event as guest or speaker, and he receives more requests than he can fill to present his slide show on Alaska. One Puget Sound friend is well-known author/pilot/artist Ernest K. Gann, who chose Tosch Aircraft Industries to restore his Bucker Jungmann biplane. Now Tosch has commissioned Gann to do a painting of a Goose flying over the Bering Sea by King Island.

Tosch relishes such relationships. "I never made a hell of a lot of money," he says. "The biggest pay I ever got in Alaska, or anywhere else, was the friendship of the people. When I made up a party list for my fiftieth wedding anniversary, I realized I was the richest son of a bitch in the world."

Dick McIntyre

— *The Good Old Days* —

WAS BUSH FLYING in the old days more satisfying than it is today? Most retired Alaskan pilots have mixed feelings on that question, including Fairbanks's Dick McIntyre.

Founder of Frontier Flying Service, one of the best-known air taxis in the Interior, McIntyre has the aviation background for some interesting opinions on the subject. Like many of his peers, he learned to fly in the Army Air Forces during World War II. In fact, he and the legendary glacier pilot Don Sheldon served together in the 96th Bomber Group in England, although they met only much later in Alaska.

Assigned to Ladd Field outside Fairbanks in 1946, McIntyre earned a Distinguished Flying Cross for locating a missing B-29 in Greenland, and another DFC for making exploratory B-29 flights over the North Pole. Military aircraft such as the B-29 customarily cruise at high altitude on instruments, and as McIntyre watched the local bush planes come and go low enough to see the bears, the hamlets, and the fireweed, he felt a bit envious. Soon he was moonlighting as a bush pilot for several Fairbanks air services.

In 1948, the U.S. Air Force (by then organized from the Army Air Forces) reassigned him Stateside to instruct in the Training Command. But Alaska had hooked him. "The first opportunity I had I got out," he says. "That was in June 1950. I came right back and have been here ever since."

McIntyre started Frontier Airways (which he later renamed

Frontier Flying Service) upon his return. Periodically the outfit won contracts for specialized activities such as firefighting, for which he leased two surplus military B-25s. "But basically, all I was interested in was bush flying," McIntyre says. And fly the bush he did. Always a line pilot, often the only pilot (he hired help as he needed it), he took off on charters all over the Interior in a Piper Pacer, a Howard, a Cessna 180, and other aircraft. His was a typical career, a mixture of routine and adventure, of disgruntlement and exhilaration.

While he never had a "real bang-up wreck," he occasionally had to prepare for one. "The weather can just terrorize you. You think you aren't going to get to the field, that you can't hang on any longer. You think you're going to crash for damn sure. Then something happens to get you out of it—the weather opens up a little bit or you come to the field you were looking for."

He didn't always make it. There was no warm eggnog or cozy hearth for McIntyre on Christmas Eve 1951, for instance. Instead, he and an Eskimo woman he had tried to fly from Fairbanks to Wiseman were shivering on the frozen Koyukuk River, where fog had forced them to land in the ski-equipped Pacer. The short winter twilight soon faded, surrounding them in hostile night. McIntyre built a fire, but fueling it kept him continually swinging an ax: you don't let your fire go out when it's forty below. Nor do you dare to sleep. He started the Pacer's Lycoming now and then to prevent the engine from turning into a block of ice.

In midmorning, twilight finally returned, along with enough visibility to complete the flight.

McIntyre also made an unscheduled landing one March on a solo flight from Fairbanks to Ruby, when carburetor icing sapped power from both engines of his brand-new Piper Apache. Unable to hold altitude, he bellied the twin onto the frozen Yukon River. Props bent, McIntyre unhurt. Pilot Alden Williams landed and picked him up. Later, McIntyre returned with a mechanic, installed skis and new props, and flew the Apache home.

Another time one summer, a sudden wind change at the

Fairbanks airport float pond robbed him of lift just as he was taking off. Before he could abort, the 180 floatplane skimmed off the water and onto the bank. The floats were dinged. So was his pride.

But there was plenty of routine flying between such incidents, plenty of time for gazing at the northern lights, looking down on wolves chasing caribou, exploring valleys where perhaps no one had flown before. . . .

By 1974 McIntyre, then fifty-seven, was thinking of retiring from commercial flying. The trans-Alaska pipeline project had created a hot market for air transportation, so he sold the company for a nice profit and turned his concentration to the Frontier Sporting Goods store he had founded the same year as his air service.

The mounted heads of moose, bear, African sable, leopard, mountain goat, bison, sheep, musk-ox, and many other big game greet me from the upper walls of the store when I walk in to meet him. Half a dozen customers browse along shelves of fishing, camping, and shooting paraphernalia. His son Edward runs the business now and has things under control, so McIntyre takes me to the restaurant across the street, where we can talk with less distraction.

Although he grew up in the 1920s and '30s in a part of the Kentucky mountains where folks got around by packhorse and wagon, McIntyre is no hillbilly. Thoughtful and modest, he knows almost as much about Africa and India as he does about Alaska. Behind his glasses, his eyes exude the intelligence and astuteness that helped make him successful in both of his businesses.

Over a third cup of coffee, I ask him to compare bush flying then and now. He pushes back his blue Fairbanks Hangar QB (Quiet Birdmen) cap. "Well, I've seen a lot of changes in aviation, and most of them have been for the worse. The FAA has a lot more control now, with all the regulations and everything. It used to be that you could do any damn thing you were big enough to do and get away with it. I was just talking to the guys out at the airport, and it's much, much worse than when I got out. They [federal inspectors] sit out there in the field and watch you when you go out, and if you

Dick McIntyre on a North Country big game hunt in 1952.
Courtesy of Dick McIntyre

have a propane tank or something they nail you. They're haunting the guys with the schedules now."

Practically every older bush pilot shares such resentment to some degree. For years, pilots in Alaska flew with only their judgment as copilot. From experience—which included lots of mistakes and close calls—they discovered their personal limits and those of their machines. They filled the seats and baggage compartments according to what they knew could be hauled without damage, regardless of the numbers listed on the manufacturer's weight and balance form. In questionable weather, they based go/no-go decisions solely on their ability to handle the elements.

Then, like a city council introducing traffic lights into a community, the government began imposing restrictions on bush pilots. Regulations now prohibited them from flying commercially with less than 500 feet of altitude or two miles of visibility, although they had been doing so comfortably and routinely for years. Pilots now were required to get an instrument rating, even those who never operated on instruments and had demonstrated competency at seat-of-the-pants flying through thousands of hours aloft. They now had to get out of the cockpit after logging eight hours on any given day, even if they were alert and energetic enough to keep going.

Of course, the FAA was trying to promote safety, to set professional standards. But McIntyre and his peers believe the regulations are too conservative. Like a highway speed limit geared toward the least capable driver, aviation regulations fail to allow adjustments for experience.

Ironically, modern times have also brought deregulation of the aviation industry. "When I was flying, there was no way you could get a schedule to anyplace," McIntyre says, referring to the government's previous discouragement of competition through tight control of scheduled routes and mail contracts. "I just lived for the day when they deregulated and I could get some of that mail pay, but it never happened while I was involved." Deregulation passed Congress four years after he sold Frontier Flying Service.

McIntyre got out too soon for the scheduled routes he coveted, but he was in business long enough to appreciate technological progress. "Equipment now is vastly improved," he continues. "For instance, in range. The Cessna 180 or 185 carries more than eighty gallons. You can go somewhere and get back. It used to be, when you had thirty-six gallons in the Aeronca Sedan or Piper Pacer, you were always fighting the gas battle, carrying gas cans with you so you could get back. Before they built the airport float pond, floatplanes had to take off on the Chena River. We'd go on one float around one bend and up on the other around the other bend, and then when you couldn't get off you'd chop the throttle and throw off a can of gas. Then we'd try it again, and if you didn't make it off in a couple of bends you'd throw another can off, until you finally got off. Now you've got range and you've got docks and places where you can taxi up and get gasoline, and in that respect it's a lot better than it used to be."

Many of McIntyre's 20,000-plus hours are on floats. He knows to lift one float with a heavy load to help break the suction with the water, and he knows to leave the water rudders down for a moment while taking off in a strong crosswind to establish directional control. But some of his fellow pilots were ignorant of such techniques. They had never learned them—and weren't required to.

"Pilots in the old days didn't have the training the guys now do," says McIntyre. "There were a lot who knew nothing about flying. They just picked it up. I know guys who have gone through the process of taking examinations half a dozen times before they could pass, and in the meantime they were flying steady and getting away with it. A lot of them were just zilch on training. They barely had enough to solo and they became full-fledged bush pilots. In the old days facilities didn't exist to train pilots."

Today, stiffer certification and insurance requirements and periodic checkrides help weed out the buffoons. Modern flight schools, many with simulators and audiovisual aids, provide aspiring pilots with solid knowledge and skills.

"But I long for the old days," McIntyre admits. So do most other retired bush pilots. It's a longing that transcends a yearning for a more colorful aviation era. It's really a nostalgia for the old Alaska, for a time before McDonald's arches and summertime tourists, an aching for lost friends, lost opportunities, lost youth.

You won't find McIntyre languishing in the past, though. People attracted to bush flying in the first place have an innate spirit of adventure that usually keeps them active throughout their lifetimes. McIntyre still flies privately in his 185 floatplane. An avid hunter (he shot the second recorded polar bear ever taken in Alaska with bow and arrow, which is still the world's record with a bow), he's looking forward to his fourth safari in Africa. The weekend before I arrived he had shot 600 rounds in local skeet and trap tournaments (he won at skeet). He's a downhill skier, and he recently went scuba diving in the Truk Islands of the Western Pacific, where he had a chance meeting with Southeast pioneer pilot Bob Ellis. He also owns and drives three BMW motorcycles. Bike expeditions have taken him over most of the roads of Alaska and the Northwest Territories as well as back home to Kentucky.

Was bush flying more satisfying in the old days? In some ways, sure, and all retired pilots like to reminisce. But guys like McIntyre live in the present.

Shell Simmons

— *Talk of the Town* —

Atlin Flight Made by Shell

Shell Simmons hopped to Atlin yesterday afternoon with the Alaska Air Transport Lockheed, taking two passengers roundtrip and bringing four from Atlin to Juneau.

—*Juneau Empire,* June 6, 1938

THIS NEWS ITEM seems so bland today that someone browsing through old issues of the Juneau daily paper would likely look it over again, searching for a punch line. Juneau residents of the day probably reread it too—but with fascination. Flying then was still a wondrous novelty in Southeast's mountainous, watery world, and people tuned in like modern soap opera fans to find out who had ventured aloft and to what points. This particular item went on to provide passengers' names and other details.

As one of only two pilots operating commercially out of Juneau in 1938, Shell Simmons made especially good copy for journalists. A solid six feet and 200 pounds, dark hair smoothed back, eyes alert, and grin broad, Simmons radiated confidence. After starting his own flying service in 1935, he had become the first pilot in Southeast to fly year-round; more experienced pilots in the milder climate of Ketchikan, 200 miles south, had been locking their hangar doors in winter. "They said you can't fly here in winter," pioneer Southeast pilot Bob Ellis recalls. "Well, Shell Simmons proved you could."

In only his fifth year as a bush pilot, Simmons was the most sensational of the handful of flyers in Southeast, most of them based in Ketchikan. He humbled them with his tireless aggressiveness. While they waited for customers, he strode into saloons and other establishments to solicit business. When fog or snow cut visibility to near zero, he was usually out in it, step-taxiing if necessary. He flew at night, transported roving prostitutes, air-dropped mail and Christmas turkeys to miners, and once flew the Juneau marshal to a gun battle at a fish trap.

"Shell never knew when to turn around," comments Lloyd Jarman, a noted retired Southeast mechanic who accompanied many pilots in 1930s Alaska. "He used up several different airplanes—some just weren't strong enough for his demands, and we had two or three narrow escapes together. But he was one of the best pilots I ever flew with."

Jarman adds that in the early days Simmons was chronically broke, a condition that probably added fire to his drive. Yes, Shell Simmons was news. Even the name had the right ring, a name a writer might choose for the hero of adventure books.

> **Shell Carries Ten Yesterday with Lockheed**
>
> Air Transport Company pilot Shell Simmons took the Lockheed out twice yesterday, carrying a total of 10 passengers, and went out again this morning with four passengers.
>
> —*Juneau Empire*, June 20, 1938

Simmons, whose 1908 Idaho birth certificate names a midwife but no doctor, sought adventure long before he learned to fly. As a sixteen-year-old he left his Yakima Valley home in Washington State to sail to the Orient on a freighter. And in 1929 he and a buddy ventured 2,400 miles—from Whitehorse down the Yukon River, all the way to Siberia—in a fourteen-foot skiff.

After that voyage, Simmons worked at a variety of jobs in several western-Alaska communities. In Candle, he helped bulldoze a landing strip, and he watched in fascination as bush pilots began

Shell Simmons, center, and his wife, Bernice, have just landed at Tulsequah, B.C., in a Fokker Super Universal in the early 1940s. A local musher is on the right. *Courtesy of Lloyd Jarman*

touching down there in Fairchilds, Stinsons, and other aircraft. Flying seemed much more exciting than driving a tractor, he decided.

One fur buyer he met in Candle had also become interested in aviation, but for a practical reason: he wanted a quicker mode of transportation among villages than the traditional dog sled could provide. The fur buyer promised to buy a Travel Air and hire Simmons as his personal pilot if the eager young man would learn to fly at his own expense. Simmons agreed and returned to Washington to take flying lessons. After logging just five minutes of solo time, however, he received a message that the 1929 stock market crash had wiped out the fur buyer's market and thus the man's need for an airplane.

Simmons then headed north again, this time to Juneau, where he got a job in the Alaska-Juneau Mine. But flying had gripped his spirit. Too impatient to wait for adequate training, he test-flew a World War I Jenny seaplane (purportedly the only Jenny ever put on floats) that he and two partners had converted. To overcome an extreme tail-heaviness and get the plane back on the water, he yelled at his passenger to lean forward to shift the center of gravity.

Later, with a commercial license, he participated in practically all the dramatic, headline-producing search-and-rescue flights of the era. It was he who found Juneau pilot Gene Meyring and two surviving passengers after their Lockheed Vega crashed on Chichagof Island in 1934. Simmons flew the three injured back to Juneau in a Stinson with a faltering engine, limping in after dark.

The following year, his intuition helped rescue a honeymooning couple stranded in the wilderness. Al Almosolino and his bride had left Seattle for Southeast in a new Curtiss Robin floatplane, but they failed to show up at any station after Butedale, British Columbia. The only airplane in Ketchikan available for a search crashed on takeoff.

The Coast Guard then hired Simmons up in Juneau. When he reported no sign of the Robin in the Ketchikan area, the search was canceled. But stubborn Simmons refused to give up. Still a low-time fledgling himself, he had already made several flights up the Inside Passage from Seattle. Almosolino, he reasoned, might have flown into one of the dozen fjordlike inlets south of Ketchikan trying to escape bad weather.

On his own time, battling early-spring snow showers, Simmons and an observer scoured those inlets in his Stinson. It's a wonder they thought they had a chance. The inlets stretch on and on for miles, indented by countless coves and bights, distracting you with verdant valleys and waterfalls cascading off mile-high cliffs. Even if you know pretty much where to look, a hundred-foot yacht seems amazingly puny when you finally spot it. Simmons and his observer were operating on a mere hunch in quest of a two-seat floatplane that might have been anywhere.

Yet, incredibly, they found it. In Princess Bay off Behm Canal, they sighted what appeared to be two parallel logs—unnaturally parallel, the pair agreed. After landing alongside, they realized the "logs" were actually the Robin's upside-down floats.

Simmons stripped, dove into the water (about forty-five degrees, according to oceanographers), and groped unsuccessfully for the Almosolinos' bodies.

Later that day, investigating Simmons' report, crewmen on the Coast Guard cutter *Cyane* discovered the couple, cold and hungry but alive, on a beach a mile from their airplane. It had capsized a week earlier after plopping down in heavy snowfall.

"The people of this community think you did a mighty fine thing when you came down here and conducted a search for the plane of pilot Almosolino, resulting in the saving of two lives," wrote the Ketchikan Chamber of Commerce in a 1936 letter addressed to Mr. Sheldon Simmons of Juneau.

> **Simmons Up Entire Day in Lockheed**
>
> The plane that roared over town at 1:15 this morning was the Alaska Transport Lockheed piloted by Shell Simmons, ending a day's work that began at 9 in the morning.
>
> Total flying time was close to 10 hours.
>
> —*Juneau Empire,* June 25, 1938

In his most famous exploit, Simmons' persistence again saved lives. When the cargo ship *Patterson* ran aground near Cape Fairweather (geography's greatest misnomer), 130 miles northwest of Juneau, in a December 1938 Gulf of Alaska storm, rescue seemed impossible. Day after day, three Coast Guard cutters maintained a consternated vigil offshore, unable to evacuate the eighteen survivors (two crewmen had died abandoning the ship) because of monstrous coastal swells whipped by winter gales.

Driving snow and sleet grounded even Simmons on some days. When he could fly, he air-dropped food and supplies to the camp the survivors had established near the ship. But he too felt powerless to help further. The beach was too small for a wheelplane, and there was no body of water large or calm enough to accommodate a

As a flight instructor in 1933, Simmons gives tips to student Clarence Ferguson in an Aeromarine Klemm. *Photo by Lloyd Jarman*

seaplane. "I could get within a hundred feet of them, because there was nothing to run into," Simmons recalls today. "My God, you could see the color of their eyes, but you couldn't do a damn thing about it."

In his frustration, he probably shouted more poignant invectives at the turmoil below. Southeasterners could understand the military's ineffectiveness—ordinary boys from Minnesota and South Carolina. But Simmons was the Territory's most intrepid airman, an ace bush pilot who once had nursed a Bellanca seventy-five miles back to town from Cape Fanshaw after a stabilizer strut broke and threatened catastrophic inflight structural failure. Come on, Shell, public sentiment seemed to urge; those poor men have been out there wet and cold for almost two weeks now. Do something!

The rest of the country waited as well. News of the *Patterson* crew's plight had spread nationwide, and each day people in the Lower 48 listened to their radios and read their newspapers to find out if the stranded crewmen had been rescued way up there in stormy, isolated Alaska.

"That was the one time that the pressure was on me the most," Simmons admits now. Pressure has always been the bush pilot's insidious enemy. Those who cannot ignore it had better be pretty good.

One day, after dropping food, he noticed that every sixth or seventh wave would break completely over the beach and create a temporary lagoon by the ship. Was it deep enough for a seaplane? Could he land in it before the water receded? Again and again he circled in his Vega, observing, calculating.

Back in Juneau, Simmons picked up outdoorsman Nels Ludwigson, who was familiar with the coast, flew back to the ship, and circled until a lagoon formed. "To our awe and amazement, Simmons . . . took a turn out to the end of the spit and landed his plane just inside the line of breakers," wrote *Patterson* third mate Steve Johnson, who had caught pneumonia at the camp. "How he managed the split-second judgment that was required to make that dangerous landing without cracking up his plane and killing himself, I don't know, but I do know that that man sure can fly!"

The steady thirty-knot onshore wind slowed the Vega almost instantly after touchdown. Simmons dropped off Ludwigson to guide the sixteen ambulatory crewmen fifteen miles down the beach past sweeping glaciers to Lituya Bay, where Coast Guard vessels could pick them up.

Then, with Johnson and another sick man on board, Simmons restarted the engine. "The next wave breaking over the spit washed our pontoon free from the sand, and at that instant the pilot opened the throttle," Johnson reported. "By the time he had lifted the plane from the water, he was already up to the camp, and I'll swear that our pontoons didn't clear the brush around the camp by more than five feet!"

Simmons landed at Lituya Bay to refuel from a supply he had cached there, then headed for Juneau. All eighteen survivors spent Christmas in civilization. Although headlines from clippings in his scrapbook proclaim him a hero, he pooh-poohs the attention. "I had it entirely planned out," he says. "The waves were so high, but when I got down there it wasn't as bad as it looked."

What the press failed to report was that throughout his flights to the scene, he was wearing a face mask to protect healing wounds. Just weeks earlier, on a trip from Juneau to Chichagof Island, the engine of his Fairchild 71 had quit after a fuel tank ran dry. When he switched to another tank, the engine remained silent. Simmons stretched the glide to a bay, but by then the 71 had slowed too much to control, and it crashed. Simmons' face slammed into the radio, practically ripping off his nose. Despite the blood and pain, he dove into the water and pulled out one of five passengers who had gone down with the airplane. He then stumbled up the beach for help.

There were other injury-producing incidents, as well. Once, he carelessly landed a Seabee on the water in Juneau with the wheels extended. The amphibian flipped over, and Simmons again swam underwater to rescue his sole passenger, a priest. Approaching

Juneau at night on another occasion, he suddenly got a faceful of glass, blood, and feathers when a sea gull crashed through the windshield. He landed safely.

Plastic surgery restored much of his nose, but scars still show today as Simmons discusses the old days in his house on Juneau's Evergreen Avenue.

Pilots and mechanics who worked for his Alaska Coastal Airlines, a 1939 merger of Alaska Air Transport and Juneau's Marine Airways, would notice some changes in the Simmons of today. Of course, there are the physical ones that typically come with longevity. More significantly, ex-employees would find a mellower man than the uncompromising, hard-driving boss who wanted to prove he could be as successful behind a desk as in the cockpit. Since his retirement in 1968, when Alaska Coastal joined Alaska Airlines, he's learned to throttle back emotionally. The pressure's gone.

Gone, too, is the almost daily newspaper attention. When the *Juneau Empire* mentions him today, it's to report his presence at an Alaska Airlines board of directors meeting (he's a member emeritus) or a historical-aviation conference. Simmons says he enjoys his relaxed pace, but like most retired bush pilots he lingers wistfully over photos and clippings in his scrapbook.

"They thought I was pretty reckless," he chuckles. "Guess I did take a few chances. But I always had a plan. I always had a plan."

ACKNOWLEDGMENTS

ANY TRAVELER who wants to say thanks after a trip through Alaska will have a long list. Alaskans have always extended warm hospitality to visitors, a tradition unchanged by progress.

My list includes all the pilots and mechanics profiled in this book. Although I arrived during the busy season, each put aside other projects and obligations to talk aviation with me. Each loaned me photos and memorabilia (many of them irreplaceable), offered invaluable tips and advice, and cheerfully endured follow-up phone calls.

Many pilots also volunteered special help. Emitt Soldin provided a room in his home and the use of a car during my ten days in Anchorage. Ruth Jefford flew me in her Bonanza from Anchorage to Soldotna. Several pilots drove me to various research sources. And everyone made sure that I was kept well fed and plied with coffee.

In the Puget Sound area, transplanted Juneauite Lloyd Jarman generously made his extensive aviation files and photographs available to me, and aeronautical expert Peter Bowers patiently answered my endless technical questions about historical aircraft.

Perhaps most important, through their stories, photos, and friendship, these veteran aviators confirmed the rewards of a flying career.

Glossary of Aviation Terms

Aeronca C-3: a two-seat trainer in production from 1931 to 1936. Virtually a powered glider, the C-3 had a gross weight of only 875 pounds and was difficult to get off the water on floats due to its tiny, two-cylinder, thirty-six-horsepower engine. Wire bracing on both the top and bottom of the wings gave the airplane an ungainly appearance.

American Pilgrim: a large single-engine airplane of the early 1930s. The ten-place Pilgrim used a 575-horsepower engine and had a tubby appearance because of baggage/freight compartments under the cabin floor. Most Pilgrims, manufactured by the American Airplane and Engine Corporation, flew for American Airlines before Alaskan operators began acquiring them in the mid-1930s. Cruise speed was about 100 knots.

amphibian: an airplane that can operate from either land or water. Although amphibians offer operational flexibility, they're heavier and more expensive to maintain than wheelplanes or seaplanes of comparable size. Many people erroneously think amphibian is synonymous with seaplane.

angle of attack: Stick your hand out the window of a moving car and you'll feel airflow, or relative wind. The wing of an airplane also encounters relative wind as it moves through the sky. Angle of attack is the angle at which the wing meets this relative wind; it has nothing to do with the natural wind.

asymmetrical thrust: Most twin-engine aircraft have an engine on each wing. As long as each engine is producing the same amount of power, thrust is straight ahead. But with differential power or one engine shut off, thrust is uneven, since each engine is offset from the centerline; the airplane turns in the direction of the powerless engine. A pilot can compensate for asymmetrical thrust with rudder pressure.

attitude: Climb, descent, turn, level—these are possible attitudes for an airplane.

Beechcraft Bonanza: a low-wing, four- to six-seat, single-engine airplane distinctive for its V-shaped tail. Introduced in 1947, the Bonanza later came in conventional T-tail versions as well. As with all Beechcraft models, Bonanzas are noted for quality and performance. Over the years, horsepower for the Bonanza ranged from 185 to 285.

Beechcraft 18: a highly successful all-metal twin-engine airplane (resembling the Lockheed Electra 10) that was manufactured for thirty-two years, beginning in 1938. Beech Aircraft built almost 9,000 Beech 18s with 300- to 450-horsepower engines. Most versions were taildraggers, and many saw duty on floats in Alaska and Canada.

Bellanca Pacemaker/Skyrocket: a monoplane in production from 1927 to 1939 and, briefly, in 1946. With accommodations for five to seven passengers, the airplane was named Pacemaker with a Wright engine and Skyrocket with a Pratt & Whitney Wasp powerplant. A 550-horsepower Skyrocket could climb to 25,000 feet and (on wheels) cruise at 165 knots.

Boeing 247: a twin-engine, ten-passenger airliner that appeared in 1933. It set the standards of the day for speed and comfort (facilities included a toilet and galley), but the DC-3 preempted its popularity in Alaska and elsewhere. The 247 cruised at almost 135 knots and had a maximum takeoff weight of 12,650 pounds. It used a pair of 550-horsepower engines.

breakup: the transition between winter and spring, when ice and snow begin to melt, or break up. It occurs in April or May, depending on latitude. In the Northland, breakup can last several weeks and is a terrible period for pilots. River and lake ice is too thin for skis but too thick for floats, and strips can be too muddy and slushy for skis or wheels.

bush: any remote, sparsely settled, largely undeveloped region, such as parts of Alaska, Africa, and Australia.

bush pilot: a pilot who flies regularly in bush country and thus often operates from crude or natural facilities such as unpaved strips, gravel bars, lakes, and the like. The earliest Alaskan aviators were true bush pilots because they had practically no aviation facilities to use. Their descendants, today officially called "air taxi pilots," have an easier job; most Alaskan villages now feature airports, often with paved runways, and those that don't usually provide a dock for seaplanes. But modern Alaskan air taxi pilots still log many off-airport, seat-of-the-pants hours.

Cabin Waco: a single-engine biplane produced from 1931 until the early 1940s in a variety of models. The cabin Waco was somewhat anomalous because most biplanes had open cockpits, and biplanes in general were becoming old-fashioned when the Waco was introduced. Pilots of float-equipped cabin Wacos had to keep an eye on the lower wing when docking or beaching.

carburetor icing: In an engine with a float-type carburetor, fuel vaporization and a drop in air pressure within the carburetor venturi cause a sharp decrease in carburetor air temperature. Under certain atmospheric conditions, ice can form in the carburetor, reducing engine power. From the cockpit, the pilot can apply heat to the carburetor, preventing or eliminating such ice.

Cessna 140: a two-place, side-by-side, ninety-horsepower taildragger manufactured in the late 1940s. Intended as a trainer and recreational airplane, it saw some commercial bush use in Alaska. The 140 had a fuel capacity of twenty-five gallons, cruised at about 100 knots, and weighed 1,500 pounds when fully loaded.

Cessna 170: a 1948–56, four-place taildragger beloved by many bush pilots for its 145-horsepower engine, which provided both performance and economy. The B model was especially popular due to larger flaps and beefed-up landing gear. Cessna ended production of the 170 with the marketing of a nosewheel version, the 172.

Cessna 175: a single-engine, four-seat airplane built in the late 1950s and early '60s. The airplane never achieved much popularity because its geared 175-horsepower engine seemed prone to problems.

Cessna 180: a four-place, single-engine taildragger that has gained wide acceptance in the bush for both commercial and private uses. It's powerful enough to haul reasonable loads, small enough to be economical. Cessna produced 6,193 between 1953 and 1981. Most versions have a 230-horsepower engine. Bush pilots considered the float-equipped 180 to be the first truly adequate four-place seaplane, previous four-seaters being a bit underpowered.

Cessna 185: the Cessna 180's big brother. Manufactured from 1961 to 1985, the 185 remains a principal component of the North Country air taxi fleet. With a 300-horsepower engine (early versions had 260 horses), it can carry five passengers, and an optional 300-pound-capacity cargo pod beneath the fuselage adds versatility. Fuel injection in the powerplant means no carburetor icing.

Cessna T-50 "Bamboo Bomber": a twin-engine airplane introduced in 1940 for the general aviation market. Most Bamboo bombers, also called "Double-Breasted Cubs," served the military with the designation AT-17 as trainers and light transports during World War II and weren't available to civilian operators until after V-J Day. The majority had 245-horsepower Jacobs engines.

cheechako: Alaskana for tenderfoot or greenhorn.

Civilian Pilot Training Program: As World War II loomed, President Roosevelt fretted over a possible shortage of American pilots. The resulting CPTP, sponsored by the government, trained thousands of college students and young adults to fly.

Consolidated PBY Catalina: a large, twin-engine airplane that earned distinction in many theaters of World War II, including the Aleutian Islands campaign, for its toughness and transcontinental range. In the postwar years, several Alaskan operators acquired PBYs. For years Alaska Coastal–Ellis Airlines used them on scheduled flights in Southeast, where they handled storms, icing, and rough water with nonchalance. Powered by a pair of 1,200-horsepower engines, the PBY was produced in both flying boat and amphibious versions.

Curtiss C-46 Commando: a popular cargo carrier in Alaska after service in World War II, mostly as a transport. With two 2,000-horsepower engines, the C-46 can haul huge amounts of fuel oil, camp machinery, or whatever else bush residents need flown in. A taildragger, it handles off-runway operations as easily as a Super Cub. You'll still find C-46s hard at work in the Interior.

Curtiss Jenny: the most famous airplane of the early 1920s. The Jenny, a name derived from the official designation "JN," was the principal Army trainer during World War I. This biplane was also involved in Alaska's first crash, when Clarence O. Prest, a former circus motorcyclist, had to make an emergency landing near Fort Yukon in 1922 while trying to fly a Jenny from New York to Nome.

Curtiss Robin: a single-engine, three-seat cabin monoplane designed for private pilots. Introduced in 1928, the Robin needed extra-long float struts for propeller clearance when used as a seaplane. The famous ninety-horsepower OX-5 engine powered many Robins, but customers could select other engines. An OX-5 Robin sold for about $4,000 in 1928 and cruised at 74 knots. It was a Robin that "Wrong Way" Corrigan flew in 1938 from New York to Ireland, after announcing a California destination.

dead-reckoning: to navigate by compass, clock, and airspeed indicator. Example: Point B is 100 nautical miles north of Point A. To dead-reckon there in a 200-knot airplane, you would fly north at that speed for a half hour. The pilot must make allowances for wind direction and velocity and start from some reference point; dead-reckoning is meaningless if you're lost. Before the development of electronic navigation, dead-reckoning was one of only two ways to get from here to there, the other being pilotage.

de Havilland Beaver: one of the few aircraft ever designed specially as a bush plane. Canada considers its Beaver to be among the country's ten greatest engineering achievements over the last 100 years, and few Alaskan operators would disagree. Though it's slow and noisy, the eight-place, 450-horsepower Beaver can haul a load of about 1,800 pounds off a relatively short stretch of water or land. The U.S. Army used 981 of the 1,631 Beavers built between 1947 and 1967. Still the workhorse of the North.

de Havilland Twin Otter: a Canadian twin-engine airplane introduced in 1965 that quickly gained widespread use all over the North. It can carry up to twenty passengers, take off from short strips, and, with turboprop engines, shrug off the extreme cold of the Arctic. Unlike most sophisticated airplanes, it has fixed rather than retractable landing gear. The Twin Otter is almost fifty feet long.

differential power: In a multiengine airplane, a pilot normally applies the same amount of power to each engine. But unequal, or differential, power is sometimes justified. For instance, to make a tight turn while taxiing, a pilot might push one throttle forward and keep the other at the idle position. And if the airplane suddenly veers toward the edge of the runway during takeoff, differential power can help straighten it out.

Douglas DC-3: probably the most famous airplane of all time. First flown in late 1935, the DC-3 became the backbone of many airlines for years, carrying two pilots, a flight attendant, and up to twenty-eight passengers behind a pair of 1,200-horsepower engines. A sleeper version had accommodations for fourteen. More than 10,000 of these planes served allied forces in World War II as C-47s. One experimental model was fitted with floats. Some outfits in bush country continue to use the DC-3 as a cargo plane.

drag: air resistance due to an aircraft's structure (also called parasite drag). Streamlining reduces parasite drag in aircraft, just as it does in automobiles. Induced drag is a by-product of lift and increases with angle of attack.

Edo: short for Edo Corporation, the world's oldest manufacturer of seaplane floats. Edo began in 1925 at College Point, New York, as the Edo Aircraft Company and pioneered the all-metal float; previously, floats had been constructed of wood. The company estimates it has produced between 25,000 and 30,000 floats. You'll find more Edos on floatplanes than any other type of float.

elevator: the horizontal panel on the tail that makes an airplane climb or descend. When the pilot pushes forward on the cockpit wheel or stick, the elevator pivots downward; the airstream strikes it, forcing the tail up and the nose down. Pulling back on the wheel or stick causes the opposite reaction. If improper loading of passengers, cargo, or mail results in a center of gravity that's too far forward or rearward, the pilot might not have enough elevator control.

Fairchild 24: a high-wing, single-engine monoplane that came out in 1931 and ultimately was offered in sixteen models during its fifteen-year production run. Seats varied from two to four and horsepower from ninety to 200. The Fairchild 24 was used by several military services during World War II as a light utility aircraft.

Fairchild 71: a seven-seat model developed from the Fairchild FC-2; built in 1928 and 1929 with a 420-horsepower Pratt & Whitney Wasp engine. On the ground, the wings could be folded against the fuselage for easy storage or to ride out high winds. Fairchild designed the prototype for photographic and mapping missions, but most 71s spent their careers carrying passengers and cargo.

firepot: a plumber's blow pot, operating on white gas, used to preheat aircraft engines in extreme cold.

firewall: as a noun, a fire-resistant partition between the engine and the cockpit; as a verb, to apply full power to the engine by advancing the throttle all the way toward the firewall. In using the term "firewall the throttle," you imply some urgency to the situation, such as in making a go-around after a balked landing attempt.

flaps: movable panels on the wings that are adjustable from the cockpit. Flaps allow an airplane to fly slower at a steeper angle during the landing approach. In some airplanes, flaps are also used to shorten the takeoff roll.

floatplane: a seaplane with pontoons, or floats. The great majority of seaplanes are floatplanes, as opposed to flying boats.

float pond: a body of water, usually man-made, at an airport for use by seaplanes. A float pond enables seaplane pilots to deliver or pick up airline passengers right at the airport instead of having to use a lake or waterway that might be miles away.

flying boat: a seaplane that uses its hull rather than pontoons for flotation. The famous four-engine Martin M-130 China Clipper of the 1930s was a flying boat.

ground-loop: a sudden, sharp, unintended turn on the ground while an airplane is landing, taking off, or taxiing. A ground loop can be caused by a variety of factors, such as overuse of the rudder pedals, wind, a faulty brake, or a pothole. It rarely happens with tricycle gear. In especially severe ground loops, centrifugal force can cause a wing or the tail to strike the ground.

Grumman Goose: a twin-engine, ten-place amphibian produced over an eight-year period beginning in 1937. Popular because it can operate off land or sea and carry a big payload with its 450-horsepower engines. Wingspan is forty-nine feet; length, thirty-eight feet, four inches. Some Goose pilots swear that the airplane can handle any water conditions the much larger PBY can. The military air arms of the United States and eleven foreign countries used the Goose for various purposes during and after World War II, and some air services and government agencies in Alaska still have the airplane in their fleet.

Grumman Widgeon: a junior version of the Goose, produced throughout the 1940s. The six-place Widgeon originally had 200-horsepower Ranger engines, which many operators later replaced with more powerful 260- or 270-horsepower Lycomings. Alaskans liked the Widgeon because it was more economical than the Goose, yet still offered the advantages of a twin-engine amphibian. A Widgeon with Ranger engines cruised at about 120 knots.

hangar-fly: to casually discuss flying, airplanes, pilots, and other aviation subjects. A hangar is a frequent site for such conversations, which often take place during bad weather or work breaks.

Hughes 500D: a modern, five-to-seven-seat, turbine-powered helicopter widely used in Alaska. Pilots appreciate the 500D for both its speed—about 140 knots—and its ability to lift off with heavy loads. The rear compartment can accommodate two fifty-five-gallon drums, and bulky loads can be carried using an external cargo hook.

line pilot: a regular, full-time pilot who flies a company's schedules and routes and is uninvolved in administrative or managerial duties.

Lockheed Electra 10: a twin-engine, twin-tail, ten-passenger airliner popular in the 1930s and 1940s. Most Electras in Alaska had 450- or 550-horsepower engines, and some flew on skis. Amelia Earhart was flying a modified version when she disappeared on an around-the-world flight in 1937. Production ceased in 1941 after 149 Electras had been built. Not to be confused with the mid-1950s four-engine turboprop of the same name.

Lockheed Vega: a single-engine, all-wood airplane loved by Amelia Earhart,

Wiley Post, and many other pilots for its performance and docile handling. Built from 1927 to 1932, the most advanced version could carry six passengers and cruise at about 147 knots on wheels. The cantilevered (no struts) wings and fuselage streamlining gave the Vega a sleek, graceful appearance. Vega floatplanes continued in scheduled service in Alaska until about 1960.

Lower 48: literally, the contiguous forty-eight states of the U.S. (loosely including Hawaii), all of which fall below Alaska in latitude.

Monocoupe: a two-seat, single-engine monoplane noted for its rugged design and long production run (1928 to the late 1940s). The earliest model used a sixty-horsepower Velie engine, while the last had a 115-horsepower Lycoming. Seating was side by side, instead of the more usual tandem arrangement of pre–World War II designs.

navaid: short for navigational aid, usually the electronic kind.

Ninety-Nines: a national organization formed as a club in 1929 by a group of women pilots at old Curtiss Field on Long Island, New York, to promote the role of women in aviation. They solicited membership from all 117 licensed U.S. women pilots at the time and agreed to name the club for the number who responded by a certain deadline. Since then, the Ninety-Nines has evolved into one of aviation's most prestigious organizations, with about 7,000 members around the world. Amelia Earhart was a charter member.

Noorduyn Norseman: a Canadian single-engine plane designed in the mid-1930s specifically for the bush. It had a 600-horsepower Pratt & Whitney engine, a maximum takeoff weight of 7,400 pounds, and, with a special seating arrangement, a passenger capacity of nine. Although the Norseman could accommodate wheels, it was one of the few aircraft built with floats and skis in mind. Most floatplanes and skiplanes were adapted from airplanes designed specifically for wheels.

Outside: any place beyond the borders of Alaska and the northern areas of Canada. A subtly pejorative term, it connotes less beauty, freedom, and adventure, but also implies more opportunities in the world of technology and escape. For instance, Alaskans might go Outside for advanced training or a vacation; when they get tired of the traffic and tinsel, they come home.

OX-5: a famous ninety-horsepower, eight-cylinder, water-cooled engine, developed prior to World War I, that powered a number of early airplanes. The 4,000-strong OX-5 Aviation Pioneers organization includes pilots, mechanics, engineers, and others who were involved with the engine before 1940. Contemporary historians interested in the engine may also join.

pilotage: navigation by orientation with landmarks, the bush pilot's most common way of getting from point A to point B. Pilots who know the country can use pilotage in very low visibility, needing only glimpses of creeks, hillsides, islets, or other features, to update their position. Pilots in unfamiliar areas have to have better weather and a chart.

Piper Apache: A four- to five-seat, low-wing twin introduced in 1953 and used primarily as a trainer and personal airplane. A few air services in Alaska put the Apache to work on charters, but pilots considered the 150- and 160-horsepower models underpowered. A later version with 235-horsepower engines performed better.

Piper J-3 Cub: There are still some older Americans who equate "Piper Cub" with every small airplane. The Piper assembly line produced 14,125 of the little two-seat Cubs (their empty weight was just 680 pounds) from 1939 to 1947, with time out for World War II. Thousands of pilots learned to fly in them, including Alaskans. The lack of an electrical system meant you had to spin the prop by hand to start the sixty-five-horsepower engine.

Piper Super Cub: a two-seat taildragger, resembling the J-3 Cub, that for years was a favorite with bush pilots because of its ability to get in and out of tight places on wheels, skis, or floats. It can be slowed to forty knots and still stay in the air. Piper built more than 9,000 Super Cubs from 1949 into the 1980s in 90-, 125- and 150-horsepower versions, and the airplane remains popular with North Country private pilots, some of whom put extra-large "tundra" tires on their Cubs for especially rough or soft fields. To many people, the airplane is synonymous with bush flying.

propping: starting an airplane engine by spinning the propeller by hand. A necessary procedure for planes without a starter. Careless pilots who prop without first securing the airplane or stationing an assistant in the cockpit sometimes have to leap out of the way when the engine starts because they left the throttle too open. A few pilotless airplanes have actually taken off in such circumstances. Careless pilots have also been severely injured while propping. Despite its risks, propping is a useful bush pilot skill for those times when the airplane's starter or electrical system breaks down miles from nowhere.

puddle jumper: nickname for any old, low-powered, two-seat airplane, such as the Taylorcraft and the Luscombe 8A.

pusher: an engine installation in which the propeller is mounted in the rear and pushes rather than pulls the aircraft forward. Used on some seaplane designs to minimize ingestion of spray by the engine and prop. Pilots stepping from a conventional airplane to a pusher sometimes get into trouble, because adding power in a pusher causes the nose to drop and decreasing power makes it rise, the reverse reaction of the conventional "puller," or tractor arrangement.

Quiet Birdmen: a national low-key fraternity of pilots who gather for socializing in chapters called "hangars." Membership in the QBs, as they're known, is by invitation only.

Republic Seabee: a four-seat amphibian whose prototype made its first flight in 1944. With a bulky cabin and a pusher engine (215-horsepower), the Seabee pokes along at just 90 knots and looks a little ungraceful, but owners are devoted enough to have formed the Seabee Club International. Many Seabees that went to Alaska served in watery Southeast. Production ended in 1948.

scud: aviation slang for ominous, low-level, foglike clouds.

seaplane: an airplane designed to operate from the water, either on pontoons (floatplane) or a hull (flying boat).

seat of the pants: controlling an airplane by feel rather than reference to the instruments. Slips, skids, and other maneuvers are often most noticeable in the pilot's seat.

skiplane: an airplane equipped with skis on its landing gear.

slip: a maneuver in which an airplane is banked but prevented from turning by applying rudder in the opposite direction of the turn. In an airplane without flaps, slipping is a quick way to lose altitude if the landing approach is too high. A slip is also a common way of correcting for a crosswind while landing.

sourdough: an Alaskan old-timer. The word came from the fermented yeast mixture commonly used in the backcountry to make bread and hotcakes.

Southeast: southeastern Alaska."Panhandle" is another name for this narrow, 500-mile-long archipelago and strip of mainland.

stall: An airplane stops flying and stalls when its airspeed becomes too low for the angle of attack. If the angle of attack is changing rapidly, such as in a sudden, tight turn, a stall can occur at a high airspeed. Nonpilots, including journalists, often assume that it is the engine that stalls. No. It's the wing. In fact, when an airplane stalls on takeoff, the engine is usually at full power.

Stearman C-3B: a three-seat, open-cockpit biplane of the late 1920s, powered by the 220-horsepower Wright J-5 engine. Alaskan pilots who flew this and other open-cockpit airplanes really had to bundle up, although in winter the early cabin planes were almost as cold. Named the Sport Commercial, the C-3B had a range of about 620 miles.

step-taxi: to taxi a floatplane or flying boat at a speed fast enough so that it rides on the "step" portions of the floats or hull, skimming across the water like a high-speed boat.

Stinson Gullwing: a graceful, sturdy, single-engine airplane noted for its distinctive tapered wing, which from certain angles appeared birdlike. Some pilots called the Gullwing the "Cadillac of the Sky," for the quality of its construction. Used through the Interior from the mid-1930s until the 1950s, the airplane had four or five seats, came in a variety of engine options, and was a good load-hauler.

Swallow: an open-cockpit biplane produced by the Swallow Airplane Manufacturing Company of Wichita, Kansas, from 1924 to 1929. The majority of Swallows had three seats and a ninety-horsepower OX-5 engine. Like most airplanes of the era, this one lacked an electrical system.

taildragger: A typical airplane has two main landing gear and a smaller third wheel at either the nose or tail. Until the 1940s, virtually all planes had a tailwheel, which is why "taildraggers" are said to have conventional gear even though "tricycle" gear has been the normal arrangement for decades. Taildraggers are more prone to ground looping because the center of gravity is farther to the rear, but they can handle off-airport operations better than tricycle-gear planes. Many airmen say students develop a finer sense of rudder control in a taildragger.

Taylorcraft: a two-seat trainer and personal airplane of the 1940s and 1950s. The Taylorcraft, a product of the Taylorcraft Aviation Corporation, had a 65- or (later) 85-horsepower Continental engine, two side-by-side seats, and wheels instead of sticks. Though it was economical and easy to handle, it flew in the shadow of the more popular Piper J-3 Cub. Nonetheless, in the mid-1960s, nostalgia prompted renewed production of the Taylorcraft with a more powerful engine.

Travel Air: a rugged, three-seat, open-cockpit biplane of the mid-to-late 1920s, available with engines from the ninety-horsepower OX-5 to the 330-horsepower Wright. Travel Airs served in many roles, among them airmail carrier, flight school trainer, and cropduster. Some models resembled the German Fokker, and the "Fokkers" in several Hollywood dogfight scenes were actually Travel Airs wearing a Fokker paint scheme. Those were nicknamed "Wichita Fokkers."

trim: Elevator pressure on an airplane's control wheel changes as airspeed, load, attitude, and other flight conditions change. The pilot can neutralize, or "trim," that pressure by adjusting a wheel or other device intended for the purpose, so he doesn't have to hold the wheel constantly forward or back. More sophisticated airplanes also allow the pilot to trim pressure off the rudder and aileron.

Trimotor: Ford, Stinson, and Fokker manufactured three-engine airplanes called

"Trimotor," but the Ford version, of which 199 were built from the mid-1920s to 1932, was the best known. The Ford Trimotor was nicknamed "Tin Goose" because of its corrugated-aluminum construction. Customers could choose engines ranging in horsepower from 220 to 450. Several airlines in Alaska used the Tin Goose, which carried ten to fourteen passengers.

variation: the difference in degrees between the magnetic north pole and the true north pole (the geographic pole). The two poles are about 1,300 miles apart. Variation changes according to longitude. Courses on charts are measured in relation to true north, but the compass points to magnetic north. In Alaska, a pilot who plans to navigate by chart and forgets to account for variation can end up thirty degrees or more off course.

Weeks Field: an airport that used to be in what is now downtown Fairbanks. Built in 1923, Weeks Field was the most famous airport in Alaska and served as the hub of aviation in the North Country until mid-century.

weight and balance: For safety, an aircraft manufacturer establishes limitations on the maximum weight and weight distribution with which a particular model can take off. Distribution means where the weight of fuel, passengers, or anything else carried is placed fore and aft. Exceeding either parameter is risky as well as illegal. For instance, an overloaded airplane might not be able to climb fast enough to clear trees at the end of the strip, and too much weight ahead of or behind the balance envelope means the loss of some elevator control.

wheelplane: an airplane with wheels, as opposed to floats or skis.

wheel/skis: a type of landing gear containing both wheels and skis, enabling the pilot to land on either snow or a hard surface.

More Books About Bush Flying

Bruder, Gerry. *Northern Flights.* Boulder, Colo.: Pruett Publishing Company, 1988.

Callison, Pat. *Pack Dogs to Helicopters: Pat Callison's Story.* Vancouver, B.C.: Evergreen Press, 1983.

Cole, Dermot. *Frank Barr.* Edmonds, Wash.: Alaska Northwest Publishing Company, 1986.

Day, Beth. *Glacier Pilot.* New York: Holt, Rinehart and Winston, 1957.

de Goutiere, Justin. *The Pathless Way.* Vancouver, B.C.: Douglas & McIntyre, 1968.

Ellis, R. E. *What—No Landing Field?* Haines, Alaska: Lynn Canal Publishing Company, 1969.

Garner, Lloyd. *Canadian Bush Pilot.* Vancouver, B.C.: Gordon Soules, 1990.

Gleason, Robert J. *Icebound in the Siberian Arctic.* Edmonds, Wash.: Alaska Northwest Publishing Company, 1977.

Greiner, James. *Wager with the Wind: The Don Sheldon Story.* Chicago: Rand McNally, 1974.

Harkey, Ira. *Pioneer Bush Pilot: The Story of Noel Wien.* Seattle: University of Washington Press, 1974.

Helmericks, Harmon. *The Last of the Bush Pilots.* New York: Alfred A. Knopf, 1969.

Hirschmann, Fred, and Kim Heacox. *Bush Pilots of Alaska.* Portland, Ore.: Graphic Arts Center, 1989.

Janson, Lone E. *Mudhole Smith.* Edmonds, Wash.: Alaska Northwest Publishing Company, 1981.

Jefford, Jack. *Winging It!* Bothell, Wash.: Alaska Northwest Books, 1990.

Kennedy, Kay J. *The Wien Brothers' Story.* Fairbanks: Wien Air Alaska, 1967.

Lerdahl, Herman, with Cliff Cernick. *Skystruck.* Bothell, Wash.: Alaska Northwest Books, 1989.

Mason, Roy. *Ice Runway.* Vancouver, B.C.: Douglas & McIntyre, 1984.

Mills, Stephen E., and James W. Phillips. *Sourdough Sky: A Pictorial History of Flights and Flyers in the Bush Country.* New York: Bonanza Books, 1960.

Satterfield, Archie. *Alaska Bush Pilots.* New York: Bonanza Books, 1969.

———. *The Alaska Airlines Story.* Edmonds, Wash.: Alaska Northwest Publishing Company, 1981.

Stevens, Robert W. *Alaska Aviation History.* Des Moines, Wash.: Polynyas Press, 1990.

Time-Life Books editors. *The Bush Pilots.* Alexandria, Va.: Time-Life Books, 1983.

Turner, Dick. *Wings of the North.* North Vancouver, B.C.: Hancock House, 1980.

Whitesitt, Larry L. *Flight of the Red Beaver: A Yukon Adventure.* Coeur d'Alene, Idaho: Century Publishing Company, 1990.

Whyard, Florence. *Ernie Boffa: Canadian Bush Pilot.* Edmonds, Wash.: Alaska Northwest Publishing Company, 1984.

Wilson, Jack. *Glacier Wings and Tales.* Anchorage: Great Northwest Publishing, 1988.

Worthylake, Mary M. *Up in the Air.* Bend, Ore.: Maverick Publications, 1988.

INDEX

Boldface type in all capitals indicates aircraft companies;
boldface indicates aircraft model and model number. *Italic* page numbers indicate photographs.
All sites are in Alaska unless indicated otherwise.

About the Author

Gerry Bruder has written extensively about aviation as a free-lance writer and as a staff member of *Flying* magazine, *Business & Commercial Aviation* magazine, and *Western Flyer.* He's also been a general assignment reporter for the *Ketchikan Daily News* and the *Anchorage Times.*

In his flying career, Bruder has logged more than 14,000 hours in floatplanes in Alaska, Washington, and Canada. His first book, *Northern Flights,* is an account of his experiences as an Alaskan bush pilot.

Bruder has degrees from Hanover College and Ohio State University and lives in Seattle, Washington.